SYNCOPATED RHYTHMS:

20th-Century African American Art from the George and Joyce Wein Collection

JOYCE WEIN • (1928–2005)

The opening of the exhibition of the George and Joyce Wein Collection of African American Art is a joyous occasion for me, even though Joyce is not with me today. The sadness of not having her here is lessened, because I knew the pride Joyce had in looking forward to this day. The depth of our love for each other never became more apparent than when I realized that she would no longer be at my side. Knowing of her love for the paintings and the artists that are involved in our collection doesn't erase that sadness, but it allows me to enjoy the moment of what is a memorable celebration of our life.

Joyce Alexander Wein passed away August 15th, 2005.

—George Wein

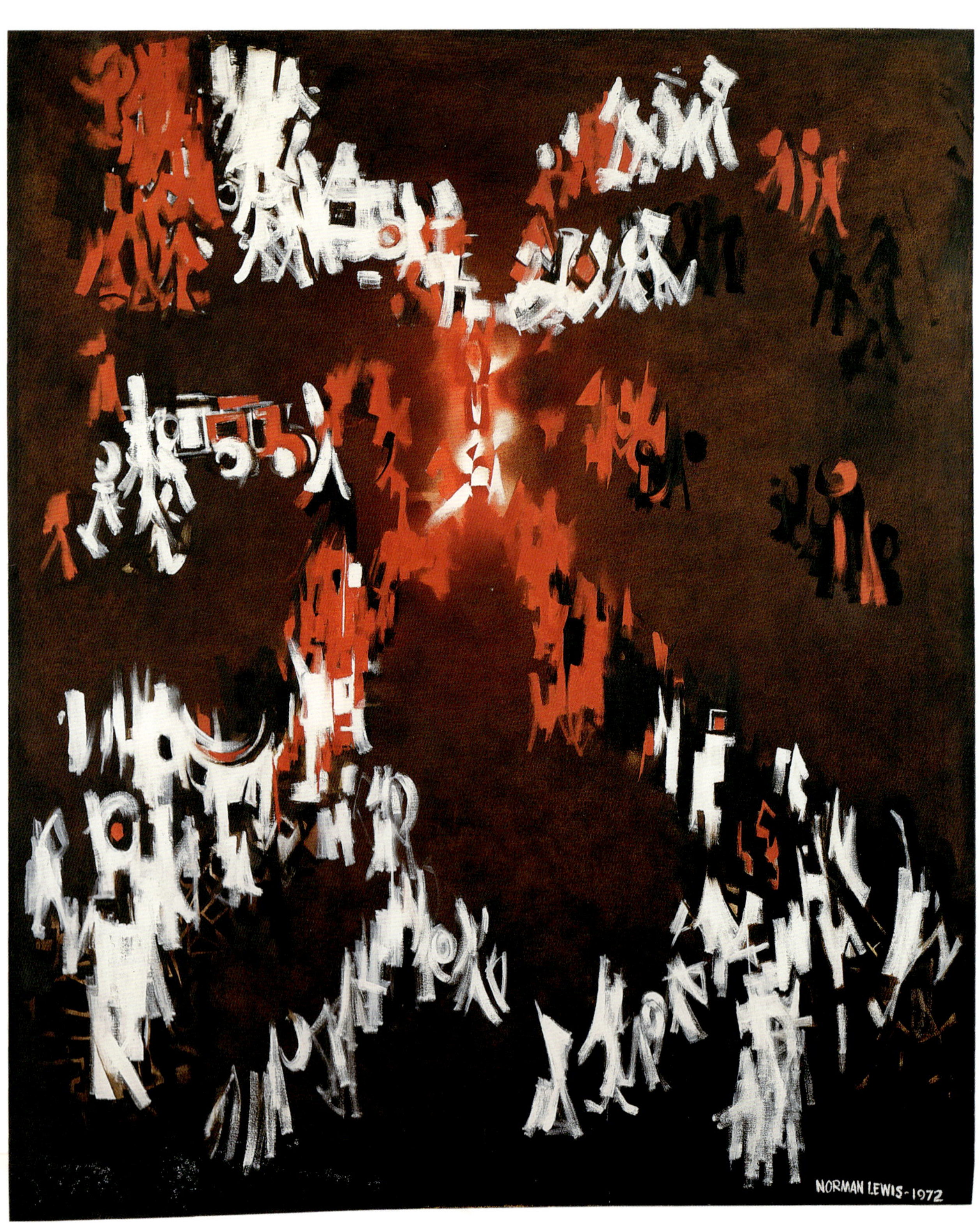
NORMAN LEWIS-1972

SYNCOPATED RHYTHMS:

20th-Century African American Art from the George and Joyce Wein Collection

Exhibition and Catalogue by
PATRICIA HILLS and **MELISSA RENN**

Foreword by
ED BRADLEY

BOSTON UNIVERSITY ART GALLERY
BOSTON · 2005

FRONTISPIECE: Norman Lewis, *Triumphal*, 1972. Oil on canvas, 87 x 73 in. (220.9 x 185.4 cm).

Exhibition Dates
November 18, 2005–January 22, 2006

Boston University Art Gallery
855 Commonwealth Avenue
Boston, Massachusetts 02215
617-353-3329
www.bu.edu/art

Distributed by University of Washington Press
P.O. Box 50096
Seattle, Washington 98145–5096
www.washington.edu/uwpress

Printed in the United States of America
Library of Congress Control Number: 2005928366
ISBN: 1–881450–23–6

CONTENTS

ACKNOWLEDGMENTS

SYNCOPATED RHYTHMS: *20th-Century African American Art from the George and Joyce Wein Collection* continues the Boston University Art Gallery's long-standing mission to pursue an interdisciplinary interpretation of art and culture and to provide a culturally inclusive viewpoint that expands the boundaries of the museum. As a publication and exhibition, *Syncopated Rhythms* adds to the growing body of scholarship on African American art and presents important yet previously unpublished information and images. We are privileged to have the opportunity to work with the George and Joyce Wein Collection on this significant project, the first public exhibition and publication on the collection itself. A project of this kind allows us to take a fresh look at the history of African American art in a more personal and pointed way, through one focused, private art collection.

George and Joyce Wein have been gracious and accommodating in allowing us access to their collection and to their lives. When I first visited the Weins in their New York apartment with Patricia Hills to discuss the possibility of this exhibition, I was impressed by the quality of their knowledge. I realized then that we were going to learn quite a lot from them, as well as from their fine collection. We are grateful to George and Joyce Wein for their enthusiasm on this project. We are all saddened that Joyce Wein passed away on August 15, 2005, just as this publication went to press, and was not with us to see the project to completion.

We thank Deborah Ross, assistant to George and Joyce Wein, for her availability and dedicated presence from the start, and for providing every aspect of the raw data needed to produce the exhibition and publication. She supplied us with an image and information for each artwork, did research on individual objects, made calls on our behalf, and continuously offered welcome advice. This project would not have been possible without her support.

We offer additional thanks to Bearle Bowen, Andrezj Gluchowski, Carolyn McClair, Melanie Nañez, and Lee Weissman of Festival Productions, Inc. We also wish to thank Ed Bradley for providing his personal history of the Weins' collecting for the foreword.

Patricia Hills, Boston University Professor of Art History, and Melissa Renn, a Jan and Warren Adelson Curatorial Fellow in American Art and Ph.D. Candidate in Art History, provided the intellectual vigor, experience, and determination to push this project to completion. I thank them for their commitment to the project and for ensuring its success. Boston University Art Gallery Assistant Director Rebekah Pierson was the driving force behind the exhibition and accompanying catalogue, directing all aspects of planning and production related to the project. She worked directly with The Stinehour Press to conceive and craft this publication and its excellence is ultimately a testament to her efforts.

Patricia Hills would like to thank those scholars with whom she discussed this project: Ann Eden Gibson, Theresa Leininger-Miller, Diana Louise Linden, Gwendolyn DuBois Shaw, Jeffrey Stewart, and Margaret Rose Vendryes. She would also like to thank the artists she interviewed: Benny Andrews, William T. Williams, and John Wilson.

Melissa Renn would like to thank Félicie Balay, Joshua Buckno, Meghan Dorney, William Fagaly, James Mitchell, Chris Newth, Luz Rodriguez, Martha Severens, and Albert Sperath for assisting her in her research; Ernie Barnes, Oliver Johnson, Michael Kelly Williams, and Richard Yarde for taking the time to be interviewed; and Robert Renn, Nancy Renn, and Robert Zeiller for their continual support throughout the production of this catalogue.

We are grateful to Michael Rosenfeld and Maggie Seidel at the Michael Rosenfeld Gallery in New York for their generous guidance and assistance, as well as Carol Freeman at Boston University's Office of Publications Production for her initial input on the exhibition catalogue. The curators would like to acknowledge the study by Romare Bearden and Harry Henderson, *A History of African-American Artists from 1792 to the Present* (New York: Pantheon Books, 1993), an indispensable resource for research on the artists presented here.

For their assistance with securing copyright permissions, the Boston University Art Gallery would like to thank: Amalia Amaki, Brooke Anderson, Félicie Balay, Avis Berman, Patricia Sue Canterbury, Lynne Clifford, Jackie Cox-Crite, Lisa L. Crane, Susan Earle, Charles Eldredge, Karen Fairbank, Margo Feiden, Tarin M. Fuller, Ann Eden Gibson, Eric Hanks, Sarah Henrich, Janet Hicks, Bill Hodges, Stella Jones, Joshua Kaufman, Amy Kurtz Lansing, Tammi Lawson, Theresa Leininger-Miller, Samella Lewis, Richard Long, John Magill, Grace Matthews, Paula Mazzotta, Mary Fernanda Meza, Nancy Mirsky, Caitlin Miller, Sandy Paci, Wendy Wick Reaves, Michael Rosenfeld, Luise Ross, Maggie Seidel, Grace Stanislaus, Marty Stein, Cledie Taylor, Sherry Washington, Janie Welker, and C. Ian White.

For their excellent work on this publication, we thank Paul Hoffmann, John Stinehour, Dan Craven, and the entire staff of The Stinehour Press in Lunenburg, Vermont. Patricia Johnston, Gwendolyn DuBois Shaw, Jeffrey Stewart, and Kevin Whitfield read all or some of the manuscripts with care. We would also like to thank Chris Pierson for editing the text. We are grateful to Jan and Warren Adelson for their generous support since 1997 of the graduate students studying American art at Boston University. We thank Jeffrey Henderson, Dean of the College of Arts and Sciences at Boston University, for his continued support. Katherine T. O'Connor, Director, Frances Heaton, Administrator, and the Humanities Foundation, College of Arts and Sciences and Graduate School of Arts and Sciences at Boston University, generously sponsored this publication.

STACEY McCARROLL
Director & Curator
Boston University Art Gallery

MY FRIENDS GEORGE AND JOYCE WEIN

By Ed Bradley

GOING TO DINNER at Joyce and George Wein's apartment is like visiting a jewel of a museum that specializes in African American art. Their collection runs the gamut from A to Z. I mean that literally, because you will see everything from the Harlem Renaissance painter Charles Alston to that wonderful chronicler of life in Harlem, the photographer James Van Der Zee. Even when you've been there a dozen times, there is often something that will catch your eye and give you the feeling that you are seeing one of their paintings for the first time. It's like visiting old friends and learning something new and wonderful about them.

The first painting they bought was Romare Bearden's *New Orleans Farewell*. It resonated with George because his life had been so involved with New Orleans, both the music and the politics. George and Joyce helped end segregation in that city through their first Jazz and Heritage Festival in 1970, which brought musicians and patrons, black and white, together in the same venue. In those days that was revolutionary because New Orleans was one of the most segregated cities in the country. Bearden opened the door of his life to George and Joyce, and in walking through that door they took a stroll not just through his history but through the history of the world of African American art. It was no coincidence that Bearden was so involved in jazz, and that was the connection that drew them together. Look at the back of the bus in the painting by Jacob Lawrence and you know that George knew what that life was like because of his pioneering work with musicians. In those days, they had to ride in the back of the bus or in their own cars.

George and Joyce did their homework; collecting art was like collecting knowledge. They didn't just buy paintings. They studied the artists and *then* they bought their art. As their knowledge grew, so did their collection. They read about William Johnson and then one day Joyce noticed a painting in the corner of a gallery. Today it hangs in their dining room. Faith Ringgold had an exhibition of her quilts, including *Matisse's Chapel*. Well, that chapel is just five minutes from the Weins' home in Vence. Of course they had to buy it; it was a natural. Bob Thompson was a great friend of the musicians Ornette Coleman and Charlie Haden. There is a lyrical quality to his work. It fit well in George and Joyce's collection. Look at all of their art today and you will see the music in their lives; you will see the broad sweep of their knowledge, their collection, and their taste.

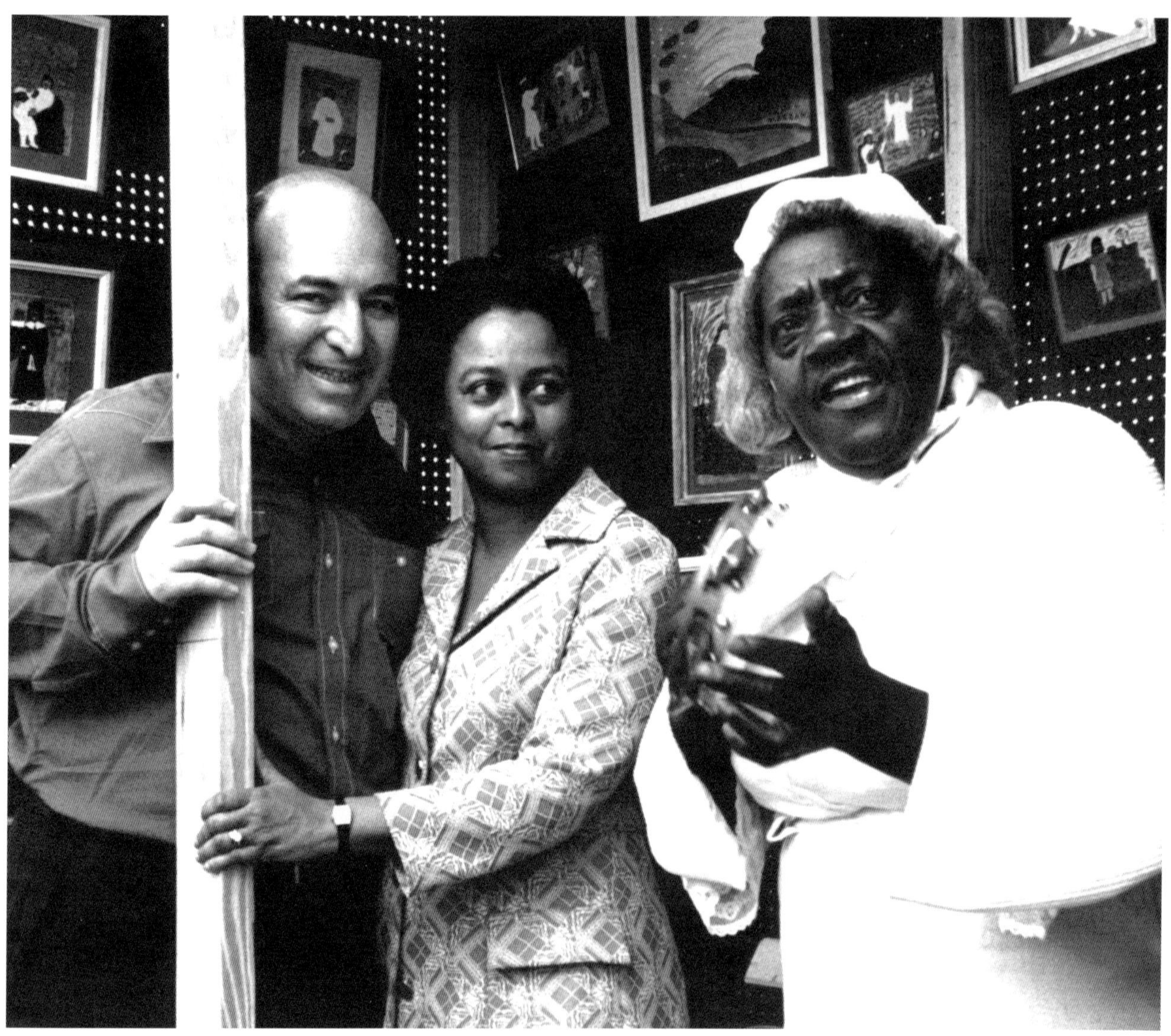

Jules Cahn, *New Orleans Jazz Festival: Sister Gertrude, George and Joyce,* 1973. George and Joyce Wein with Sister Gertrude Morgan in her booth at the New Orleans Jazz & Heritage Festival in the New Orleans Fairgrounds.

THE EXPRESSIVE MODERNISM OF 20TH-CENTURY AFRICAN AMERICAN ART

By Patricia Hills

WILLIAM T. WILLIAMS, one of the artists in the exhibition *Syncopated Rhythms: 20th-Century African American Art from the George and Joyce Wein Collection*, recalls George Wein's visit to his New York studio a few years ago. Wein took time to look carefully through the racks of paintings in Williams's studio: "It's rare to have an experience with a collector . . . where he had been so involved in the thing that involved me so much—music. It was like a validation of the paintings for me. There was something that Wein connected to in the work. And I hope that *something* is a continuum of the humanity he connects to in the music as well."[1] For Williams, Wein had grasped the expressive modernism of *Carolina Shout* that the artist had worked to achieve in his paintings, just as Wein has always understood the essential modernity of the jazz tradition. Jazz changed American culture. An active life in music had prepared George Wein to recognize the jazz "soul" within Williams's painting and within the many other works in the collection he and Joyce Wein have gathered in the last few decades.

George Wein is well known as the founder of the Newport Jazz Festival, back in the summer of 1954. Joyce Alexander Wein has helped him organize many other jazz and music festivals over the years, throughout the world.[2] Less known are their love of the visual arts and their efforts to assemble what is clearly a museum-quality collection of African American art. George comes to his appreciation of art through his family. The paintings of Boston artist Louis Kronberg, a distant cousin, hung in the Wein family's home in Brookline, Massachusetts. Kronberg, who lived abroad in his later life, took the young Wein to Paris galleries and lectured him on art. Later, as a Boston University undergraduate, Wein took an art history class. Joyce, a Simmons College student when she met George at a jazz concert in 1947, knew artists at the School of the Museum of Fine Arts, just a few blocks from Simmons. After a long courtship they married in March 1959, just before they were to embark on the first European tour of the Newport Jazz Festival.

The Weins made their first purchase of artwork by an African American when they bought Romare

1. William T. Williams, taped interview with Patricia Hills, 12 July 2005.
2. See George Wein with Nate Chinen, *Myself Among Others: A Life in Music* (Cambridge, Massachusetts: Da Capo Press, 2003).

Bearden's *New Orleans Farewell*. They had already purchased many modern European works, including paintings by Jean Dubuffet and Joan Míro, but Bearden opened their eyes to African American art—its characteristics and possibilities. Bearden, in turn, was close to Stuart Davis, an early twentieth-century modernist who was about twenty years older and a jazz enthusiast. From Davis, Bearden learned to listen to the "intervals" (the steps or breaks) in an Earl Hines piano composition and to apply the lessons of jazz—coloration, rhythms, intervals—to painting. Bearden told one biographer: "Stuart used to say, 'You've got to look at varying things. Say you have people walking—you have to consider these things as musical beats; you don't want to have just dot dot dot dot.' . . . Most people differentiate color and form. But for Stuart, these things were one: color, form—all of them affecting each other. . . ."[3] About Davis's lesson on intervals, Bearden elaborated: "[T]he interval is what you're leaving out. But . . . these intervals . . . reinforce the more solid forms and objects. . . . [I]t is the spacing of what you leave out that makes what is *in* there."[4] Davis came to his ideas about art-making through his experiences as a youth frequenting the barrelhouses of Newark, where he heard ragtime and other music coming North with the Great Migration. When the two artists got to know each other in the 1940s, Davis was taking the pictorial structures of his early compositions from the 1920s and riffing over them with new color combinations, creating jazzy pictures like *Hot Still-Scape for Six Colors—Seventh Avenue Style*, 1940 (Museum of Fine Arts, Boston).[5] Davis's and Bearden's understanding about intervals is essentially an update to the Cubists' interest in "negative spaces," where the shapes of space between forms take an emphasis equal to or exceeding the forms themselves. In other words, what should be unstressed gets stressed.

This brings us to what is perhaps the defining practice of ragtime— "syncopation"—which the Random House dictionary defines as "a shifting of the normal accent, usually by stressing the normally unaccented beats."[6] The generation of African American artists who came of age in the 1920s, when ragtime was evolving into jazz and our story begins, did just that in their art. They shifted the beats and emphasized subjects (African Americans in American life) rarely shown in American museums and art galleries. In their styles also, they probed the images and sensations of their memories of African American cultural practices to produce the unexpected. Beginning with Palmer Hayden and continuing with Jacob Lawrence, up to the present day with Benny Andrews, many African American painters, even those academically trained as artists, consciously gravitated to off-beat syncopated styles—such as folk styles, simplified forms, and silhouetted shapes, rather than the Western tradition of chiaroscuro painting. Some, like Bearden in the early 1960s, embraced a cubist collage style, knowing full well that African art had inspired the early French Cubists, who themselves had rejected academic art. Bending the rules, skipping the felicities of academic painting techniques, choosing often to incorporate collage elements into their work, and expressing their lived experiences all characterize the modus operandi of many of these artists. Hayden, who won prizes for his seascapes, later stated that artists could be

3. Quoted in Myron Schwartzman, *Romare Bearden: His Life and Art* (New York: Harry N. Abrams, Inc., 1990), 107.
4. Ibid., 111.
5. See Patricia Hills, *Stuart Davis* (New York: Harry N. Abrams, 1996), 18–21.
6. *The Random House Dictionary of the English Language: The Unabridged Edition* (New York: Random House, 1966).

ruined by too much academic training. By rejecting "art as usual" the artists in the Wein collection transformed themselves into modernist artists—but, like jazz, it was a modernism on their own terms.

* * *

What the artists in the Wein collection share is a common struggle to become modern artists—with many having to surmount daunting obstacles, including poverty and bigotry. But all of them also had a parent, a teacher, several teachers, or older, more seasoned artists, who served as role models, gave them books to read, and encouraged them. In Harlem, Arthur A. Schomburg, curator of the 135th Street branch of the New York Public Library, mounted exhibitions of African and African American art on the walls of the reading room that made an impression on young artists, such as Jacob Lawrence. The artists discovered patrons and organizations that would hire them to work at jobs related to their art training, or that would provide funds so they could travel to Europe, Mexico, or the Caribbean, where they might find a more congenial and stimulating environment in which to study and make art than the one in the United States. Artists encouraged each other. Many knew each other from art school, from showing in the same exhibitions, from frequenting the same Paris cafés, from joining artists' associations, from walking the union picket lines during the 1930s, or from protesting the exclusionary policies of the big museums during the 1960s and 1970s.

In addition to Bearden, many of the artists in the Wein collection associated themselves with musicians and found inspiration in music. Some made jazz the subject of their art; others simply listened while they painted.[7] In the 1920s Joseph Delaney frequented jazz spots in Chicago and painted portraits of Eubie Blake, Mahalia Jackson, and others. In the 1930s Charles Alston knew jazz singers Billie Holiday, Ethel Waters, and Bessie Smith, and sketched singers and musicians during recording sessions in New York. Some worked in the music industry. Miles Davis, the great jazz trumpet player, began making abstract paintings in the 1980s. During the 1950s Romare Bearden associated with musicians and even wrote lyrics for popular songs. Bearden and Benny Andrews designed record album jackets for jazz groups; Ernie Barnes designed a Motown jacket for Marvin Gaye. And as a young artist, Hughie Lee-Smith performed as a modern dancer in Cleveland.

It comes as no surprise that African art inspired a number of these artists. Howard University philosophy professor Alain Locke, a major figure in the Harlem Renaissance, collected and wrote about African art. In his essay "The Legacy of the Ancestral Arts," published in *The New Negro* (1925), an anthology he edited, Locke urged artists to study African art and learn from its "wealth of decorative and purely symbolic material" and its discipline: "But what the Negro artist of to-day has most to gain from the arts of the forefathers is perhaps not cultural inspiration or technical innovations, but the lesson of a classic background, the lesson of discipline, of style, of technical control pushed to the limits of technical mastery. . . . If, after absorbing the new content of American life and experience, and after assimilating new patterns of art, the original artistic endowment can be sufficiently augmented to

7. Richard J. Powell in his exhibition catalogue *The Blue Aesthetic: Black Culture and Modernism* (Washington, D.C.: Washington Project for the Arts, 1989) argues that a "blues aesthetic" is not confined to only one race, and he includes Stuart Davis in this category.

express itself with equal power in more complex patterns and substance, then the Negro may well become what some have predicted, the artist of American life."[8] To Locke, African American artists would then take their rightful place at the center of modernism, not at its margins.

Charles Alston recalled first seeing African art in Locke's collection and being overwhelmed by its strength and beauty. Eldzier Cortor, as a student at the School of the Art Institute of Chicago, spent his time in Chicago's Field Museum studying African art, which he credits for influencing his own stylistic development. A major event for artists in Harlem was the large exhibition of African art held at the Museum of Modern Art in 1935, which both Bearden and Lawrence saw as young artists. Lawrence even began to carve wooden sculptures like the ones he had seen in the exhibition.[9] African art, like African music, challenged the imperial authority of the Western canon and in doing so jump-started the creation of modern twentieth-century culture.

The history and contemporary culture of African Americans generated subjects for many artists, who realized that through art they could communicate some of their own experiences as well as those of communities affected by the Great Migration. This migration of African Americans from the South to the North from about 1910–70 relocated more than six and a half million people,[10] which resulted in a blending of expressive cultural styles and a consolidation of community. A witness to the early waves of the migration, Locke remarked in 1925: "Each group has come with its own separate motives and for its own special ends, but their greatest experience has been the finding of one another."[11] Blues and jazz came up with the migrants from the Delta and flourished in those communities in the North created by the Great Migration.

Artists wanted to tell this important, but largely invisible, story in United States history. Jacob Lawrence, after painting his series celebrating the lives of African American heroes, tackled the subject of the Great Migration in sixty paintings done in 1940–41. In the 1940s Palmer Hayden and William H. Johnson followed with their history series. The three artists also painted scenes of the everyday community life of African Americans. Eldzier Cortor sought to paint the beauty of African American women, and Charles White painted the struggles of African Americans to achieve justice and civil rights. John Biggers brought the patterning of quilts and African textiles to his scenes of Southern shotgun houses. Bearden painted his memories of the farms, gardens, and sporting houses of the South as well as his experiences of the music played by his jazz friends. Even in art school, Benny Andrews chose to sketch the African Americans living on Chicago's South Side rather than school models. Self-taught artists Sister Gertrude Morgan, Minnie Evans, and Bruce Brice worked in their own unique styles to express their religious experiences (Morgan), visions (Evans), and social experiences of life in New Orleans (Brice). Memories of the cultural practices of their own communities generate even the most abstract paintings in the collection—those done by Norman Lewis and William T. Williams.

8. Alain Locke, "The Legacy of the Ancestral Arts," in *The New Negro: An Interpretation*, Alain Locke, ed. (New York: Albert and Charles Boni, 1925), 256.

9. Ellen Harkins Wheat, *Jacob Lawrence: American Painter* (Seattle: University of Washington Press, 1986), 36.

10. Nicholas Lemann, *The Promised Land: The Great Black Migration and How It Changed America* (New York: Alfred A. Knopf, 1991), 6.

11. Locke, 6.

Artists who achieve recognition and fame do so because of the encouragement from individuals who taught them the techniques of art-making, bolstered their self-confidence, and paved their way to recognition. The artists in this exhibition were no different from others in the history of art except—and this is a big exception—that they continuously had to confront the racism that kept them at the margins—in the general culture's negative space. The women artists had to confront gender discrimination as well. Yet teachers and mentors were there for them, showing them the way to the center. Artists Charles Hawthorne and George Luks raised funds for William H. Johnson to study in Europe; W.E.B. Du Bois, the editor of the NAACP journal, *The Crisis*, sought to do the same for Augusta Savage. Sometimes a private patron, such as Alice M. Dike, stepped forward to provide needed funds, as she did for Hayden.

Philanthropic institutions played a large role in supporting specifically African American artists. The Julius Rosenwald Fund, founded by and named for the president of the Sears Roebuck Company in 1917, sought to promote the education of racial minorities—by creating libraries and public schools in the South, establishing YMCA/YWCA branches in urban African American communities, and setting up a fellowship program for writers, artists, and public leaders.[12] In 1930 the directors were so impressed with Savage's *Gamin*, hung in a Harmon Foundation exhibition, that they gave her a fellowship to study in Europe. The Fund also awarded fellowships to Richmond Barthé, Aaron Douglas, Eldzier Cortor, Jacob Lawrence, Joseph Delaney, and Elizabeth Catlett.

Like the Julius Rosenwald Fund, the Harmon Foundation was run by white philanthropists focused on helping the careers of African American artists. Founded in the 1920s by William E. Harmon, a real estate developer, the Foundation was run with an iron hand by his assistant, Mary Beattie Brady, who set up a series of group exhibitions in New York in 1928, 1929, 1930, 1931, 1933, and 1935, with traveling shows for the years 1932 and 1934–35. In addition, the Foundation gave cash awards for "Outstanding Achievement" to civic leaders and creative artists. The artists who received gold or bronze medals included Hayden, William H. Johnson, and Hale Woodruff—all three of whom lived in Europe, in part because of Harmon Foundation support. Those exhibiting in the New York shows included Douglas, Savage, Barthé, Hayden, Johnson, Woodruff, Ellis Wilson, Loïs Mailou Jones, Beauford Delaney, and Allan Rohan Crite. Several African American artists, however, leveled harsh but legitimate criticism at Brady. Savage criticized her for using white jurors; Bearden, for "coddling and patronizing" the artists and using standards "that are both artificial and corrupt."[13]

During the mid- to late-1930s, in response to artists' demands, the federal government stepped in to support artists in need of relief. In December 1933 the first federal project set up to help artists was the Public Works of Art Project (PWAP). In New York Juliana Force, the Director of the Whitney Museum of American Art, took charge of the program, which operated until about April 1934. The Trea-

12. See "The Julius Rosenwald Fund," Special Collections Department, University of Virginia Library, posted on http://www.lib.virginia.edu/speccol/jdavis (7 August 2005).

13. For Brady and the Harmon Foundation see Romare Bearden and Harry Henderson, "Mary Beattie Brady," in *A History of African-American Artists from 1792 to the Present* (New York: Pantheon Books, 1993), 250–59; and Gary A. Reynolds and Beryl J. Wright, *Against the Odds: African-American Artists and the Harmon Foundation*. exh. cat. (Newark, New Jersey: The Newark Museum, 1989). Bearden's critique was published in "The Negro Artist and Modern Art," *Opportunity* 12 (December 1934): 371–72.

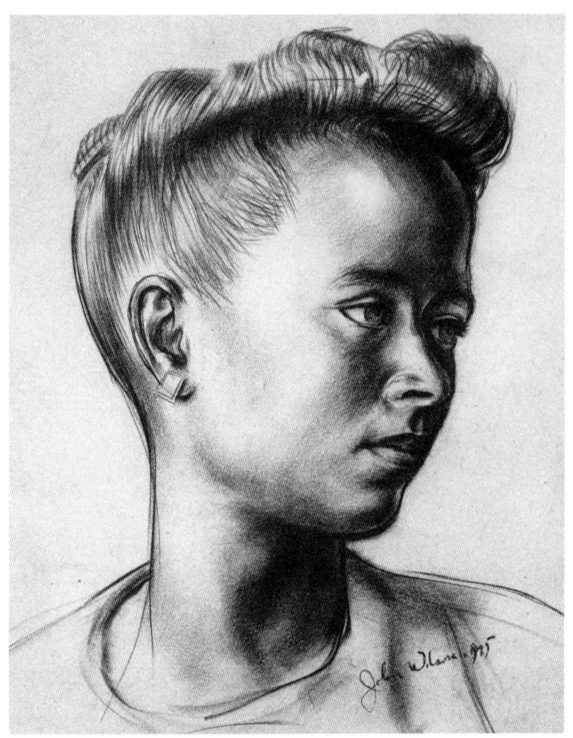

John Wilson, Joyce, *1945, pencil on paper, 18½ x 15 in. (46.9 x 38.1 cm).*

sury Department set up other programs, one of which (the "Section") commissioned artists to paint murals on the basis of juried competitions. The most ambitious program was the Federal Art Project (FAP), organized in August 1935 under the Works Progress Administration, which hired professional artists needing relief. Audrey McMahon, who was director of the College Art Association, and who knew Mary Brady, was put in charge of the New York FAP office. McMahon was well aware of the numerous African American artists qualified to work for one of the eight divisions under the FAP, including the Index of American Design and the separate divisions for easel painting, sculpture, prints, and murals, and she offered them jobs. The FAP artists received regular paychecks to work as artists; they had the satisfaction of seeing their work shown to the general public; and they developed a solidarity by working together within a multiracial group of artists and union organizers, many of whom were political radicals.[14]

Artists also generated their own organizations, which sustained them psychologically and spiritually. When the Harlem Artists Guild was founded in 1935, seventy-five artists joined; Douglas was elected president and Savage, vice-president. The Guild held their exhibitions at the Harlem YMCA and agitated government officials to permit African American artists to hold jobs as FAP supervisors. Charles Alston thus became the first black supervisor, in charge of the Harlem Hospital mural project.[15] Many Guild artists also were members of the Artists Union, and Douglas delivered a paper, "The Negro in American Culture," at the first American Artists Congress, held in February 1936.

During the 1960s, when the Civil Rights movement became a daily matter of concern, artists' organizations again became political, as they had in the 1930s. Romare Bearden held the first meeting of the artists' group *Spiral,* in February 1963 in his Canal Street studio. Woodruff, Alston, Lewis, James Yeargans, Felrath Hines, Richard Mayhew, and William Pritchard attended the meeting. Other artists, such as Emma Amos, subsequently joined the group to discuss the role of artists in Civil Rights struggles, and to plan an exhibition. In January 1969 Benny Andrews helped organize the Black Emergency Cultural Coalition (BECC) to protest the *Harlem on My Mind* exhibition at the Metropolitan

14. For a general history of the projects, see Richard D. McKenzie, *The New Deal for Artists* (Princeton, New Jersey: Princeton University Press, 1973).
15. Bearden and Henderson, 238.

Museum of Art. In 1971 Faith Ringgold and others organized an exhibition of the art of African American women, called *Where We At.* Meanwhile, when the Studio Museum in Harlem was founded in the late 1960s, with the participation of Bearden, the trustees called on William T. Williams to set up the Artists-in-Residence program. Michael Kelly Williams was later a Fellow in the program. On the West Coast Betye Saar was active in both the feminist and Black Arts movements.

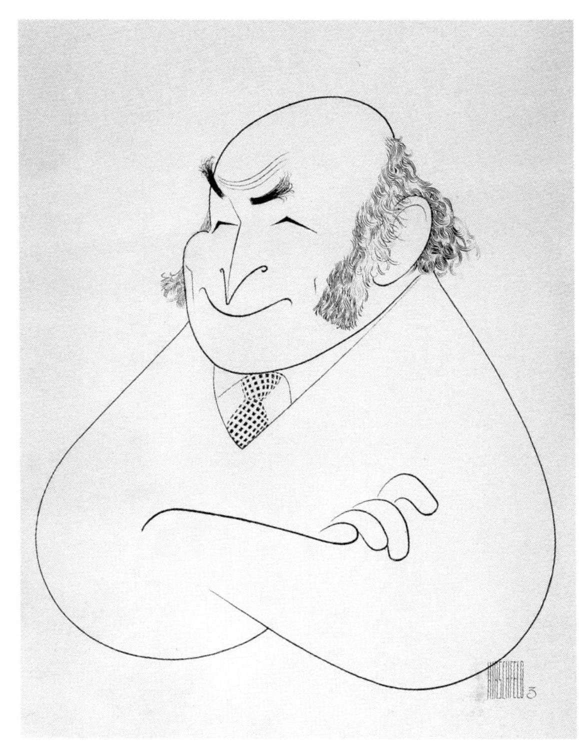

Al Hirschfeld, George Wein, *n.d., pen on paper, 25 x 19 in. (63.5 x 48.3 cm).*

Artists also initiated their own workshops: "306" was the address on West 141st Street in Harlem where Alston and Henry W. Bannarn taught FAP art classes in the 1930s, while Savage was teaching at her own Savage Studio of Arts and Crafts. Many artists went on to found or teach in art departments in historically black colleges: Loïs Mailou Jones at Howard University; Hale Woodruff at Atlanta University; Elizabeth Catlett at Dillard University; and Aaron Douglas at Fisk University. During the early 1970s Andrews and Ringgold also taught art to prisoners at Riker's Island.

The post–World War II years saw an exodus of African American artists going abroad, especially after returning soldiers described Europe to them. Many chose Paris, where there were art treasures to be seen, internationally known teachers to study with, cheap living, and an escape from American Jim Crow segregation compounded by a hostile Cold War cultural environment. Bearden studied in Paris for many months during 1950. Beauford Delaney lived the expatriate life in France beginning in 1953 and developed close friendships with James Baldwin and others; he died there in 1979. Bob Thompson went to Paris in 1960 and lived in Europe off and on until his death in Rome in 1966. Miles Davis went to Europe as a musician; his quintet played in Louis Malle's 1957 film noir *Ascenseur pour l'échafaud* (*Elevator to the Gallows*). Wifredo Lam spent decades in Europe, away from his native Cuba; we now consider him a key player in the Surrealist movement.

More radical artists wanting to continue the tradition of political commentary such as Elizabeth Catlett, Charles White, and John Wilson, went to Mexico in the late 1940s and 1950s, where they studied the art of the leftist Mexican muralists and participated in print workshops. And still others who wanted to learn about African culture, such as John Biggers and Jacob Lawrence, went to Africa for extended stays; Michael Kelly Williams and William T. Williams had shorter sojourns in Africa.

The Weins have developed personal relationships with many of these artists, with music often providing the occasion for socializing. Joyce Wein has known John Wilson since her days at Simmons College; it was she who introduced Wilson to classical music by insisting he attend concerts at the Boston Symphony Orchestra. Richard Yarde recalls frequenting George Wein's Storyville club in Boston during the 1950s.[16] Oliver Johnson once went with Wein to hear Miles Davis, and another time they heard Benny Goodman.[17] Sister Gertrude Morgan set up a booth to sell her work during the New Orleans Jazz & Heritage Festival, which George Wein organized.

George Wein also had a special and long-term relationship with Miles Davis. Davis played at Wein's Storyville nightclub and at the Newport Jazz Festivals. In his book, *Myself Among Others: A Life in Music*, Wein recalls many encounters with Davis, including gifts of paintings. In 1991, the year Davis died, the musician/artist gave Wein a painting at dinner following a ceremony inducting the two into the French Légion d'Honneur.[18]

George and Joyce Wein know how to listen to artists. George, in a conversation in early 2005, maintained that viewing a painting is a different experience to him from listening to music, but in each case he listens to the voice: "An artist compromises when he finds his voice . . . and then stops searching. Picasso never stopped searching. How many voices do you have to have in life? If you have one voice, that's original, that's something. Picasso had six or seven. Very few jazz musicians can do that. Erroll Garner was one of the great piano players of all time, and people say he didn't do anything new, but what he did was one of the most original."[19]

The artists in the Wein Collection exemplify those who have a single, strong original voice, such as Jacob Lawrence and Hughie Lee-Smith, and those who developed several strong voices, such as Norman Lewis and Romare Bearden. Together the Weins have changed the way we respond to music—by hearing jazz as modern, as vernacular, as intellectual, and as vital to our culture. The art they have collected does that too, and shows that the works of African American artists were central to twentieth-century expressive modernism.

16. Richard Yarde, taped interview with Melissa Renn, 19 July 2005.
17. Oliver Johnson, telephone interview with Melissa Renn, 26 July 2005.
18. Wein, 470–71.
19. George Wein, taped interview with Patricia Hills, 4 February 2005. Regarding Garner, see Wein, 89–90.

CATALOGUE

CHARLES ALSTON • (1907–1977)

Untitled, 1952

Oil on canvas, 20 x 16 in. (50.8 x 40.7 cm)

Charles Henry Alston was born on 28 November 1907 in Charlotte, North Carolina, the youngest of five children of Primus Priss Alston, an Episcopalian minister, and Anna Elizabeth Miller Alston. Alston's father died when he was three, and his mother married Henry Bearden, an uncle of Romare Bearden. In 1915 the family relocated to New York, but Alston stayed in Charlotte with his grandparents to finish the school year. In subsequent years he spent his summers in Charlotte.

Alston graduated from DeWitt Clinton High School in New York, where he served as the art editor of the school magazine. In 1929 he enrolled at Columbia University. After graduation he won a scholarship for the Master's program at Columbia Teachers College. During his student years he supported himself by working at an after school program, Utopia House, where he taught Jacob Lawrence.

Romare Bearden and Harry Henderson, who interviewed Alston in 1969, emphasize the point that a major influence on Alston in the 1920s was African art, which he got to know through Alain Locke, who invited Alston to help install an exhibition of African art at the 135th Street Public Library. At the same time, at Columbia, Charles Martin was teaching him both old-master European painting techniques and a modern art outlook.[1] The result was not so much a synthesis of these influences as an eclectic approach to experimenting with art styles throughout his career. Over the course of his career the various influences on his art included Modigliani, Picasso, El Greco, Jules Pascan, the Mexican muralists, and Egyptian and Oceanic art. This eclecticism made him an excellent teacher who refused to dictate styles to his students.

During the Depression of the 1930s Alston took a leadership role in developing Harlem as an exciting art milieu. His studio at 306 West 141st Street, which he shared with Henry Bannarn, became a center where young artists came to work, talk, and socialize. He was also active in the Harlem Artists Guild. When the Federal Art Project (FAP) of the Works Progress Administration (WPA) was created in August 1935, Alston joined the easel division but later transferred to the mural division as a supervisor. He took charge of assigning artists to various mural projects within the Harlem Hospital complex. His own pair of murals, *Magic in Medicine* and *Modern Medicine*, created for the lobby entrance at 136th Street, at first generated a negative response from the Superintendent of New York City Hospitals, who claimed they had too much "Negro subject matter" which might offend future residents.[2] At Harlem Hospital Alston met his future wife, Dr. Myra A. Logan. In 1938 he left the FAP and spent the next two years painting in the South on a Julius Rosenwald Fund fellowship.[3]

Also during the 1930s Alston came to know leading jazz musicians and singers, such as Billie Holiday, Ethel Waters, and Bessie Smith, whom he sketched at recording sessions. The famous jazz record producer John Hammond credits Alston for introducing him to musicians and cutting-edge concepts: "He quite literally changed my life, helped me to insights I would never have discovered on my own."[4] Blues singers and groups became part of his repertory of subjects, and he also designed record jackets.

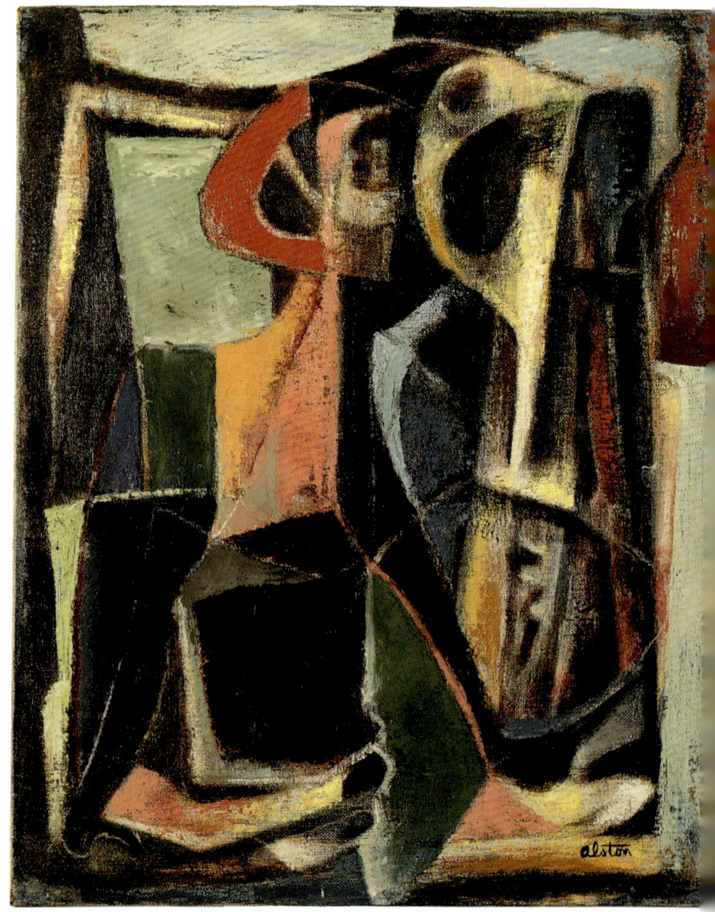

When World War II began Alston worked for the Office of War Information designing posters and drawing cartoons. Although drafted into the infantry, he never finished basic training, because his commanding officer immediately gave him a desk job that drew on his art training—producing visual training aids.

Following the war Alston decided to be a commercial artist. He took art courses at Pratt Institute and began working for major advertising agencies and book publishers, but soon grew dissatisfied. The commission he, along with his friend Hale Woodruff, received to design and paint a large mural on the contribution of African Americans to California's history for the headquarters of Golden State Mutual Life Insurance Company in Los Angeles must have stiffened his resolve to leave the commercial art business. In 1950 the Metropolitan Museum of Art purchased one of his abstract paintings out of its contemporary art exhibition. During the remainder of the 1950s Alston painted and sculpted as well as taught—at the Art Students League, from 1950–71, and then at City College of New York until 1977. He responded to political events in some of his paintings, such as *Walking*, 1958 (Private Collection, Chicago), which recalls various civil rights marches; others were abstractions. At the end of his life he received awards and recognition. In 1969 Mayor John V. Lindsay appointed him to the New York City Art Commission. He stayed active until his death from cancer, on 27 April 1977.

Untitled, in the Wein collection, typifies his 1950s abstract works. In 1969 he described his working methods to Bearden and Henderson:

> All of my paintings start very abstractly. I just throw some color on the canvas, push it around, and then sit back and relax and look at it, and various patterns become suggestive and sometimes an idea reveals itself with a great deal of strength. You look at it and then you push the painting in that direction. Then it becomes a conscious thing.
>
> The first part is completely intuitive, just pushing around paint the way you feel, and then you look at the shapes and features and they suggest things in terms of what you are thinking about, or that are unconsciously on your mind. When you see it, you begin developing it. That's the way most of my painting begins.[5]

In *Untitled* the viewer can begin to think of the work as Alston might have, and, indeed, Alston would have encouraged the viewer to use her or his imagination. What seems to emerge within the composition are two forms that are not quite figures. We perhaps see a shoulder at the left with perhaps a dark blue sleeve cascading vertically down to a shape that might be an arm resting on a ledge or table. Perhaps a head attached to that shoulder leans to the right, inclining toward what might be a second figure. Where is the head of that figure? Is it a void? Or is it the small blue oval shape that recedes into the background in the upper right? Perhaps Alston in *Untitled* is commenting on our propensity to bring humanity, if not order, to our abstract meditations. P.H.

BIBLIOGRAPHY

Alston, Charles. Interview with Dr. Harlan Phillips, 28 September 1965, Archives of American Art, Smithsonian Institution, Roll 4210.

Bearden, Romare and Harry Henderson. "Charles H. Alston," in *A History of African-American Artists from 1792 to the Present*. New York: Pantheon Books, 1993.

Linden, Diana. "Charles Alston's Harlem Hospital Murals: Cultural Politics in Depression Era Harlem," *Prospects: A Journal of American Studies*, v. 26 (2001): 391–422.

1. Bearden and Henderson, 261–62.
2. See Linden.
3. Charles Alston, interview with Dr. Harlan Phillips, 28 September 1965, typescript, p. 16, Archives of American Art, Smithsonian Institution, Roll 4210.
4. John Hammond, letter to Aida Winters Wishonant (Alston's half sister), 19 May 1977, read at a funeral service, quoted in Bearden and Henderson, 263.
5. Quoted in Bearden and Henderson, 269.

BENNY ANDREWS • (born 1930)

Angel, 1977

Collage of painted acrylic, canvas, cloth, rope and terry cloth on canvas
76 x 45 in. (193.1 x 114.3 cm)

Benny Andrews grew up on a farm near Madison, Georgia, where he was born on 13 November 1930, the second of ten children. His father, George Andrews, a tenant farmer at the onset of the Depression, had talents in music and art. His mother, Viola Andrews, had instilled in her children ambitions to go into the arts. During the Depression, George and Viola moved into a two-room house, residing there from 1935–43. George got a job on the Works Progress Administration digging ditches, the best he could do in the South at that time. Benny's brother Raymond, who later became a novelist, recalled the family's cultural obsession with reading magazines and newspapers, such as *The Atlanta Constitution*, read daily, and other publications when they could get them, such as *Life, Look, Collier's, The Saturday Evening Post,* and the black publications *Ebony, The Chicago Defender,* and *The Pittsburgh Courier*.[1]

In 1948 Andrews, the first in his extended family to finish high school, left home for Fort Valley State College on a partial scholarship. After two years he joined the U.S. Air Force, serving in the Korean War. In 1954, following his discharge, he entered the School of the Art Institute of Chicago. While going to school he found work illustrating record covers and spent his free time sketching people living on Chicago's South Side. In Chicago he also met Mary Ellen Jones Smith, and they later married. In 1958, with his B.F.A. in hand, the couple moved to New York's Lower East Side, where their first son was born a week later.

New York was a congenial place where Andrews met other artists, such as Bob Thompson, Red Grooms, Mimi Gross, and Lester Johnson, but it was a struggle to make ends meet. Mary Ellen went to work, and Andrews stayed home to care for the two boys (the second was born in 1959) and to paint. He was making only modest sales, although beginning to show his work—at the Pennsylvania Academy of the Fine Arts, the Detroit Institute of Arts, and finally a solo exhibition at Paul Kessler Gallery in Provincetown, Massachusetts. In 1962 his solo exhibition at the Forum Gallery garnered praise from critics at *The New York Times* and *The Herald Tribune*. More exhibiting opportunities came his way, and he moved into a larger loft studio. In 1964 his daughter was born, and he had another solo show at the Forum Gallery. In 1966 he started to teach drawing and painting classes at the New School for Social Research in New York, then moved to Queens College in 1968.[2]

At this time he began to be involved in the protests against the escalating Vietnam War. He met artists Rudolf Baranik, Irving Petlin, and Leon Golub, and participated in the "Collage of Indignation" exhibition held at the Loeb Student Center of New York University in 1967. He participated in demonstrations against the Metropolitan Museum's *Harlem on My Mind* exhibition, which opened in January 1969, and he helped organize the Black Emergency Cultural Coalition (BECC). The BECC met with officials of the Whitney Museum of American Art to protest its policies of discrimination, and also formed an alliance with the Art Workers Coalition.

In the early 1970s he divided his time between political action, painting, teaching, and exhibiting. With Baranik he put together the *Attica Book*, which included prison poetry and reproductions of works by artists protesting the handling of the riots at Attica Prison in 1971. His *Bicentennial Series* was exhibited at the High Museum in Atlanta in 1975, and subsequently traveled the country.

In 1977 he was elected to the Board of Directors of the College Art Association, and in 1982 he accepted a year's appointment as Director of the Visual Arts Program at the National Endowment for the Arts, where he hoped to make positive changes for women and African American artists. He stayed on at the NEA for a second year, then left to devote himself to his art, though he continued to be active in a number of artists' organizations. In 1986 he and Mary Ellen divorced, after years of separation. That summer he married sculptor Nene Humphrey. He continued to teach at Queens College until his retirement in 1997. Today he works in his loft in Brooklyn, and in Connecticut.

In 1985 Andrews held an exhibition with his father, George Andrews, a self-taught artist, at the Madison-Morgan Cultural Center; another joint exhibition followed at the Memphis Brooks Museum of Art in 1990, traveling to six other museums through 1992. Andrews has an affinity to his father's art, and credits his early family experiences for his desire to work in collage: "Ever since I can remember, Dad and I have made do with what we had, and we had about as close to nothing as one could imagine.

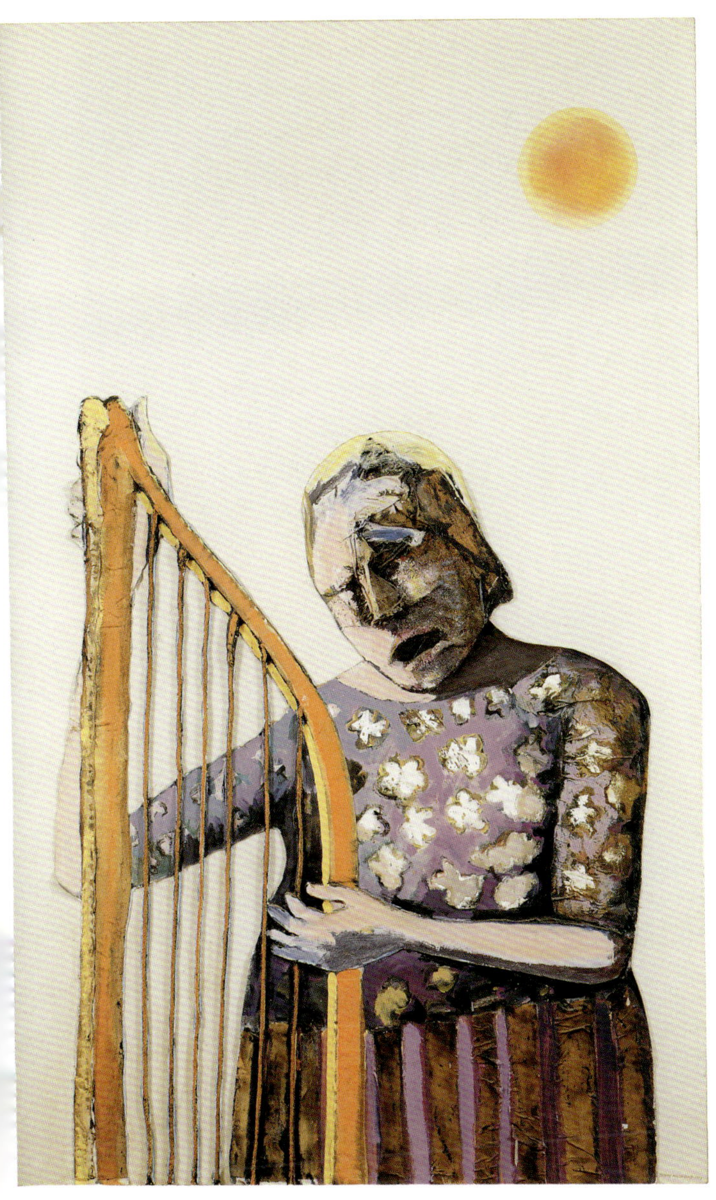

In fact, I'm sure that's why I started using collage, and continue to use it, because it allows me to take a seemingly nondescript scrap of fabric and create something artistic."[3]

Andrews works in two media. His pencil drawings are elegant outlines of figures, motifs, and landscape elements. His paintings, on the other hand, often are built up of pasted canvas, cardboard, and thick paint, as exemplified by *Angel*. He chose the subject from memories of his relatives telling children about how a recently deceased person would pass to heaven, where he or she would play the harp and enjoy the presence of other angels.[4] To create this image he used various found objects: the harp strings are lengths of rope, a piece of terry cloth forms one side of the angel's face, a fold of canvas creates the angel's nose. Not for the conventional person expecting angels to look like old master renderings, the image nevertheless has its own special beauty. His words from a 1990 interview are apt here: "I didn't want to lose my sense of rawness. Where I am from, the people are very austere. We have big hands. We have ruddy faces. We wear rough fabrics. We actually used the burlap bagging sacks that seed came in to make our shirts. These are my textures."[5] Like Palmer Hayden and Romare Bearden, Andrews is drawn to a vernacular tradition that evokes the cultural practices and treasured memories of plain folk working hard, living their lives, and enjoying themselves.

P.H.

BIBLIOGRAPHY

Bladon, Patricia P. *Folk: The Art of Benny and George Andrews*. exh. cat. Memphis: Memphis Brooks Museum of Art, 1990.

Fax, Elton C. *Seventeen Black Artists*. New York: Dodd, Mead and Company, 1971.

Gruber, J. Richard. *American Icons: From Madison to Manhattan, The Art of Benny Andrews, 1948–1997*. exh. cat. Augusta, Georgia: Morris Museum of Art, 1997.

1. Raymond Andrews, *The Last Radio Baby* (Atlanta: Peachtree Publishers, 1990), 180, noted in J. Richard Gruber, *The Dot Man: George Andrews of Madison, Georgia* (Augusta, Georgia: Morris Museum of Art, 1994), 13.
2. Much of this information is gleaned from Andrews's "Chronology," included in Gruber, 239–55.
3. Quoted in Judd Tully, "A Collage of Painterly Roots," Bladon, 28.
4. Benny Andrews, telephone interview with Patricia Hills, 9 July 2005.
5. Quoted in Bladon, 28.

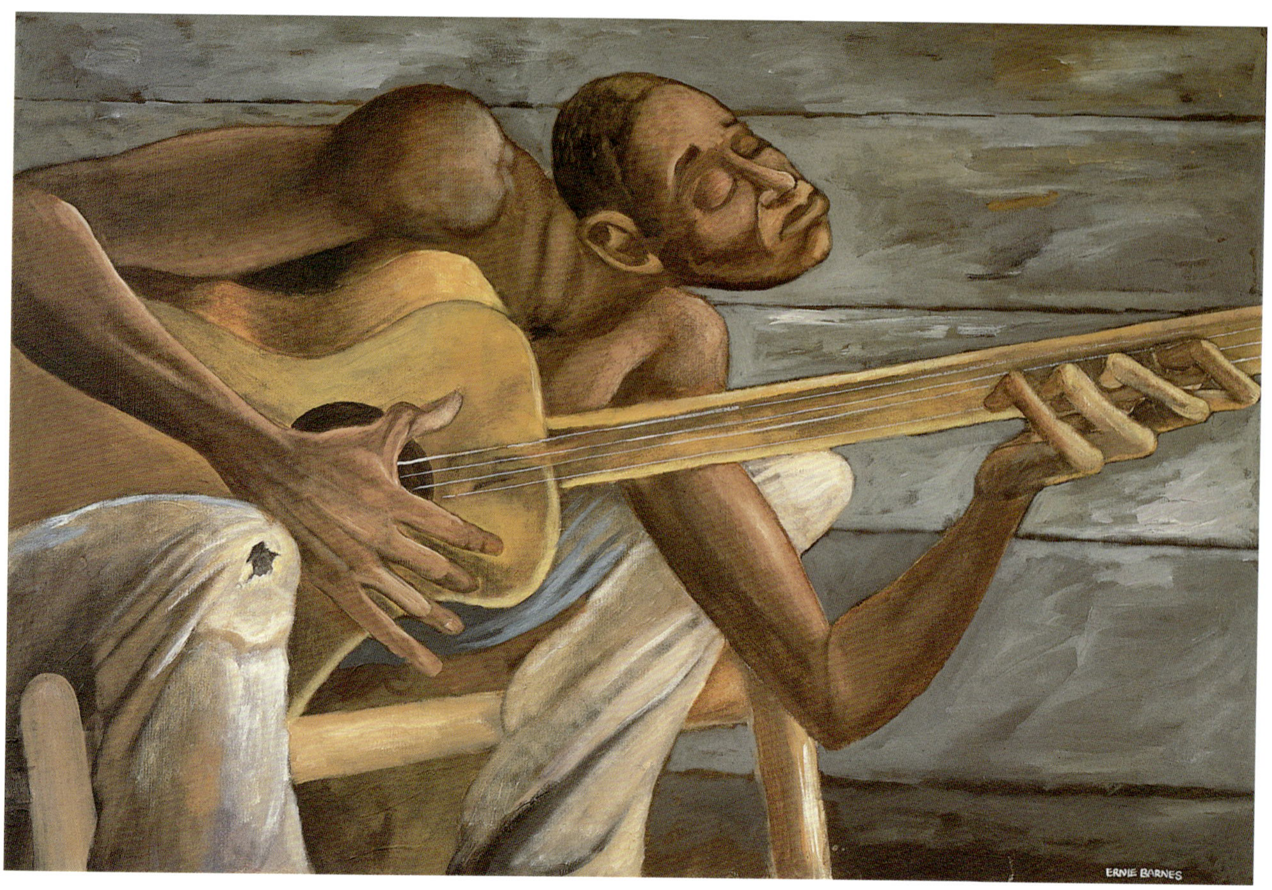

ERNIE BARNES • (born 1938)

Song of Myself, n.d.

Oil on canvas, 24 x 36 in. (60.9 x 91.4 cm)

The leading painter of sports subjects in the United States, Ernest Eugene Barnes, Jr., was born on 15 July 1938 in Durham, North Carolina. His father, Ernest Barnes, Sr., worked as a shipping clerk at Liggett Myers Tobacco Company; his mother, Fannie Mae Geer, was employed as a domestic. Barnes loved to draw and paint from an early age, but excelling in sports was much more respected in the African American community where he was raised. He attended Hillside High School, which was known statewide for its excellence in sports. With some reluctance, he joined the high school football team and became captain. When he graduated from high school in 1956, he had twenty-six scholarship offers to play football at the collegiate level, but none from his hometown college, Duke University, or the nearby University of North Carolina at Chapel Hill, as they did not recruit African American athletes at the time. Barnes therefore enrolled at the historically black North Carolina College (now North Carolina Central University), where he received a full four-year athletic scholarship.

Although he continued to participate in athletics, Barnes's passion was art. In college Barnes majored in Fine Art, studying with artist Ed Wilson, whom he credits as his greatest artistic influence. He had one of his first experiences with an art museum when Wilson took him on a tour of the recently desegregated North Carolina Museum of Art. He recalls, in his autobiography, how he asked a docent where the paintings by African American artists were located. Surprised by the question, the docent replied: "I'm afraid your people don't express themselves this way." When they got back to school, Wilson said to the class: "Now you know what you are up against,"[1] and proceeded to show slides of works by Henry Ossawa Tanner, Edmonia Lewis, Archibald J. Motley, Jr., Robert Duncanson, Hale Woodruff, and Palmer Hayden.

Upon graduation in 1960, Barnes was drafted into the National Football League as an offensive guard for the Baltimore Colts. He went on to play for the New York Titans, the San Diego Chargers and the Denver Broncos. Although he was an exceptional athlete, Barnes's primary interest was art: "Throughout my five seasons in the arena of professional football, I remained, at the deepest level of my being—an artist."

Barnes's interest in the human figure and depictions of movement stem from his lifelong experiences as an athlete. He is fascinated by "the tension caused by conflict and paradox," which informs many of his works. Many of his figural drawings and sports paintings depict athletes, both at play and at rest. Moreover, he chooses to work in a style he describes as neo-mannerist. He likes "the challenge of capturing movement. . . . The mannerist style lends itself to distortion, in order to reveal a truth that is difficult to capture in any other way. . . . For that reason the mannerist style appeals to me."[2] Barnes's subjects, characterized by elongated figures with an emphasis on movement, were greatly influenced by the Italian mannerist painters as well as by American painters George Bellows and Thomas Hart Benton. The works of Charles White also influenced Barnes. In his autobiography, Barnes recalls a significant moment while browsing in a Harlem bookstore when he came across a portfolio of reproductions of White's work. He was drawn to the confident, proud, and positive images of African Americans in White's drawings.

In addition to sports paintings, Barnes paints genre scenes depicting the everyday life of African Americans. His *Song of Myself*, painted in the 1970s, depicts a seated man playing a guitar. He describes the central figure as the kind of man

> . . . that I was exposed to when I was growing up in my hometown of Durham, North Carolina. It reveals, I think . . . the way that people who sang the blues, sang as a way of solving the blues. . . . I've become aware that music is an investigation of the black mind and reveals the inner world of what is really an oral culture. . . . [The title] is quite correct. The only thing [the guitar player] is exposed to is his own feelings. Singing was an avenue, of course, of expressing those feelings.

Barnes's genre scenes are well known. His 1976 painting *Sugar Shack* (Private Collection), which depicts a roadhouse dance scene, was featured in the credits for Norman Lear's popular 1970s television series *Good Times*, as well as on the cover of Marvin Gaye's 1976 album *I Want You*.

Barnes's first national exposure as an artist came in the early 1960s when *Sports Illustrated* reproduced his painting *The Bench*. In 1966 Sonny Werblin, owner of the New York Jets, helped organize a solo exhibition at Manhattan's Grand Central Art Galleries. Barnes retired from football in the early 1970s and moved to Los Angeles to pursue his dream of becoming a professional artist. He has received many honors as both an athlete and an artist, including his appointment as the official artist of the American Football League in 1966 and being named the first "Sports Artist of the Year" by the United States Sports Academy in 1984. That year, Barnes was also elected the Official Sports Artist for the Olympic Games in Los Angeles. In 1990, his alma mater, North Carolina Central University, gave him an honorary Doctorate of Fine Arts, and in 1993 he was chosen for the Sheridan Black Network's "All-Time Black College Football Team." In 2004 the American Sport Art Museum and Archives named Barnes "America's Best Painter of Sports."

Barnes currently lives in Studio City, California, with his wife, Bernadine, and continues to paint figurative works in his well-known neo-mannerist style. His recent work has commented on events in contemporary society, including his 1995 *A Dream Deferred* (Collection of Troy and Tommie Vincent), a visual response to the concept of repentance and return to responsibility as expressed in the Million Man March.[3] Most recently he has been commissioned to do a variety of works for prominent African Americans in the music industry, including a 1998 portrait of actor-singer Will Smith and his son, as well as a 2005 painting of musician Kanye West's near-death experience in a car accident, titled *A Life Restored*.

M.R.

BIBLIOGRAPHY

Barnes, Ernie. *From Pads to Palette*. Waco, Texas: WRS Publishing, 1995.

Riggs, Thomas, ed. "Ernie Barnes," in *St. James Guide to Black Artists*. Published in Association with the Schomburg Center for Research in Black Culture. Detroit: St. James Press, 1997.

1. Quoted in Barnes, 15.
2. Ernie Barnes, telephone interview with Melissa Renn, 6 July 2005; all subsequent quotations are from this interview.
3. Luz Rodriguez, e-mail to Melissa Renn, 3 August 2005.

RICHMOND BARTHÉ • (1901–1989)

Feral Benga (Benga: Dance Figure), 1935

Bronze, 18½ in. high (39.4 cm)

Sculptor James Richmond Barthé was born to Richmond Barthé, Sr., and Marie Clementine Robateau in Bay St. Louis, Mississippi, on 28 January 1901. A active participant in the Harlem Renaissance, Barthé was one of the first African American male sculptors to portray the black experience. His sculptures range from portrait busts of African American leaders, intellectuals and artists, including George Washington Carver, Booker T. Washington, Paul Robeson, and Judith Anderson, to works depicting African dancers, people, and culture.

Barthé left New Orleans in 1924 to study at the School of the Art Institute of Chicago. In Chicago Barthé met Archibald J. Motley, Jr., as well as painter Charles Schroeder, both of whom influenced him as an artist. Schroeder became a mentor to Barthé and encouraged him to work in the medium of sculpture. In 1929 Barthé moved to New York and studied at the Art Students League; his work was also featured in W.E.B. Du Bois's *Crisis* magazine, the journal of the National Association for the Advancement of Colored People (NAACP). In 1929 his work won an honorable mention at a Harmon Foundation exhibition. In 1930 he returned to Chicago and had his first public solo exhibition, featuring forty of his works at the Chicago Women's City Club. In 1929 and 1930 Barthé received consecutive Julius Rosenwald Fund fellowships, which enabled him to move to New York.

Once in New York, Barthé began to exhibit widely, including a solo exhibition at the Caz-Delbo Gallery in 1931, which brought him critical acclaim. Sculptor Gertrude Vanderbilt Whitney and Director of the Whitney Museum of American Arts, Juliana Force, saw Barthé's work at the Caz-Delbo exhibition and, impressed by his sculptural skills, included him in the Whitney Museum Annuals of 1933, 1940, 1944, and 1945. Force also added three of his sculptures to the Whitney's collection. Barthé continued to have great success in the art world: his work was included in the Metropolitan Museum of Art's *Artists for Victory* exhibition of 1942; the Pennsylvania Academy of the Fine Arts's annual exhibitions of 1938, 1940, 1943, and 1944; as well as solo exhibitions at the Arden Gallery, 1939; DePortes Inter-Racial Center, 1941; and International Print Society, 1945.

In 1934 Barthé traveled to Europe, where he became associated with the Négritude movement. A parallel movement to the Harlem Renaissance, Négritude was ini-

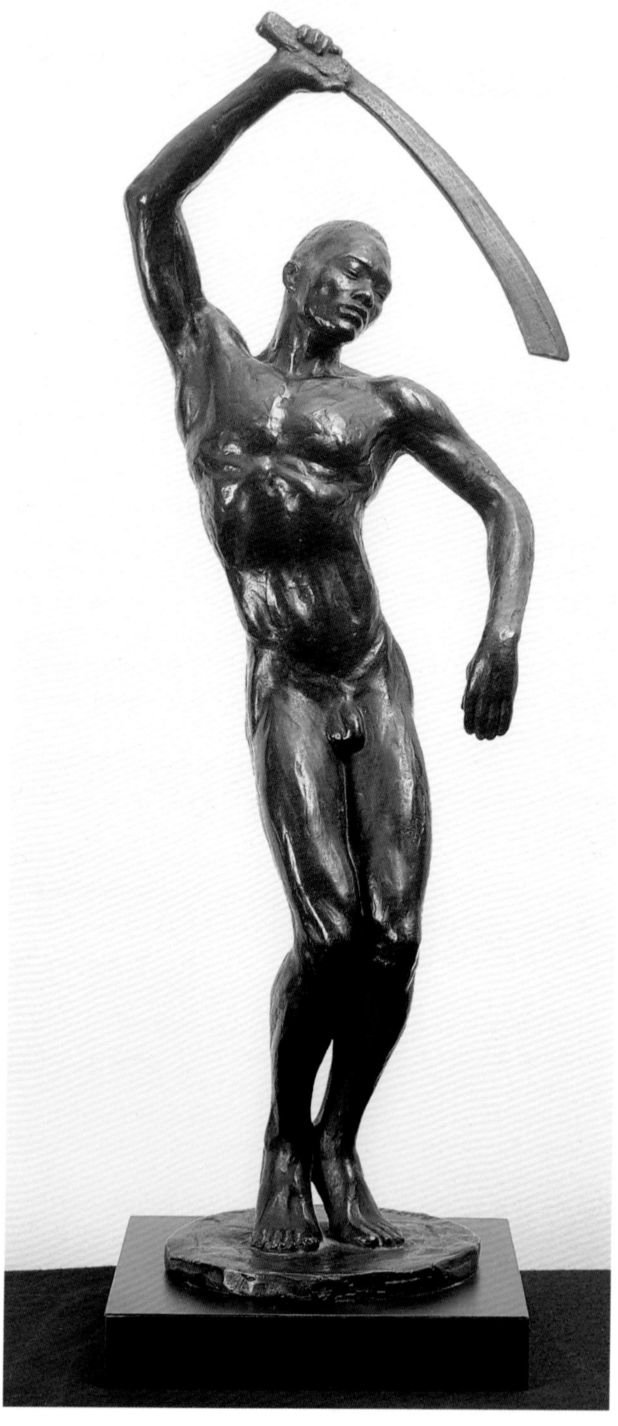

tiated by French-speaking West African and Caribbean artists and intellectuals and included artist Loïs Mailou Jones and poet Aimé Césaire. The movement, which developed in the midst of burgeoning modernism and jazz, celebrated African art and culture and believed in an exceptional "Negro personality," as well as a "mythic" pan-African soul.

One of only two known casts (the other is at the Newark Museum),[1] Barthé's *Feral Benga (Benga: Dance Figure)* embodies many qualities associated with both the Harlem Renaissance and Négritude. With a striking sensuality and expressive form, *Feral Benga* portrays Senegalese dancer François Benga (he changed his name to Feral when he moved to Paris), whom Barthé saw perform in Paris in 1934. Barthé, who was also a member of a modern dance group at Martha Graham's studio, was interested in dance, movement, and lyrical depictions of the body in sculpture. Many of his bronze sculptures, including *Feral Benga*, emphasize movement and recall ancient Egyptian forms.

Barthé received many honors throughout his career, including Guggenheim Fellowships in 1940 and 1941. In 1949 Barthé was elected to the National Academy of Arts and Letters. He was also active in many arts-related organizations, such as the National Sculpture Society, Audubon Artists, The Liturgical Arts Society, and the New York Clay Club. Barthé also participated actively in the Sculptors Guild, organizing a group showing at the 1939 World's Fair.

In 1937 Barthé was commissioned by the United States Treasury Department to create a series of bas-reliefs for the Harlem River Housing Project. During World War II Barthé made several sculptures depicting historic black generals, including Jean-Jacques Dessalines and Toussaint L'Ouverture. After the war, in 1951, Barthé left New York and moved to Jamaica. In the early 1960s he moved to Pasadena, where he continued to work until his death on 5 March 1989.

Although Richmond Barthé garnered much critical attention during the early twentieth century, during the postwar period interest in his figurative sculptures faded. Recently there has been a resurgence in critical attention to Barthé and his contributions as an African American sculptor to American art, including a forthcoming monograph by artist and art historian Samella Lewis. M.R.

BIBLIOGRAPHY

Bearden, Romare and Harry Henderson. "Richmond Barthé," in *A History of African-American Artists from 1792 to the Present*. New York: Pantheon Books, 1993.

Lewis, Samella S. *African American Art and Artists*. 3rd edition, revised and expanded. Berkeley: University of California Press, 2003.

Reynolds, Gary A. and Beryl J. Wright. *Against the Odds: African-American Artists and the Harmon Foundation*, exh. cat. New Jersey: The Newark Museum, 1989.

Vendryes, Margaret Rose. "Casting Feral Benga: A Biography of Richmond Barthé's Signature Work," from *Masters of African American Art: An Online Journal of Publications by Professional Scholars Grant Recipients*. http://www.artsnet.org/anyonecanfly/library/Vendryes_on_Barthe.html (3 August 2005).

1. Margaret Rose Vendryes, e-mail to Patricia Hills, 3 August 2005.

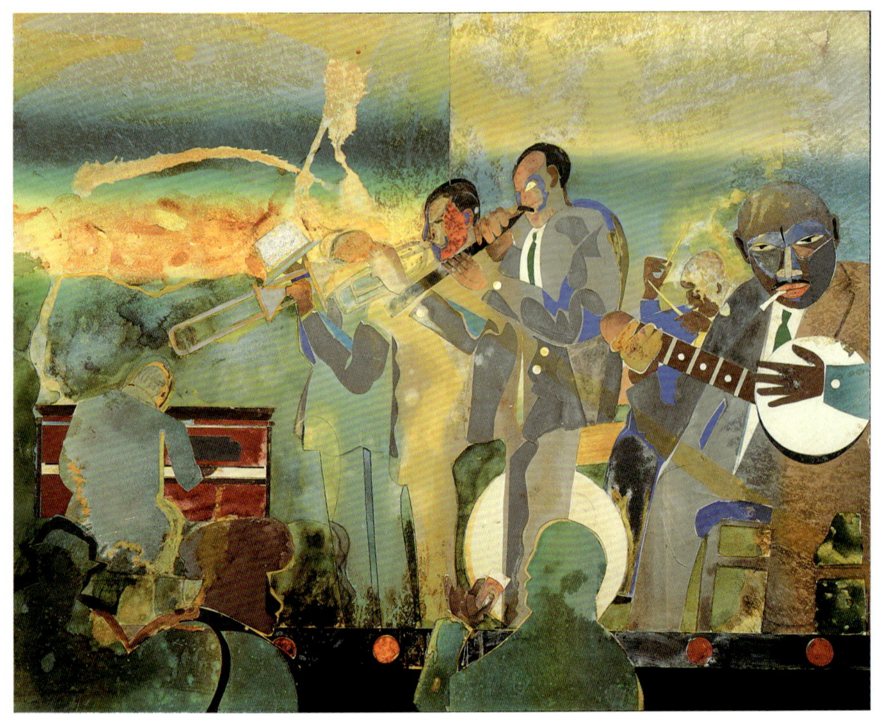

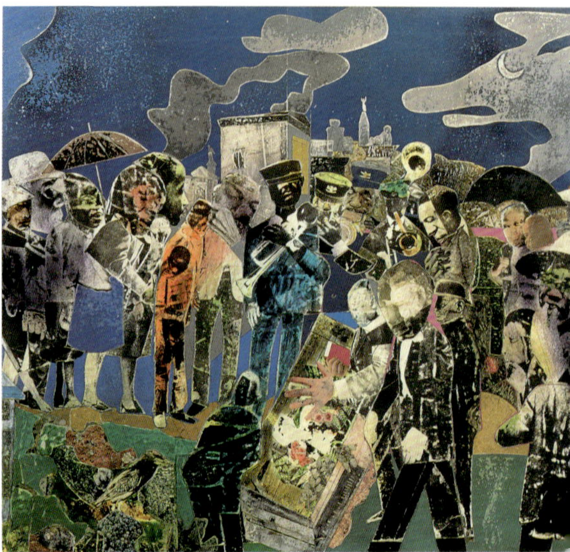

New Orleans Farewell

Uptown Sunday Night Session

ROMARE BEARDEN • (1911–1988)

New Orleans Farewell, 1974

Collage of painted photostats and acrylic on board, 44 x 51 in. (111.8 x 129.5 cm)

Profile/Part II, The Thirties: Uptown Sunday Night Session, 1981

Collage of various papers with foil, paint, ink and graphite on fiberboard, 44 x 56 in. (111.8 x 142.2 cm)

Fred Romare Harry Bearden, named after a family friend, was born on 2 September 1911 in Charlotte, North Carolina, but raised in Harlem in New York City, with summers, and even one school year, spent on extended visits to relatives in North Carolina, the Pittsburgh area, and Maryland. In New York Bearden's father, Richard Howard Bearden, worked for the city. His mother, Bessye Johnson Bearden, a journalist, educator, and community activist, wrote the New York column for *The Chicago Defender*; she also founded and was first president of the Colored Women's Democratic League and active in the Urban League and the National Association for the Advancement of Colored People (NAACP). During the 1920s and 1930s Bessye Bearden frequently entertained at home the leading writers, musicians, and intellectuals of Harlem.

From 1930–32 Bearden studied at Boston University, where he took art courses and became a star pitcher on the varsity baseball team. In 1932 he transferred to New York University, graduating in 1935. During the late 1930s he studied at the Art Students League, did political cartoons for black publications, and showed in group shows at the Harlem YMCA and the Harlem Community Art Center. When the United States entered World War II he enlisted in the Army, serving until May 1945.

Following the war's end, Bearden maintained a studio while working at the New York City Department of Social Services. From February to August 1950 he took a leave of absence from his city job and traveled to Paris under the G.I. Bill of Rights. He studied philosophy with Gaston Bachelard at the Sorbonne, as well as French and Buddhism, socialized with other expatriate artists and jazz musicians, and traveled. In 1954 he married dancer Nanette Rohan, and they lived for a time with Bearden's father on West 114th Street. In 1956 the couple moved to a Canal Street loft.

During the 1940s, 1950s, and early 1960s, his artistic style embraced a flattened figurative naturalism, influenced by School of Paris artists. At this time he actively participated in the music scene and wrote lyrics for popular songs—his most popular was "Seabreeze," sung by Billy Eckstine. In 1955 he joined the American Society of Composers, Authors and Publishers.

The Civil Rights movement of the late 1950s and early 1960s spurred Bearden and other artists to organize *Spiral,* a group that first met in 1963 at his studio on Canal Street and planned an exhibition of art by African Americans. He was active in the Harlem art scene during the 1960s and 1970s. In 1966 he retired from his full-time job, but continued part-time until 1969, leaving him time for both painting and organizing. In 1968 he was one of the founders of the Studio Museum in Harlem, and in 1969, along with Norman Lewis and Ernest Crichlow, he founded the Cinque Gallery, with a grant from the Ford Foundation. In the following year he was one of the founding members of the Black Academy of Arts and Letters; he also received a fellowship from the Guggenheim Foundation to write a history of African American art. In the summer of 1971 he and Nanette began building a house in the Antilles, where her family had originally lived. During the 1970s and 1980s they returned frequently to the Antilles and also traveled to Europe.

In the early 1960s Bearden's resolve to produce art that asserted the racial pride of his community led him to construct collages from images cut out of glossy magazines. He soon was adding watercolor, ink, oil paint, cut out pieces of colored paper, and fabric to the magazine images. During the 1970s and 1980s many of Bearden's collages were done as parts of series, with a focus often on music and rural Southern blacks. As a whole they now take their place as inventive representations of the sounds, music, and sights of African American culture.

New Orleans Farewell is one of a series of nineteen collages done in 1974 called *Of the Blues,* which trace jazz from its rural sources to the cities where it spread and developed: New Orleans, New York, Chicago, and Kansas City. The series, exhibited at Cordier & Ekstrom Gallery in February and March 1975, also includes images of performers, musical instruments, and abstract forms suggesting the sounds of jazz. Myron Schwartzman has described the techniques of this series: "Bearden was coming to exploit the improvisational possibilities of collage and other mediums in a manner that allowed him to unite a freer, more open approach to his art with his subject matter, blues improvisation. He began to brush benzene directly onto a plastic plate to 'pick out' the color, which was then allowed to splatter and disperse on the paper. The more volatile the mixture of benzene, the more quickly the plate dried."[1] This was just one technique among many that Bearden explored.

In 1981 Bearden exhibited the series *Profile/Part II, The Thirties* which included *Uptown Sunday Night Session.* The catalogue of the exhibition, held at Cordier & Ekstrom, included extended captions written by Bearden and edited by his friend, novelist and cultural critic Albert Murray. The text for this painting reads: "The Legendary Sunday nites at Leroy's on the corner of 135th Street and Lenox Avenue which also included a floor show. Unlike Connie's Inn and the Cotton Club, Leroy's was mostly off limits to tourists."[2] The caption refers to the fact that, unlike Connie's and the Cotton Club—both Harlem nightclubs that were restricted to a white paying clientele during the 1930s—Leroy's welcomed the black community. In this work the performers and the audience merge together in a colorful syncopated rhythm that embraces the viewer as well.

Awards, commissions, and honorary degrees came frequently to Bearden in the last twenty years of his life. He was elected a member of the National Institute of Arts and Letters in 1972. He was feted by Atlanta branch of the NAACP and the Urban League, and attended concerts, dinners, and award ceremonies at the White House and Gracie Mansion, the New York City mayor's residence. In the late 1980s, however, his health began to deteriorate. He spent time in the Antilles in July 1987 and died in New York on 12 March 1988. Retrospective exhibitions of his work were organized by the A.C.A. Galleries in New York in 1989, by the Studio Museum in Harlem in 1991, and by the National Gallery in Washington, D.C., in 2003. P.H.

BIBLIOGRAPHY

Fine, Ruth, ed. *The Art of Romare Bearden.* exh. cat. Washington, D.C., National Gallery of Art, 2003.

Schwartzman, Myron. *Romare Bearden: His Life and Art.* New York: Harry N. Abrams, 1990.

Studio Museum in Harlem. *Memory and Metaphor: The Art of Romare Bearden 1940–1987.* exh. cat. New York: Studio Museum in Harlem, 1991. Essays by Mary Schmidt Campbell, Kinshasha Holman Conwill, and Sharon F. Patton.

1. Schwartzman, 230. Some of the works in the series are illustrated in Schwartzman, 231–37, 239.

2. Quoted in Fine, 110.

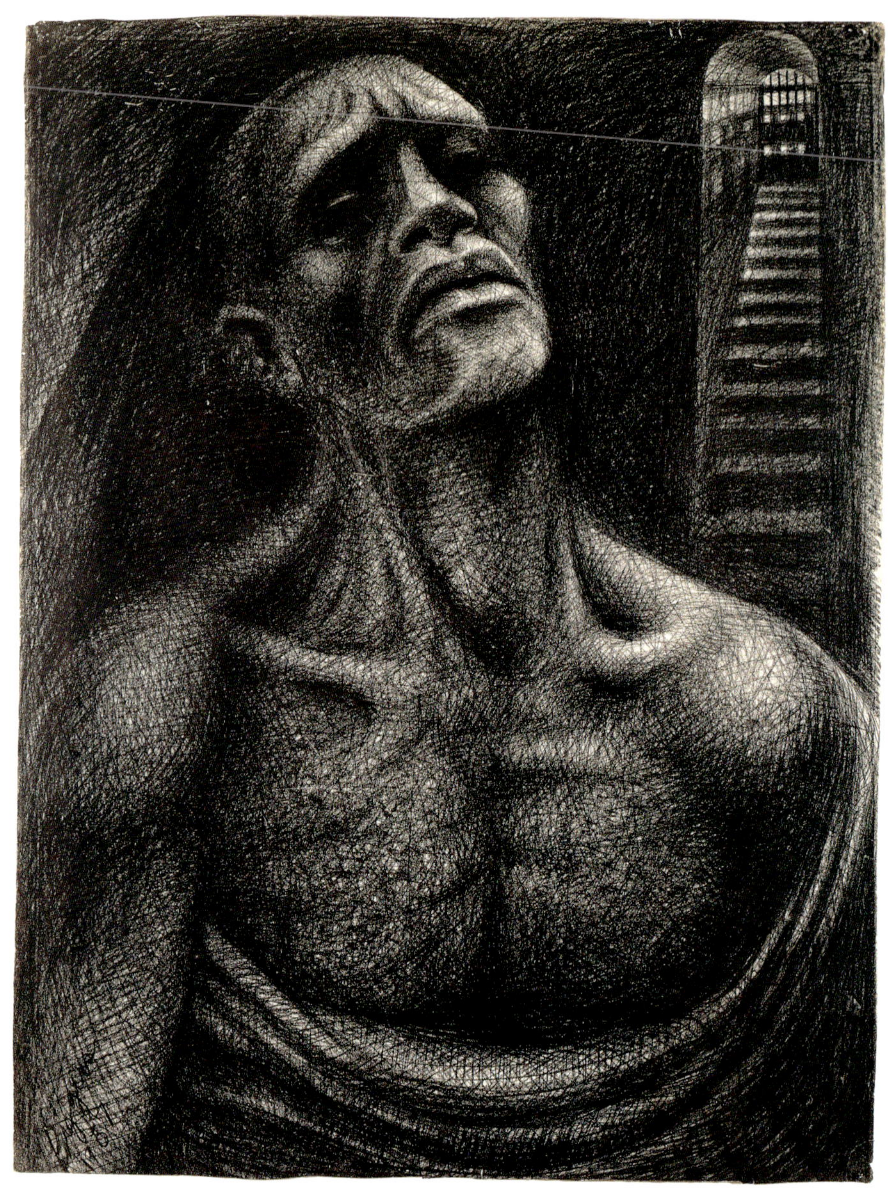

JOHN BIGGERS • (1924–2001)

Prempe II, 1957

Conté crayon, 38¼ x 29⅜ in. (97.7 x 74.6 cm)

The youngest of seven children, John Thomas Biggers was born in Gastonia, North Carolina, on 13 April 1924 to Reverend Paul Biggers and Cora Finger Biggers. When Biggers's father died in 1937, John and his brother were sent to Lincoln Academy in King's Mountain, North Carolina. In 1941 Biggers enrolled at Hampton Institute (now Hampton University), where he met Hazel Hales, whom he would marry in 1948. At Hampton Biggers studied under artist and art educator Viktor Lowenfeld and met Elizabeth Catlett, Alain Locke, Charles White, and Hale Woodruff. White's mural, *The Contributions of the Negro to American Democracy*, created while he visited Hampton as a Julius Rosenwald Fellow, greatly affected Biggers, demonstrating to him the powerful educational impact of public art. Throughout his life Biggers greatly admired muralists both African American and Mexican. In the 1960s he would travel with his wife to Mexico to see the murals of Diego Rivera, José Clemente Orozco, and David Siqueiros.

In 1943 Biggers was drafted into the Navy. Following his discharge in 1946, he returned to Hampton for a semester, then followed his mentor Lowenfeld to Pennsylvania State University. Biggers received his B.S. and M.S. in Art Education in 1948, as well as his Ph.D. from Pennsylvania State in 1954. In 1949, after teaching for a summer at Alabama State Teachers College, Biggers moved to Houston to establish the Art Department at Texas State University for Negroes (now Texas Southern University). Biggers would teach there for over thirty years.

Whether working as a muralist, educator, scholar, illustrator, draftsman, or painter, Biggers's consistent interest was in chronicling, depicting, and celebrating the lives of African Americans. His 1951 mural *Negro Folkways* for the Eliza Johnson Home for the Aged in Houston, Texas, pictures the traditional activities of the African American family. Similarly, his 1953 mural and corresponding dissertation, *The Contribution of Negro Women to American Life and Education*, celebrates and historically documents the role of black women in American life.

The most significant moment in Biggers's life as an artist was his 1957 journey to West Africa. With the aid of a UNESCO grant, Biggers was one of the first black artists to travel to Africa. His experiences there led to the publication of a book of drawings and text chronicling his travels in Ghana, Nigeria, and other parts of Africa titled *Ananse: The Web of Life in Africa* (1962). In the introduction Biggers describes his search for his own cultural heritage: "One reason was that I was traveling on a UNESCO fellowship to do an artist's study of West African life. Another reason was that I wanted to embrace Africa. I was searching for roots."[1]

The impact of his visit to Africa challenged Biggers as an artist. He further recalls:

> The impact of Africa almost paralyzed my creative efforts; the drama and the poetic beauty were devastating. Until I was able to reorient myself I was literally broken; I felt unequal to the task. . . . I was filled with fresh poignant odors, tastes, sounds, visual images; and the vigor of these new experiences aroused in me deep emotion and thought.[2]

Moved by his own experiences in both Africa and America, Biggers advocated that his students should use art as a means of expressing their own cultural heritage, including their African ancestry.

Maya Angelou has eloquently described the powerful nature of Biggers's portraits, which is certainly evident in *Prempe II*. In a poetic reflection written for Biggers's 1995 retrospective at the Museum of Fine Arts, Houston, Angelou wrote:

> John Biggers shows his people as distinct, yet will not allow them the self-consciousness of being distinct from other human beings. [His] art functions as delight and discovery. Viewers of Biggers's monumental work are made to celebrate the circumstance of life, individual and particular, and to cherish life as wondrously homogenous.[3]

Biggers's conté crayon drawing of an African man demonstrates his interest in portraying the strength and beauty that he saw in African people. With its textured cross-hatching, expressive realism, and strong modeling of the figure, *Prempe II* is a powerful image from his travels to West Africa.

Biggers retired from teaching in 1983, leaving a legacy as both an artist and educator that was recognized during his lifetime. He received Purchase Awards from the Museum of Fine Arts, Houston, in 1950, Atlanta University in 1950, 1951, 1952, and 1953, and the Dallas Museum of Fine Arts in 1952, as well as the Harbison Award for Teaching from Texas Southern University in 1968. Biggers received an honorary degree from Boston University in 1997. He died in Houston, Texas, in 2001. M.R.

BIBLIOGRAPHY

Biggers, John T. *Ananse: The Web of Life in Africa*. Austin, Texas: University of Texas Press, 1962.

Biggers, John T. and Carroll Simms with John Edward Weems. *Black Art in Houston: The Texas Southern University Experience*. College Station and London: Texas A & M University Press, 1978.

Wardlaw, Alvia J. "John Biggers—Artist: Traditional Folkways of the Black Community," in Abernethy, Francis Edward and Carolyn Fielder Satterwhite, eds., *Juneteenth Texas: Essays in African American Folklore*. Denton, Texas: University of North Texas Press, 1996.

——. *The Art of John Biggers: View from the Upper Room*. exh. cat. New York: Harry N. Abrams in association with the Museum of Fine Arts, Houston, 1995. With essays by Edmund Barry Gaither, Alison de Lima Greene, and Robert Farris Thompson.

1. Biggers, *Ananse: The Web of Life in Africa*, 4.
2. Ibid., 27.
3. Maya Angelou, "Reflections," in Wardlaw, *The Art of John Biggers: View from the Upper Room*.

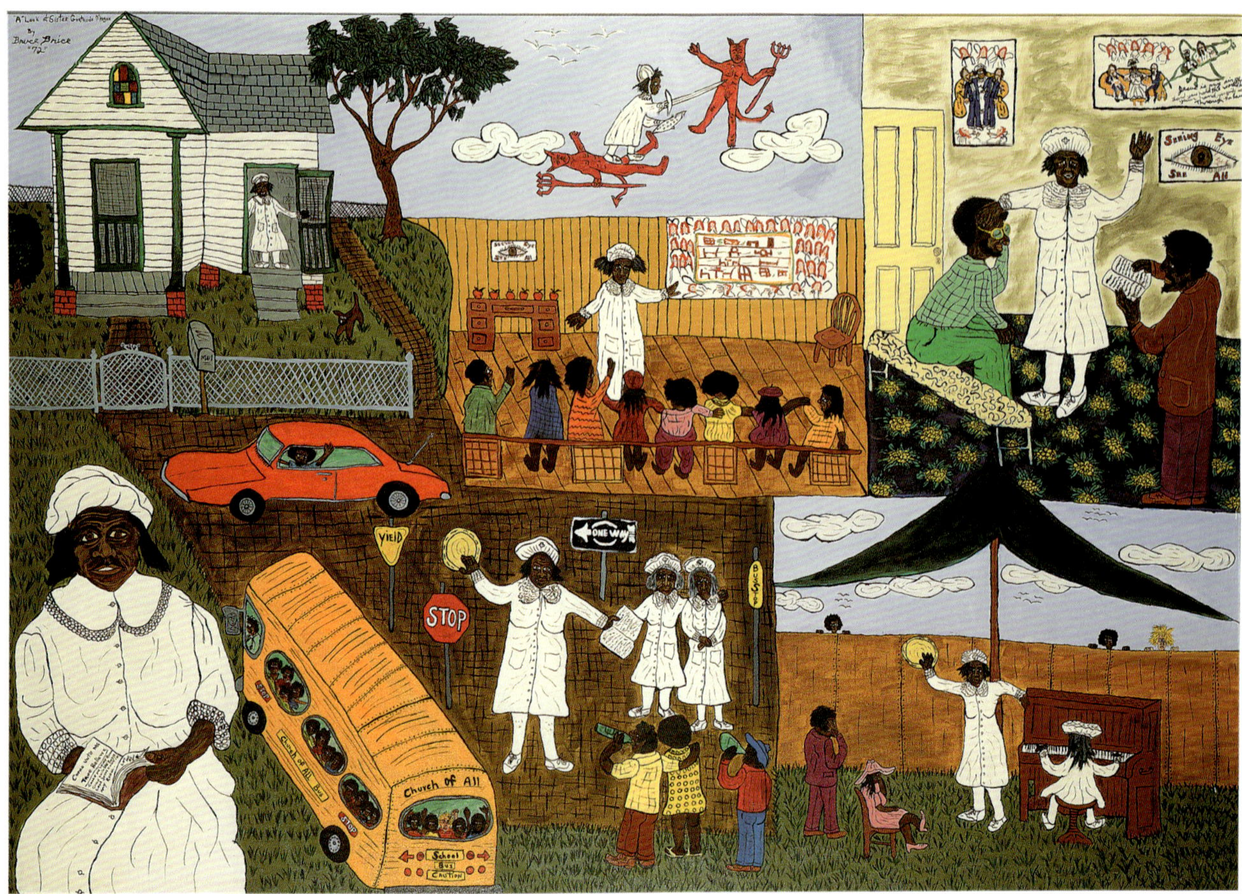

A Look at Sister Gertrude Morgan

BRUCE BRICE • (born 1942)

A Look at Sister Gertrude Morgan, 1972

Acrylic on canvas, 48 x 70 in. (121.9 x 177.8 cm)

Buster's No. 2, New Orleans, LA, n.d.

Acrylic on canvas, 48 x 70 in. (121.9 x 177.8 cm)

Folk artist Bruce Brice was born on 4 May 1942 in New Orleans, Louisiana. At the age of ten, Brice created a marionette show to earn some extra money while growing up in a housing project at the edge of the French quarter. The show was such a success that it led to a weekly television program on Channel 6 in New Orleans. After graduating from Joseph S. Clark High School in 1960, Brice worked at a coffee company, a lumberyard, and a New Orleans art gallery.

Brice's experience framing pictures at the art gallery led to his interest in painting. In 1960 he began displaying his work at the popular outdoor art show Jackson Square in the New Orleans French Quarter. Brice is best known for his lively and colorful depictions of New Orleans city life and cultural events, such as his 1978 *Mardi Gras in New Orleans* (Edward G. and Jacqueline M. Atkins Collection), which depicts the French Quarter at the height of the annual Mardi Gras celebrations. Brice chooses to paint in acrylics on either canvas or Masonite, since in the humid climate of Louisiana, acrylics dry faster. A prolific artist, Brice has painted over 1000 works, many large in scale.

Brice's 1972 *A Look at Sister Gertrude Morgan* depicts

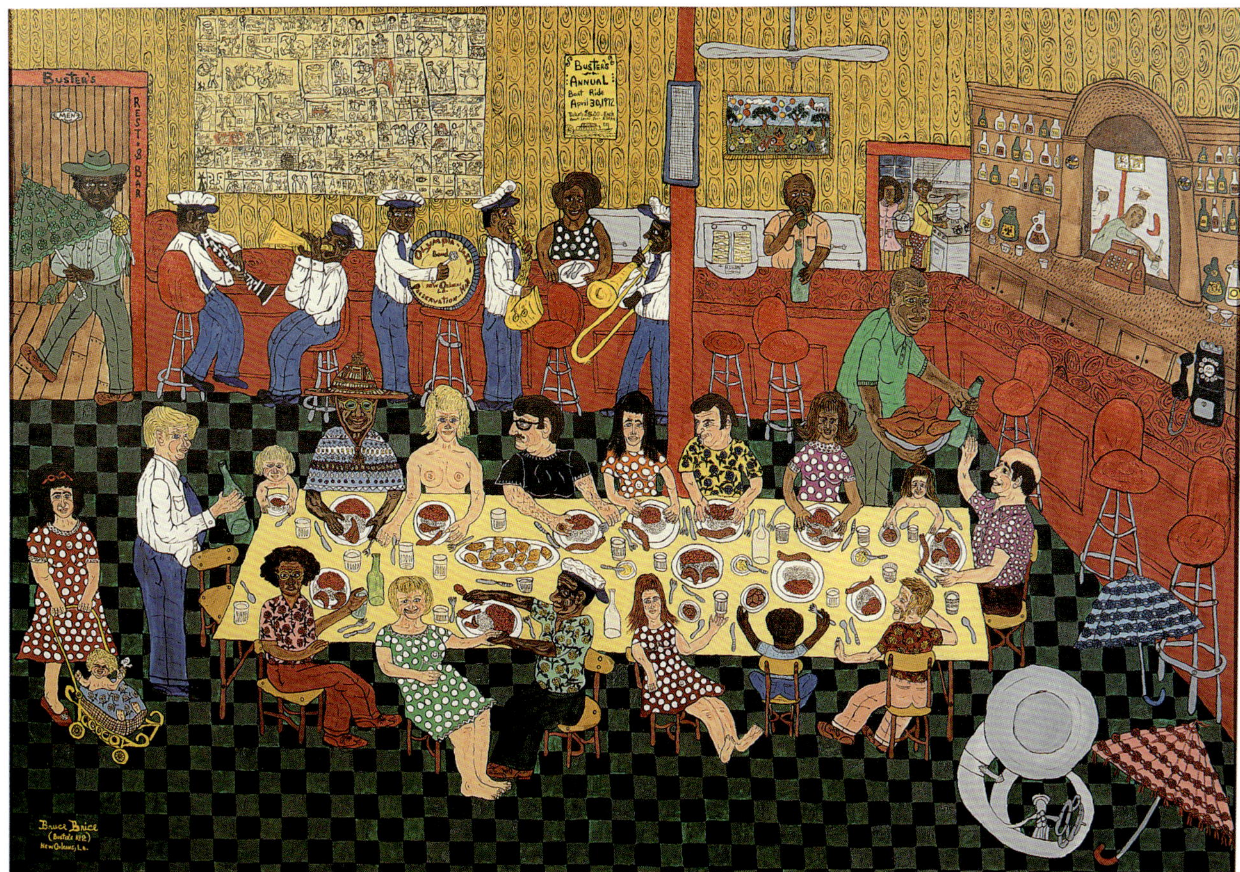

Buster's No. 2, New Orleans, LA

self-taught artist Sister Gertrude Morgan in her native New Orleans. Using bold, bright colors, Brice expertly captures Sister Gertrude in all her various roles: fighting the Devil, street preaching, running an orphanage, attending church, witnessing, healing people, singing God's praise, and showing her colorful paintings.

Buster's No. 2, New Orleans, LA depicts a local New Orleans restaurant owned by Buster Holmes. Painted in bright and festive colors, Buster stands behind the counter looking on at a table that includes both George and Joyce Wein with their friends and colleagues. George sits at the far right of the table with Joyce seated at his left, wearing a purple shirt. E. Lorenz Borenstein, owner of New Orleans's Preservation Hall, an art gallery and jazz performance center, sits to the right of the nude woman and Allan Jaffe, jazz tuba player and co-founder of Preservation Hall, is depicted at the far left of the table.

Bruce Brice's paintings celebrate and depict the cultural life of New Orleans in bold and lively colors. Brice holds the distinction of being the first commissioned artist to design the official poster for the 1972 New Orleans Jazz & Heritage Festival, organized by George Wein. He also made a series of wall murals for the Treme section of New Orleans, which are considered local landmarks. Painting is clearly Brice's passion, as he has said: "Some people read. Some people write. I paint!"[1] He continues to paint and exhibit his work at his New Orleans gallery as well as venues throughout the city, including the New Orleans Jazz & Heritage Festival. M.R.

BIBLIOGRAPHY

Artist website: http://www.brucebrice.com (27 July 2005)

Fagaly, William A. "Bruce Brice," in *Louisiana Folk Paintings*. exh. cat. New York: The Museum of American Folk Art, 1973.

Rosenak, Chuck and Jan. *Museum of American Folk Art Encyclopedia of Twentieth-Century American Folk Art and Artists*. New York: Abbeville Press, 1990.

1. Rosenak, 61.

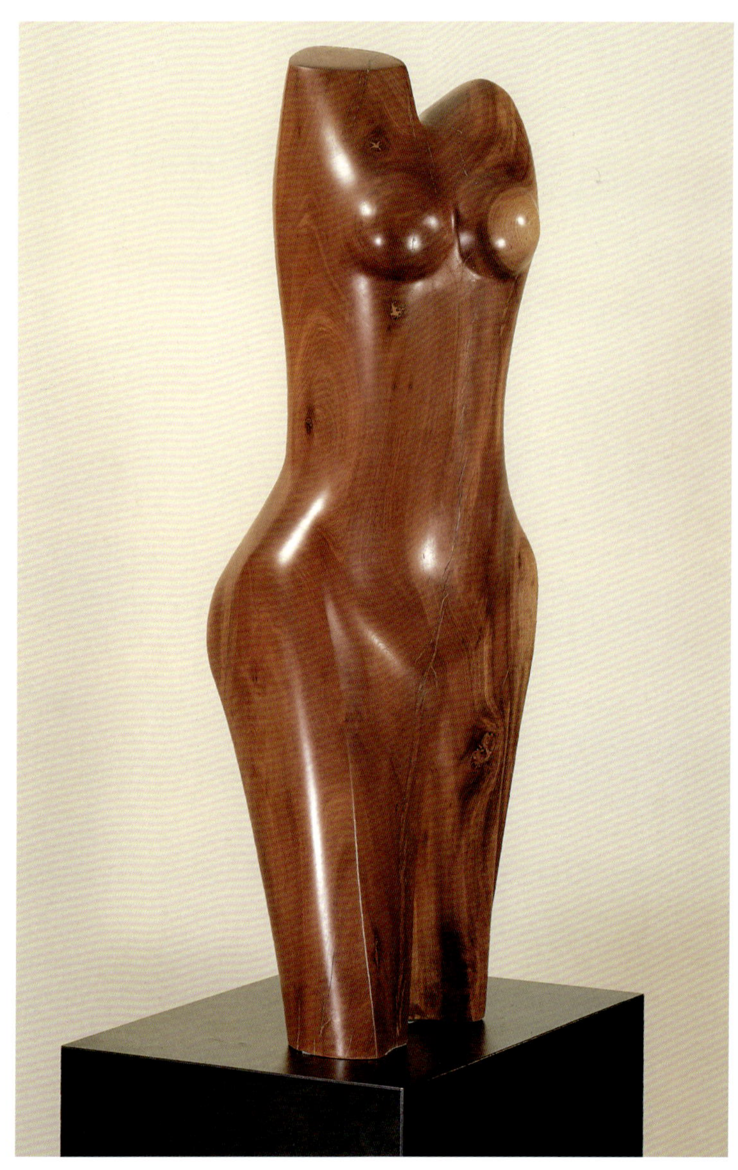

ELIZABETH CATLETT • (born 1915)

Torso, 1997

Wood (red eucalyptus), 42 in. high (106.7 cm)

Elizabeth Catlett was born on 15 April 1915 in Washington, D.C., the youngest of three children. Her mother, Mary Carson Catlett, was a school teacher and dressmaker; her father, John Catlett, taught mathematics at Tuskegee Institute and also in the Washington schools, but died shortly after she was born.[1] Although times were hard in the Catlett family, her mother always supported her ambitions to be educated and develop her considerable talents. Catlett received a scholarship to attend the Carnegie Institute of Technology in Pittsburgh, but it was revoked when authorities discovered she was African American. She then enrolled at Howard University, where she studied under artists Loïs Mailou Jones and James Porter; James Herring, her art history professor, introduced her to African sculpture. She was briefly on the Federal Art Project (FAP) of the Works Progress Administration (WPA).[2]

After graduating cum laude in 1937, Catlett taught for two years in the segregated school system of Durham, North Carolina, before enrolling in the Master's program at the University of Iowa (M.F.A. 1940). In Iowa she was fortunate to study with the regionalist painter Grant Wood, who urged her to experiment with different artistic media and to express her own personal experiences. In the summer of 1941 she enrolled in a ceramics course at the Art Institute of Chicago, where she met and later married Charles White.

Her career as a sculptor advanced when, in 1940, she received first prize in sculpture for *Mother and Child* at the American Negro Exposition, held in Chicago. She subsequently taught at Prairie View College, a black school in Texas, then Dillard University in New Orleans, where she directed the art department. Two years later Catlett and White moved to New York and she continued her studies with the sculptor Ossip Zadkine, who encouraged her to take a "humanistic international viewpoint" in her art. She later explained to Romare Bearden, "I felt the contrary—that it should begin as a nationalistic experience and be projected towards international understanding, as our blues and spirituals do. They are our experience, but they are understood and felt everywhere."[3]

In 1943 Catlett accompanied her husband to Hampton Institute (now Hampton University) in Virginia, where he had a commission to paint a large mural, and where she taught in the art department. Back in New York in 1944, she began working at the George Washington Carver School, a progressive community art center organized when the federal government closed the FAP community art centers. She taught sculpture and dressmaking. The experience of working with the poor, proud, and struggling people of Harlem made a deep and lasting impression on her.[4] She also received a Julius Rosenwald Fund fellowship, renewed in 1946.

With the Rosenwald funds she and White moved to Mexico, where she worked on the series *Negro Women*, consisting of fifteen linocuts. She also worked at the famous artists' collective Taller de Gráfica Popular, and studied the work of the Mexican muralists Diego Rivera, David Siqueiros, and José Clemente Orozco. In 1946 she divorced White. In 1947 she married the printmaker Francisco Mora, settled into life in Mexico City, and had three sons. In 1958 she became a professor of sculpture at the Escuela Nacional de Artes Plásticas (National Fine Arts School) at the Universidad Nacional Autónoma de México; she retired in 1976.

Catlett moved in the artistic and literary circles of radical politics in Mexico, and during the 1950s was harassed by Mexican government officials hunting subversives and was even jailed for two nights.[5] When she became a Mexican citizen in 1962, the U.S. government would not issue her a visa to enter the United States. The ban was not lifted until 1971, when she had an exhibition at the Studio Museum in Harlem. During the 1960s and 1970s she was outspoken on behalf of civil rights for African Americans, and much of her art, such as the sculpture *Political Prisoner*, 1971 (Schomburg Center for Research in Black Culture, New York Public Library), dealt with themes sympathetic to issues of black disenfranchisement and black empowerment. She currently divides her time between Mexico and New York.

Catlett both carves in wood and casts in bronze. Often, she will take a natural block of wood and work with it to bring out a figural form, as in *Torso*. Using her carving tools, she enhances the sensuousness of the curves and then polishes the surface to bring out the rich color of the wood. The final sculpture recalls the original tree at the same time as it presents that tree's metamorphosis into a simplified human figure, thereby suggesting the unity of nature with humankind. Her politics, her integrity, and professionalism have inspired younger artists through both her art and her example. P.H.

BIBLIOGRAPHY

Bearden, Romare and Harry Henderson. "Elizabeth Catlett," in *A History of African-American Artists from 1792 to the Present*. New York: Pantheon Books, 1993.

Gedeon, Lucinda H. *Elizabeth Catlett Sculpture: A Fifty-Year Retrospective*. exh. cat. Purchase, New York: Neuberger Museum of Art, 1998. Essays by Lowery Stokes Sims and Michael Brenson.

Herzog, Melanie Anne. *Elizabeth Catlett: An American Artist in Mexico*. Seattle: University of Washington Press, 2000.

Lewis, Samella. *The Art of Elizabeth Catlett*. Claremont, California: Hancraft Studios, 1984.

Tesfagiorgis, Freida High. "Elizabeth Catlett," in *Black Women in America: An Historical Encyclopedia*, vol. 1, Darlene Clark Hine, Elsa Barkley Brown and Rosalyn Terborg-Penn, eds. New York: Carlson, 1993.

1. Bearden and Henderson, 419.

2. The synthesis of information in this brief biography is condensed from the author's entry on Catlett for *Dictionary of Women Artists*, vol. 1, Delia Gaze, ed. (London: Fitzroy Dearborn Publishers, 1997), 371–74.

3. Quoted in Bearden and Henderson, 420.

4. Elizabeth Catlett, interview with Patricia Hills, 3 June 1995, untranscribed audio-tape, collection Patricia Hills.

5. Ibid.

ELDZIER CORTOR • (born 1916)

Nude Dressing, 1945

Ink on paper, 14 x 10 in. sight (35.6 x 25.4 cm)

Room No. 5, 1948

Oil on board, 37½ x 27 in. (95.3 x 68.6 cm)

Eldzier Cortor was born in Richmond, Virginia, on 10 January 1916. The following year his parents, John and Ophelia Cortor, became part of the Great Migration, when they moved to Chicago in search of better economic opportunities. John Cortor found work as an electrician and saved money to open a grocery store and repair shop. The family eventually moved to the West Side, an integrated neighborhood, but had to relocate to the South Side when the Depression hit.[1]

As a child Cortor copied cartoon strips from the *Chicago Defender* and received encouragement from his art teacher at Englewood High School. He left school and worked for a few years, while attending evening art classes at the School of the Art Institute of Chicago. In 1937 he enrolled full time, and under the tutelage of his art history teacher, Kathleen Blackshear, he absorbed the lessons of African sculpture on exhibit at the Field Museum in Chicago. He later recalled: "[I]t was her enthusiasm for African art that really got to me. That was the most important influence of all in my work, for to this day you will find in my handling of the human figure that cylindrical and lyrical quality I was taught by Miss Blackshire to appreciate in African sculpture."[2] Following his studies, he joined the easel division of the Federal Art Project (FAP) of the Works Progress Administration (WPA). At this time artist George Neal urged a group of young African American artists to paint the people who lived on the South Side in a social realist style. Cortor also worked at the South Side Community Art Center, teaching and working on murals. The Community Center, funded by the FAP, exposed Cortor to a dynamic group of writers, artists, and dancers, who spoke and performed there. In 1940, encouraged by Horace Cayton, co-author of *Black Metropolis*, he applied for and received a Julius Rosenwald Fund fellowship to travel to the Sea Islands, off the Georgia coast, where black Americans, the Gullah, had lived for centuries and had retained many of their African traditions. His sojourn among the Gullah intensified his resolve to paint the beauty of African American women. He returned to Chicago and was stunned by an exhibition of nineteenth-century French artists, including Jacques-Louis David, Camille Corot, and others. He vowed to give the same kind of grandeur to his own paintings. Since he was also interested in developing his printmaking skills, he moved to New York to study at Columbia University.

Cortor's most critically acclaimed paintings of the 1940s were *Americana*, 1946 (Collection Miriam and Stephen Cortor) and *Room No. 5*, 1948. Both depict statuesque black nude women in interiors with walls covered with pasted newspapers and magazine pages.[3] In *Room No. 5* we see a nude woman reflected in the mirror of a formerly elegant Victorian vanity. Magazine clippings pasted to the wall behind the vanity contain images that suggest the memories or the fears of the woman; for example, one image depicts the head and shoulders of a red-haired white man holding a pistol, which Cortor paints as aimed at the back of the nude. A cigarette lies burning at the edge of the vanity's marble top, a cat sleeps on the center, while a chipped china cup sits on the right. Peeling blue striped wallpaper and crumbling plaster define the sides of the walls. The painting combines an environment of gentility and beauty with the sense that hard times have come. *Life* magazine reproduced *Room No. 5* as a full-color page in its 20 May 1950 issue on "19 Young American Artists."

Awarded a Guggenheim Fellowship in 1949, Cortor went first to Cuba and Jamaica, and then to Haiti, where he stayed for about two years.[4] He returned to Chicago, but left again for Mexico in the mid-1950s to escape the Cold War repression fanned by Senator Joseph McCarthy and the House Committee on Un-American Activities. Romare Bearden and Harry Henderson, after conversations with Cortor, sum up that situation: "For Cortor and many other artists devoted to black subject matter, this political hysteria was a disaster. To survive, many artists eliminated black subject matter." Cortor, however, stayed the course. He learned lithography in Mexico, where he lived for a few years in a small town near Guadalajara, before returning to New York.

In 1973 he participated in a three-artist exhibition at the Museum of the National Center of Afro-American Artists in Boston. In 1988 he was in another three-artist exhibition at the Kenkeleba House, an art gallery in New York. A comment to Elton Fax sums up his approach to his

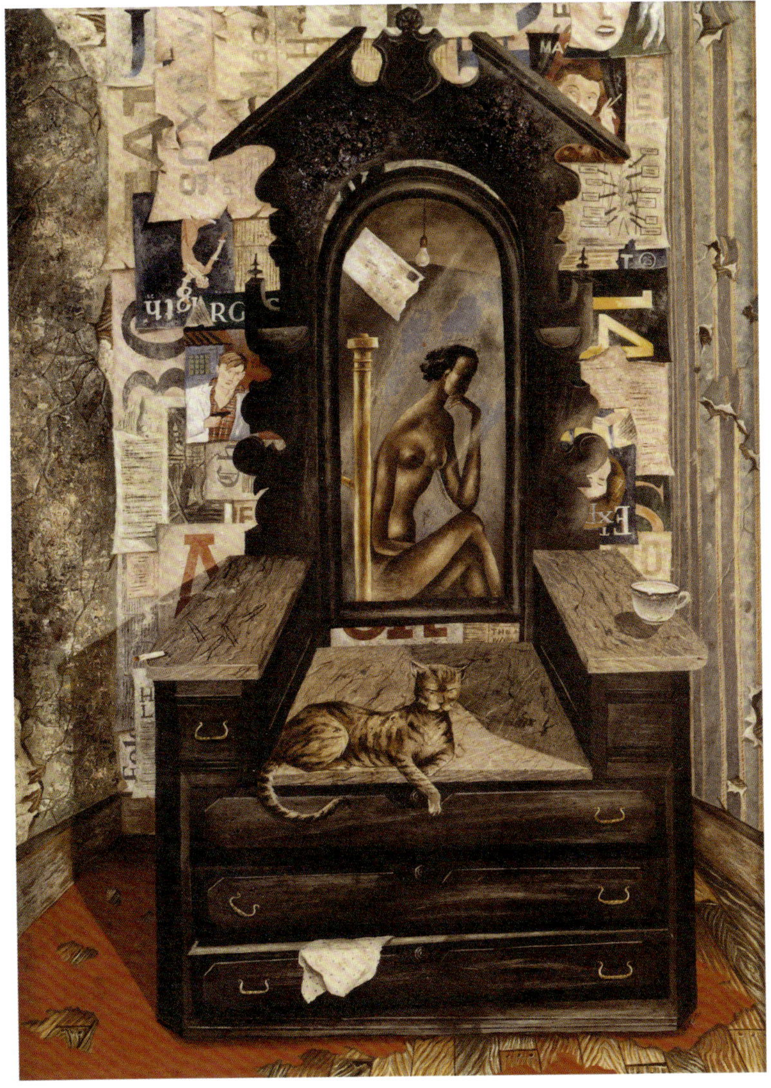

Room No. 5

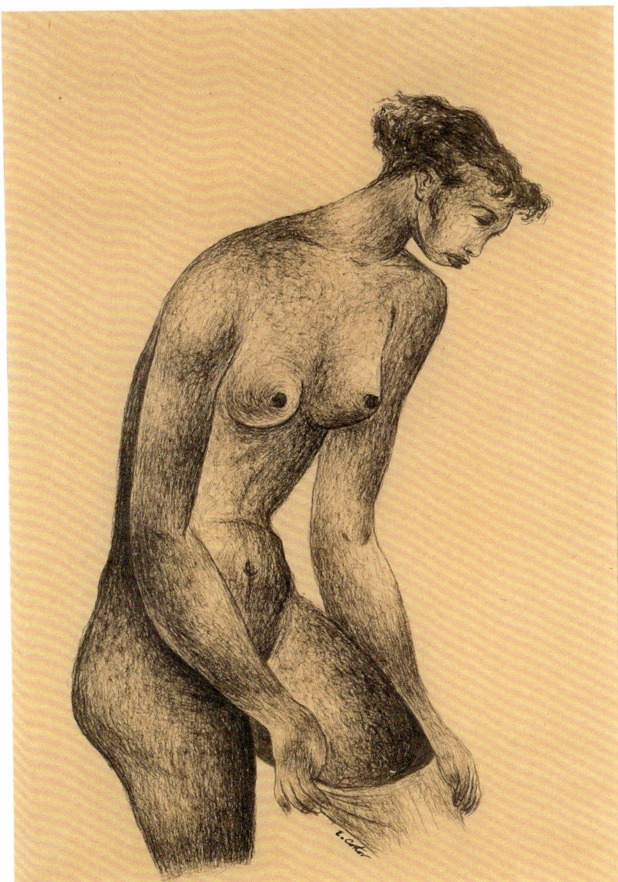

Nude Dressing

late work, but it could be readily applied to a modest early drawing such as *Nude Dressing*: ". . . I work with what's around me, though sometimes I reach back for something out of my memory. I work with what I know—what I understand—even if it's just a head. Everything doesn't have to be an epic, you know."[5] Cortor currently lives in Manhattan.

P.H.

BIBLIOGRAPHY

Bearden, Romare and Harry Henderson. "Eldzier Cortor," in *A History of African-American Artists from 1792 to the Present*. New York: Pantheon Books, 1993.

Fax, Elton C. *Seventeen Black Artists*. New York: Dodd, Mead and Company, 1971.

Kenkeleba Gallery. *Three Masters: Eldzier Cortor, Hughie Lee-Smith, Archibald John Motley, Jr.* exh. cat. New York: Kenkeleba Gallery, 1988. Essay on Cortor by Corrine L. Jennings.

1. Information in this biographical sketch is drawn primarily from Bearden and Henderson, 272–79, based on interviews with the artist conducted in 1973 and 1988.
2. Quoted in Fax, 87; date of citation not given.
3. *Americana* is reproduced in Bearden and Henderson, 277.
4. *The John Simon Guggenheim Memorial Foundation, 1925–2000, a Seventy-Fifth Anniversary Record* (New York: John Simon Guggenheim Memorial Foundation, 2001), 334, gives the date of 1949 when he received his award. Other accounts are vague.
5. Quoted in Fax, 93.

ALLAN ROHAN CRITE • (born 1910)

Tire Jumping in Front of My Window, 1936/1947
Oil on canvas, 23½ x 17½ in. (59.7 x 44.5 cm)

Surely He Hath Borne Our Griefs, 1948
Lithograph, 12 x 9¾ in. comp. (30.5 x 24.8 cm)

Family, 1980
Pencil on paper, 11¾ x 14¾ in. sight (29.9 x 37.5 cm)

The Teacher, 1980
Pencil on paper, 11¼ x 14½ in. comp. (28.6 x 36.4 cm)

Allan Rohan Crite has become a Boston institution. Although born in Plainfield, New Jersey, on 20 March 1910, he came to Boston as an infant when his father, Oscar William Crite, and mother, Annamae Palmer Crite, moved so his father could pursue a degree in engineering. He was the only one of four children to survive infancy. Educated at Boston Latin High School, he went on to the School of the Museum of Fine Arts. For more than sixty years he painted street scenes of Boston neighborhood people, particularly African Americans living in the South End, where he still resides on Columbus Avenue. In a series of interviews during 1979 and 1980 with Robert Brown, then the Director of the Boston office of the Archives of American Art, Crite elaborated on his art training and education in Boston, his religion, and his views on the pluralism of the United States and the nature of human relationships.[1]

Crite showed an early aptitude for drawing, encouraged by his mother and recognized by one astute grade school teacher, who urged the youngster to enroll at the Children's Art Center, an experimental art school founded in the early 1920s. He also took the children's classes at the School of the Museum of Fine Arts. In 1929 he was offered scholarships by Yale University School of Art and by the School of the Museum of Fine Arts. Crite chose to attend the Museum School, in order to help his mother care for his father, disabled by a stroke.

Crite stayed at the Museum School until 1936, during which time he received training in both the drawing and painting fine arts program and the design program geared to commercial art careers. His most vivid memories were of the drawing teachers, particularly the colorful Russian émigré Alexander Iacovleff, whose abilities to produce quick, large portraits were legendary. However, precision was also held in high regard by the faculty, and Crite was encouraged "to put in all the bricks" when painting his street scenes.

During the Depression, the federal government put in place relief programs to help artists. Crite enrolled in the Public Works of Art Program within two months after it began hiring needy artists in December 1933, and in 1936 he briefly joined the easel division of the Federal Art Project (FAP). During the 1930s he also developed three genres of his art: street scenes of his neighbors strolling along the sidewalks and children playing, illustrations of Negro spirituals, and religious scenes drawn from the New Testament and the High Episcopal Church liturgy. African Americans appeared in all three of these: in the neighborhood scenes because Crite wanted to show "just ordinary people as I see them," not the "Southern sharecroppers and Harlem jazz men" that usually appeared in the works of African American artists; in the illustrations of the spirituals because he "was just telling the story of Black people, and using the black figures because the spirituals are related to Black people naturally"; and in the liturgical drawings because he wanted "to tell the story of man" with the black figure, in order to make that story more universal.[2]

In the late 1930s, after closely studying Christian liturgy and the doctrinal issues within the Episcopal Church, Crite committed himself to the theological outlook of the High Episcopal Church. He then began giving lectures on the liturgical arts and worked for fourteen months in New York City for the Rambusch Decorating Company, which specialized in church decoration, where he designed a large mural for St. Augustine's Church in Brooklyn. From 1940 until 1974 Crite worked for the Boston Naval Shipyard doing technical illustrations. For a while he continued

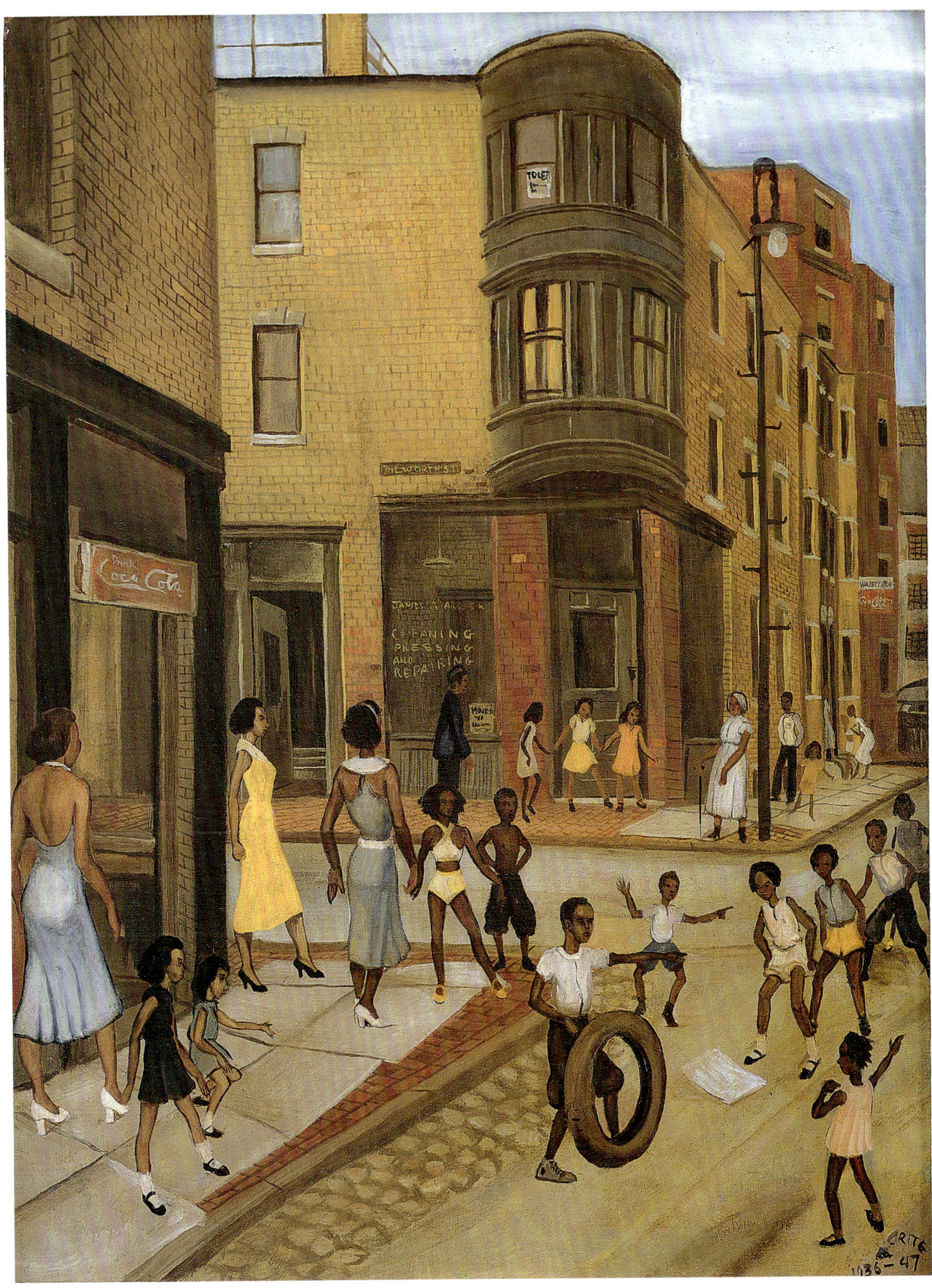

Tire Jumping in Front of My Window

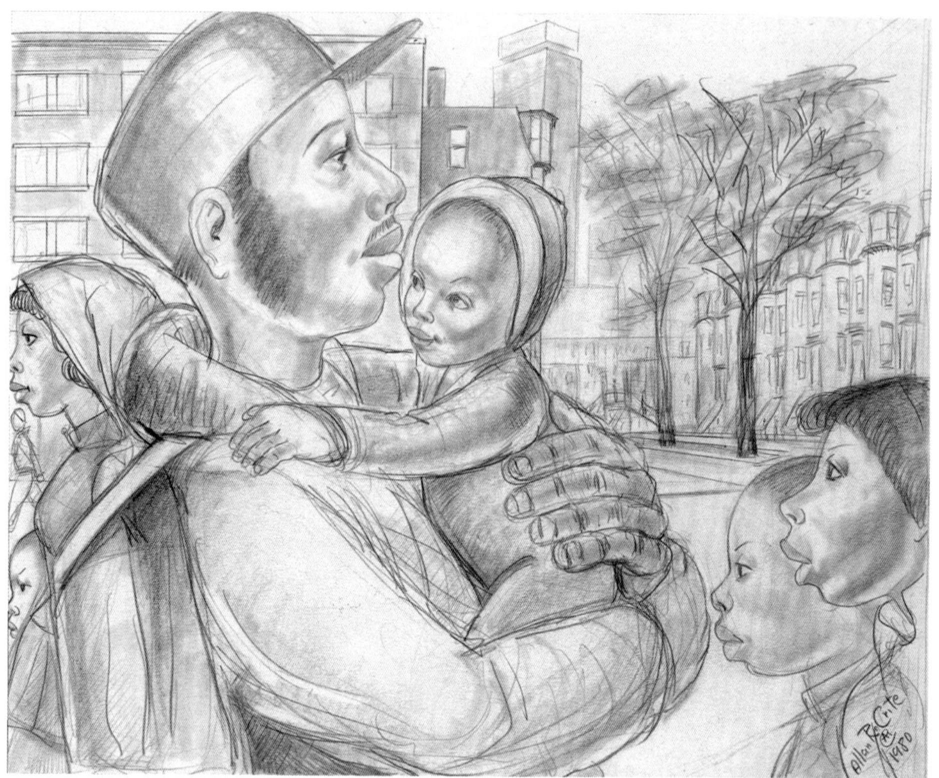

Family

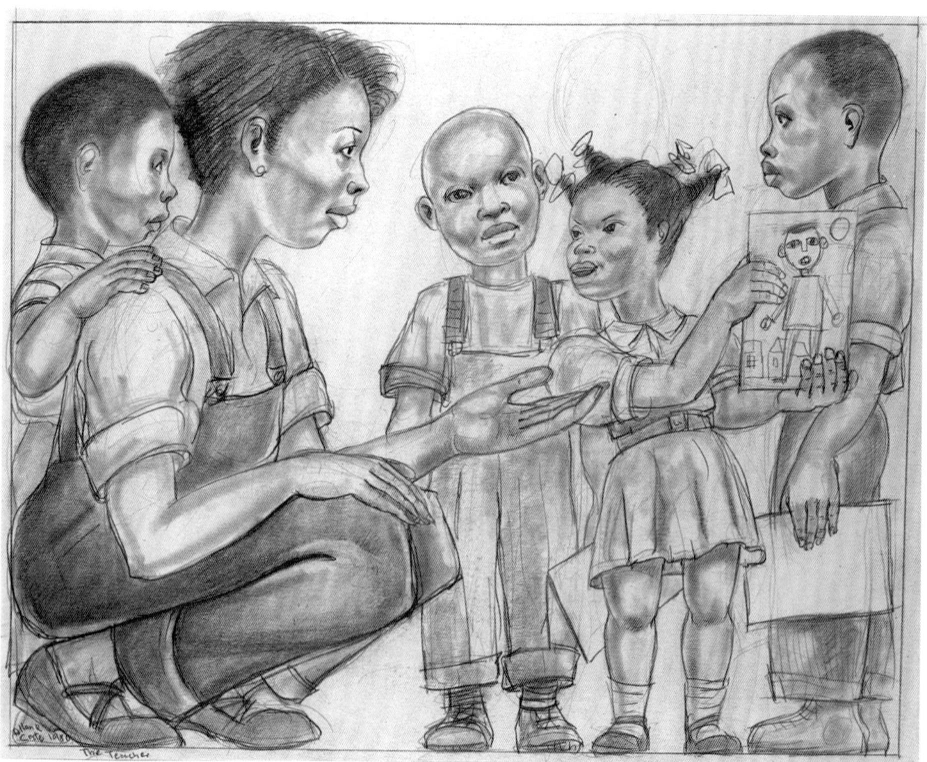

The Teacher

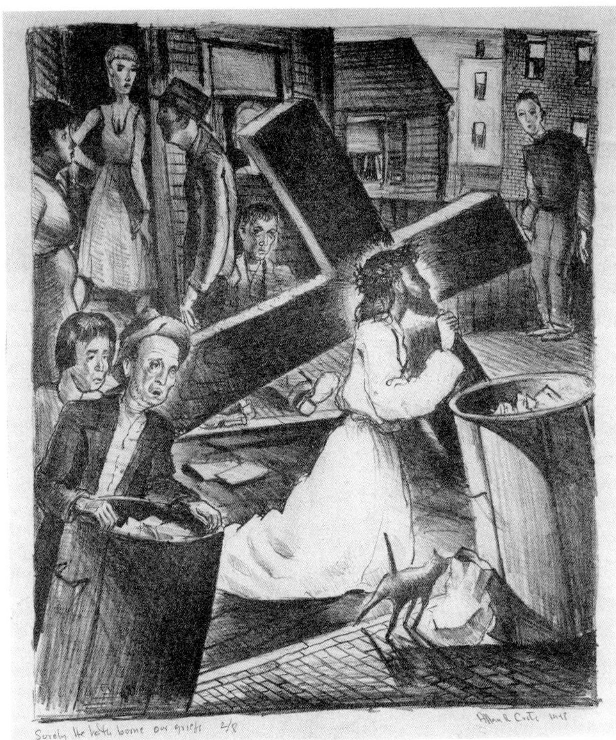

Surely He Hath Borne Our Griefs

designing church decorations part-time for Rambusch, but the distance from Boston to New York made the association difficult to continue. Nevertheless, he continued to draw, paint, and print Sunday church bulletins for a number of Episcopal churches. He also published a number of books of his drawings, notably *Were You There When They Crucified My Lord: A Negro Spiritual in Illustrations*, 1944, and *Three Spirituals from Earth to Heaven*, 1948, both published by Harvard University Press. *All Glory*, 1947, was published by the Society of St. John the Evangelist. His illustrations for the *Book of Revelation* were published by the Limited Edition Book Club, New York, in 1994. He received an A.B.E. degree in 1968 from the Harvard University Extension School, where his mother had often taken classes. He has taught at Roxbury Community College and has given private lessons in his studio, even taking the studio students on a trip to China. In 1993 he married Jackie Cox, an art and planning consultant, who has been helping him with his archives and papers.

He was always able to exhibit his work, both in Boston and nationally. His painting *School's Out*, 1936 (Smithsonian American Art Museum) was included in the *New Horizons in American Art*, a 1936 exhibition of FAP art held at the Museum of Modern Art. He was featured in Alain Locke's 1940 survey, *The Negro in Art*, and also showed regularly in Harmon Foundation exhibitions. The Boston University Art Gallery included his work in the 1983 exhibition *Social Concern and Urban Realism: American Painting of the 1930s* and the 2002 exhibition *The Visionary Decade: New Voices in Art in 1940s Boston*. In 1991 he had a major retrospective at the Museum of the National Center of Afro-American Artists, and in 2001 he had another retrospective, with an accompanying catalogue, at the Frye Art Museum in Seattle.

The works in the Wein collection characterize his oeuvre. Crite is conscious that his paintings such as *Tire Jumping in Front of My Window*, 1936/1947, have value not only as art but as historical records of Boston neighborhoods. With the urban renewal of Boston during the 1960s many of the neighborhoods in the South End and Roxbury were broken up; in fact he was evicted from his own home.

Crite's lithograph *Surely He Hath Borne Our Griefs* typifies his religious pictures. In a scene from the "Stations of the Cross," a modern Jesus carries his cross through a poor urban neighborhood that includes people loitering on the streets and a man groping through a garbage can. Crite wanted to show Jesus as a man moving through a milieu of contemporary ordinary people. His two superb drawings of 1980, *The Teacher* and *Family*, characterize his drawing style with their solid figures, firm outlines, and delicate chiaroscuro. The same theme pervades both images: the caring nature of adults towards children seen from the children's point of view. All of his works have this tender quality—whether religious or secular—that reflects the thoughtful nature of the man himself. P.H.

BIBLIOGRAPHY

Archives of American Art. Interviews with Allan Rohan Crite conducted by Robert Brown, 16 January 1979 to 22 October 1980 [99 pages]. Washington, D.C.: Archives of American Art. Posted on http://www.aaa.si.edu/oralhist/crite79.htm (17 July 2005).

Caro, Julie Levin. *Allan Rohan Crite: Artist-Reporter of the African American Community*. exh. cat. Seattle: Frye Art Museum in association with the University of Washington Press, 2001. Introduction by Mark Pomerantz; essays by Barbara Earl Thomas and Edmund Barry Gaither.

1. Most of the information in this entry is drawn from the Allan Rohan Crite/Robert Brown interviews, 16 January 1979 to 22 October 1980, Archives of American Art, Smithsonian Institution, online text at http://www.aaa.si.edu/oralhist/crite79.htm

2. Ibid., p. 40 of printout.

MILES DAVIS • (1926–1991)

Untitled, n.d.

Oil on canvas, 53 x 25½ in. (134.6 x 64.8 cm)

Untitled, n.d.

Acrylic on canvas, 57½ x 40½ in. (146.1 x 102.9 cm)

Miles Davis, best known as a jazz musician, became a serious painter in the 1980s, though his interest in both music and the visual arts was with him from childhood. Davis's keen visual sense is demonstrated in his recollection of an early memory:

> The very first thing I remember in my early childhood is a flame, a blue flame jumping off a gas stove somebody lit. It might have been me playing around with the stove. I don't remember who it was. Anyway, I remember being shocked by the whoosh of the blue flame jumping off the burner, the suddenness of it. That's as far back as I can remember; any further back than this is just fog, you know, just mystery. But that stove flame is as clear as music is in my mind. I was three years old.[1]

Born on 25 May 1926 in Alton, Illinois, Miles Dewey Davis III was the son of Miles Dewey Davis II and Cleota Henry Davis. He grew up in East St. Louis, Illinois; his father had a B.A. from Lincoln University in Pennsylvania and graduated from Northwestern University's College of Dentistry. On his thirteenth birthday, Miles was given a trumpet and lessons with his Lincoln High School teacher Elwood Buchanan. He began performing at a young age around St. Louis with Eddie Randall's Blue Devils. Jazz musicians Charlie "Bird" Parker and Dizzy Gillespie inspired Davis and led him to pursue a career as a musician. Davis describes how, for him, Parker was the "master among masters," comparing him to Spanish artist Salvador Dalí:

> Let's put it another way: There are painters and then there are painters among great painters. In this century, in my opinion, you had Picasso, Dalí. Bird for me was like Dalí, my favorite painter. I liked Dalí because of his imagination when he painted death. See, I was into that kind of imagery and I liked the surrealism in his painting. The way Dalí used surrealism always had a wrinkle in it—at least for me—it was so different; you know, like a man's head in a breast. And Dalí's paintings had a slick finish about them. But Picasso, besides his cubist work, had that African influence in his paintings, and I already *knew* what that was all about. So Dalí was just more interesting for me, taught me a new way of looking at things. Bird was like that with music.[2]

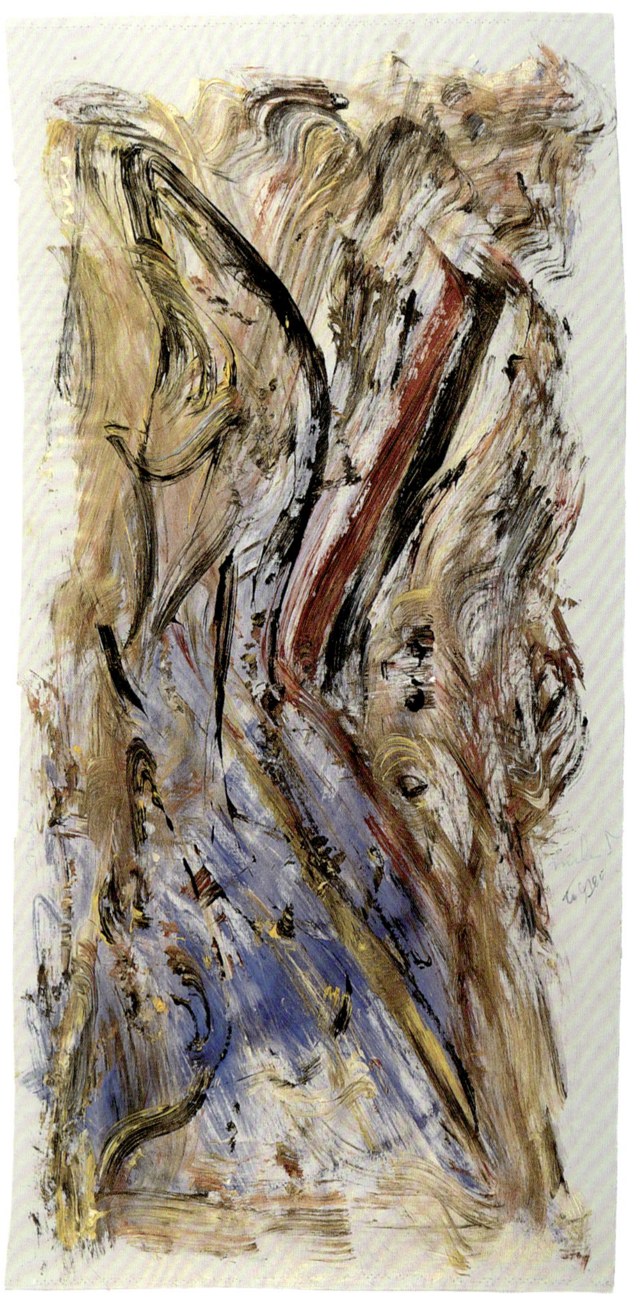

Untitled. Oil on canvas

In September 1944 Davis enrolled at the Juilliard School of Music, where he studied classical music in the daytime and played jazz at night in clubs both on 52nd Street and in Harlem; he left Juilliard in 1945 to play jazz full-time.

Davis often played with Charlie Parker and recorded one of his first be-bop sessions in November 1945. Davis made his own first recording on 14 August 1947 as a leader of a quintet that included Parker on tenor sax. In 1948 Davis began to experiment with a new style, "cool jazz." He also struggled with a heroin addiction in the early 1950s, quitting in 1954. Davis played at the Newport Jazz Festival (founded by George Wein) many times, including memorable appearances in 1955 and 1958. His albums of the 1950s are jazz classics, including *The Birth of the Cool* (1950), *Miles Ahead* (1957), *Porgy and Bess* (1958), and his best-selling album *Kind of Blue* (1959).

Davis began to express himself through visual art in the 1980s, alternating painting with playing music. He states: "I really started painting a lot in the beginning of the eighties, and now I'm spending quite a bit of time doing that. If I don't play the trumpet, I'll do that. It's always one of the two. I can't do them together."[3]

Most of Davis's paintings are untitled and undated. Davis resisted labeling his art; he believed that it limits the viewer's imagination. His earlier works contain elongated fantasy figures, especially females, as well as musicians and comic book-like forms that Davis referred to as "robots," as seen in the colorful acrylic painting depicted here, filled with faces and geometric shapes against a grid-like background.

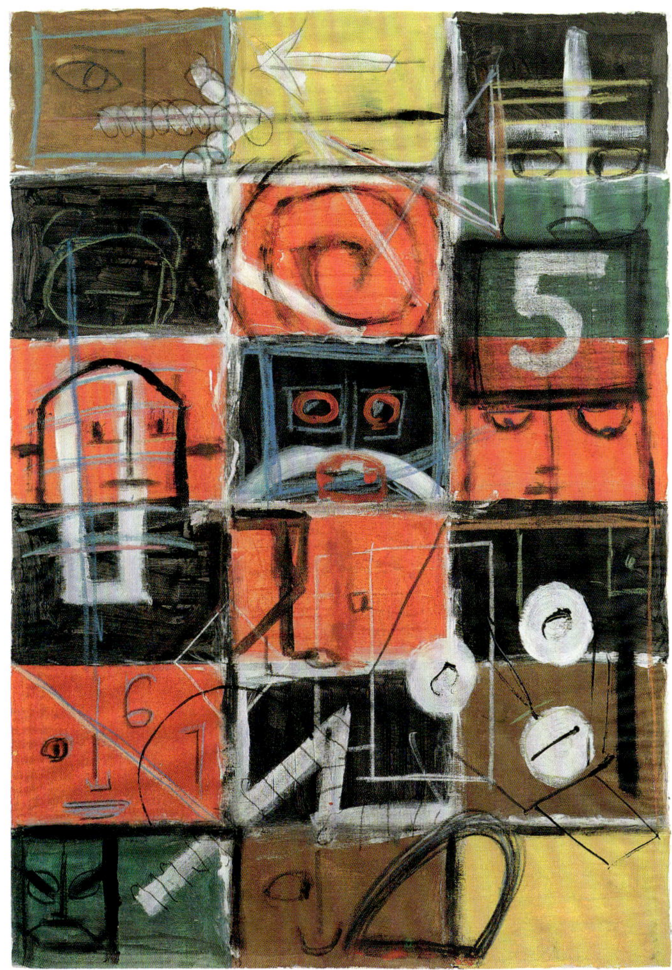

Untitled. Acrylic on canvas

In 1988, inspired by the Milan-based design movement "Memphis," Davis began painting abstract works using hot colors and clashing shapes. In the last part of his life he worked closely with New York–based artist and friend Jo Gelbard and created his signature "totem pole faces" and multimedia works that incorporated tribal masks and African art. At times they collaborated on projects; Gelbard did the cover for Davis's album *Amandla* (1989). Davis admired and was influenced by many artists other than Dalí, including Joan Miró and Jean-Michel Basquiat. Davis often painted his large canvases on the floor at his studio in California, which he preferred to New York for the quality of light.

Davis had many art exhibitions toward the end of his life, including shows in Spain, West Germany, Japan, and New York City. He died 28 September 1991 in Santa Monica, California. His works of art offer an opportunity in which to see his creativity manifest itself in visual form. Davis's figurative and abstract paintings—filled with bold, uninhibited colors, loose, improvisatory brushstrokes, and expressive gestural lines—draw a powerful parallel to his brilliant career as a jazz musician. M.R.

BIBLIOGRAPHY

Davis, Miles. *The Art of Miles Davis*. New York: Prentice Hall, 1991.

——. *Miles: The Autobiography*. New York: Simon and Schuster, 1989.

Szwed, John. *So What: The Life of Miles Davis*. New York: Simon & Schuster, 2002.

Wein, George. *Myself Among Others: A Life in Music*. Cambridge, Massachusetts: Da Capo Press, 2003.

1. Davis, Miles. *Miles: The Autobiography*, 11.
2. Ibid., 79.
3. Davis, Miles. *The Art of Miles Davis*, 6.

BEAUFORD DELANEY • (1901–1979)

Village Street Scene, n.d.

Oil on canvas, 19½ x 16 in. (49.5 x 40.6 cm)

Abstraction (Still Life with Idol), 1945

Oil on canvas, 18 x 24 in. (45.7 x 60.9 cm)

Composition, 1961

Gouache on paper, 25 x 18⅞ in. (63.5 x 47.9 cm)

Untitled, 1967

Oil on canvas, 15 x 21½ in. (38.1 x 54.6 cm)

The hallmark feature of any Beauford Delaney painting is the vibrant use of color, seen in both his figurative works and his non-representational paintings. Writer James Baldwin, a close friend, described Delaney's interest in light and color:

> I learned about light from Beauford Delaney, the light contained in every thing, in every surface, in every face. Many years ago, in poverty and uncertainty, Beauford and I would walk together through the streets of New York City. He was then, and is now, working all the time, or perhaps it would be more accurate to say that he is seeing all the time; and the reality of his seeing caused me to begin to see. Now, what I began to see was not, at that time, to tell the truth, his painting; that came later. What I saw, first of all, was a brown leaf on black asphalt, oil moving like mercury in the black water of the gutter, grass pushing itself up through a crevice in the sidewalk. And because I was seeing it with Beauford, because Beauford caused me to see it, the very colors underwent a most disturbing and salutary change. The brown leaf on the black asphalt, for example—what colors were these, really? To stare at the leaf long enough, to try to apprehend the leaf, was to discover many colors in it; and though black had been described to me as the absence of light, it became very clear to me that if this were true, we would never have been able to see the color, black: the light is trapped in it and struggles upward, rather like that grass pushing upward through the cement.[1]

Beauford Delaney, the older brother of Joseph Delaney, was born 31 December 1901 to Reverend Joseph Samuel Delaney and Delia Johnson Delaney [see entry on Joseph Delaney]. He was named for the South Carolina coastal town of Beaufort, where his parents originated. Both Beauford and his younger brother Joseph showed talent in art at an early age. After graduating from Knoxville Colored High School with honors, Beauford left the South for Boston, where he studied at the Massachusetts Normal School beginning in 1924. Delaney also studied at the Copley Society in Boston and the South Boston School of Art. He frequented the local museums, including the Museum of Fine Arts and the Isabella Stewart Gardner Museum, where he attended concerts, enjoying classical music on weekend afternoons. While in Boston he also met poet Countee Cullen, who was then studying for his Master's at Harvard.

In 1929 Delaney relocated to Harlem, where he worked as a bellboy in a midtown hotel while continuing to practice art. One of his earliest exhibitions was at the Whitney Studio Galleries in 1930. His first solo exhibition was for the 135th Street Branch of the New York Public Library in 1930, and featured five pastel portraits. Delaney painted many portraits throughout his life, sketching many jazz artists, including Louis Armstrong, Duke Ellington, and Ethel Waters. He also painted self-portraits, as well as portraits of prominent Americans, including W.E.B. Du Bois, James Baldwin, Henry Miller, and Marian Anderson.

Delaney also worked as a telephone operator and handyman at the newly founded Whitney Museum of American Art, living nearby in an apartment in Greenwich Village. Like his brother Joseph, Beauford painted city scenes, including this undated work, *Village Street Scene*, rendered in muted tones. Expressionistic brushstrokes and thick impasto characterize much of Delaney's work, as does the subject matter. While living in Greenwich Village, Delaney often portrayed the city and the people that surrounded him. Delaney studied briefly with both Thomas Hart Benton and John Sloan at the Art Students League, and attended parties at "306," the studio of

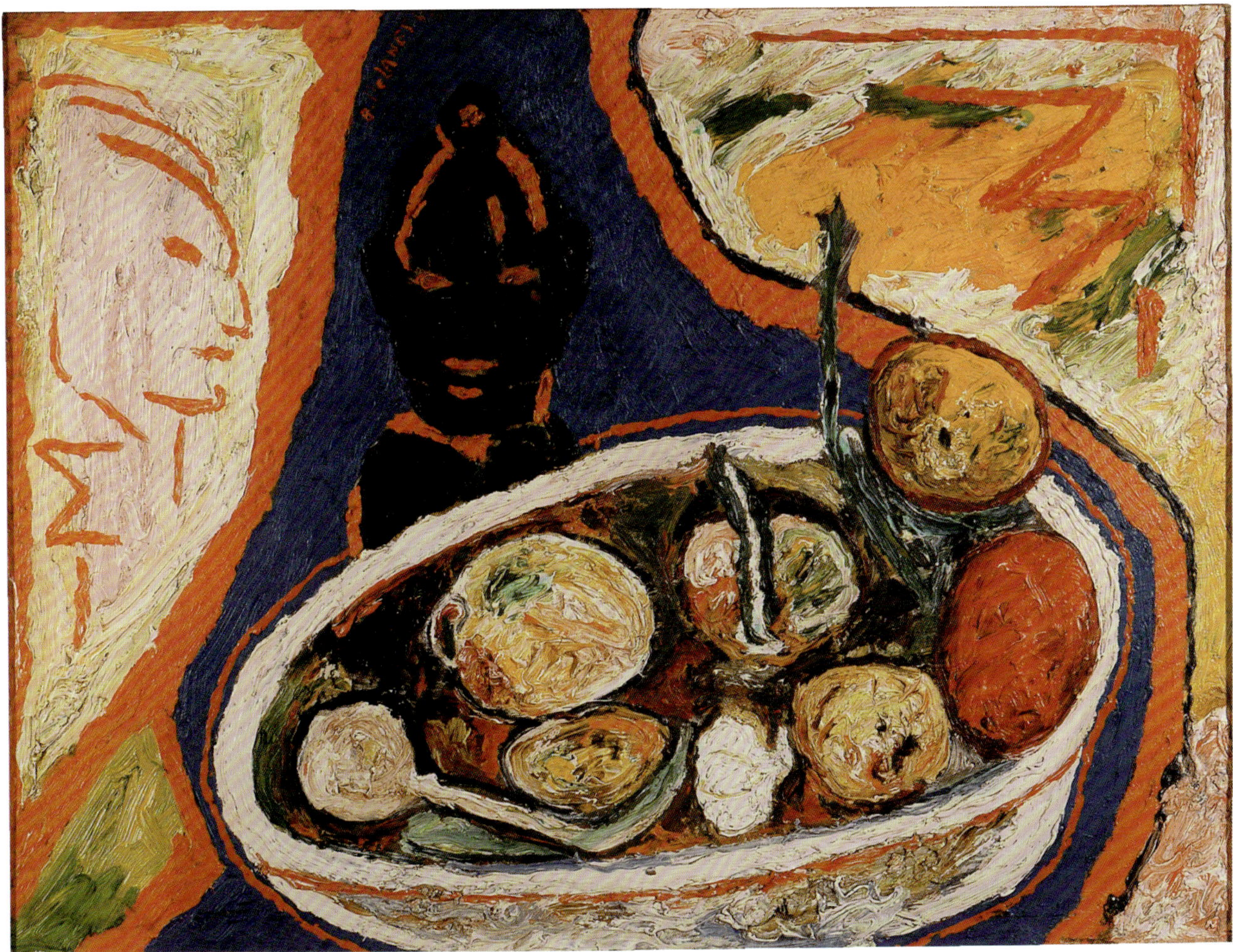

Abstraction (Still Life with Idol)

Charles Alston and Henry Bannarn. While in Greenwich Village he also became friends with artist Al Hirschfield and his wife, Dolly Haas. He was an active member, along with his brother Joseph, of the Harlem Artists Guild and, as an artist on the Federal Art Project (FAP) of the Works Progress Administration (WPA), Delaney assisted Charles Alston on his Harlem Hospital murals. His work was also included in the 1934 Harmon traveling exhibition. Delaney moved in many artist circles in both New York and Paris; Henry Miller describes Delaney's vivid paintings in his 1945 *The Air-Conditioned Nightmare*.

The swirling colors and dynamic composition of Delaney's *Abstraction (Still Life with Idol)* of 1945 energizes the image, a quality also seen in his early non-representational works.[2] As early as the late 1930s Delaney began to experiment with colorful abstractions, which, as Bearden and Henderson argue, "made him an Abstract Expressionist before that movement existed."[3]

In 1953 Delaney moved to Paris, where he met up with his friend James Baldwin and lived in a hotel on the Left Bank, then moved to Clamart, a suburb of Paris. In Clamart he painted his characteristic expressionistic works, which utilize bright colors and a heavy impasto to portray both himself and many of his Parisian friends.

Delaney alternated throughout his career between expressionistic figurative works and total abstractions. An outstanding example of his abstract work, Delaney's 1961 *Composition* shows his interest in non-representational painting. Swirling colors and forms fill the paper, seeming to bleed beyond the edge of the page. His 1967 *Untitled* exemplifies his simultaneous interest in painting landscapes, as well as city scenes and portraits. The vivid contrast of the bright yellow sky against an azure sea lends to the dramatic energy of the landscape.

Due to lack of funds and increasing alcoholism, Delaney suffered emotionally while living in France. In

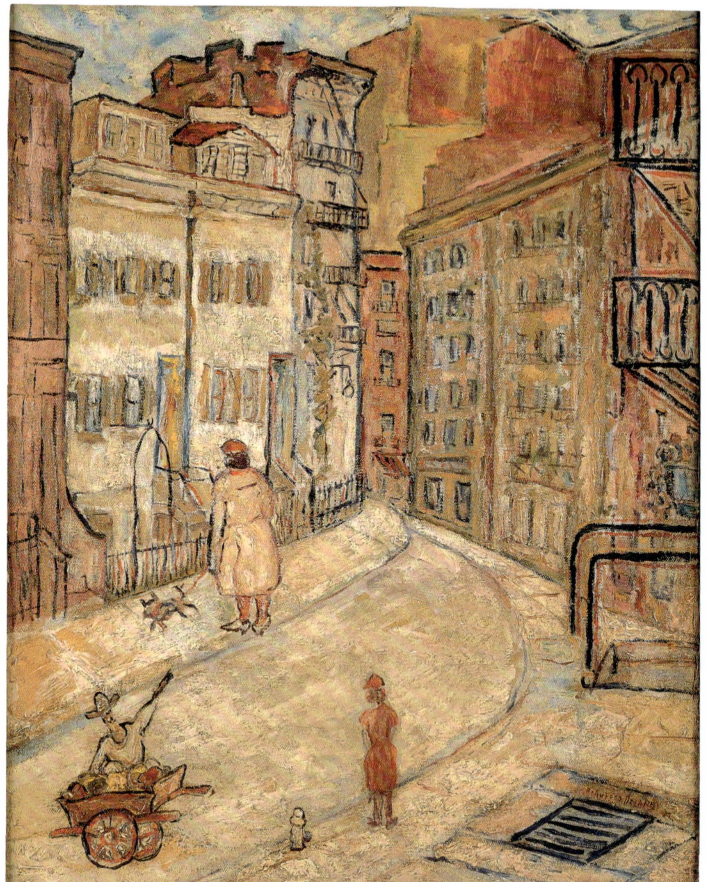

Village Street Scene

1961 while on a vacation in Greece, Delaney had a nervous breakdown. Although a 1964 Fairfield Foundation Grant temporarily relieved his financial anxiety, his mental instability persisted and in the early 1970s he started to show signs of dementia. In 1971 Delaney was hospitalized in France, and remained so until his death on 26 March 1979. A year earlier, in 1978, a major retrospective of his work was held at the Studio Museum in Harlem, organized by Dr. Richard Long, then chair of African American Studies at Atlanta University. Though Delaney did not benefit from many solo exhibitions in his lifetime, a renewed interest in his life and work has brought much recent critical attention, including a 2004 exhibition, *Beauford Delaney: From New York to Paris* at the Minneapolis Institute of Arts, which is traveling to the Philadelphia Museum of Art in November 2005. M.R.

BIBLIOGRAPHY

Baldwin, James. "On the Painter Joseph Delaney," *Transition*, No. 75/76, The Anniversary Issue: Selections from *Transition, 1961–1976* (1997), 88–89.

Bearden, Romare and Harry Henderson. "Beauford Delaney," in *A History of African-American Artists from 1792 to the Present*. New York: Pantheon Books, 1993.

Canterbury, Patricia Sue. *Beauford Delaney: From New York to Paris*. Minneapolis: The Minneapolis Institute of Arts in association with the University of Washington Press, 2004. With essays by Henry Louis Gates, Jr., Ann E. Gibson, Patricia Sue Canterbury, and Michael D. Plante; chronology and bibliography by Sylvain Briet.

Leeming, David. *Amazing Grace: A Biography of Beauford Delaney*. New York: Oxford University Press, 1997.

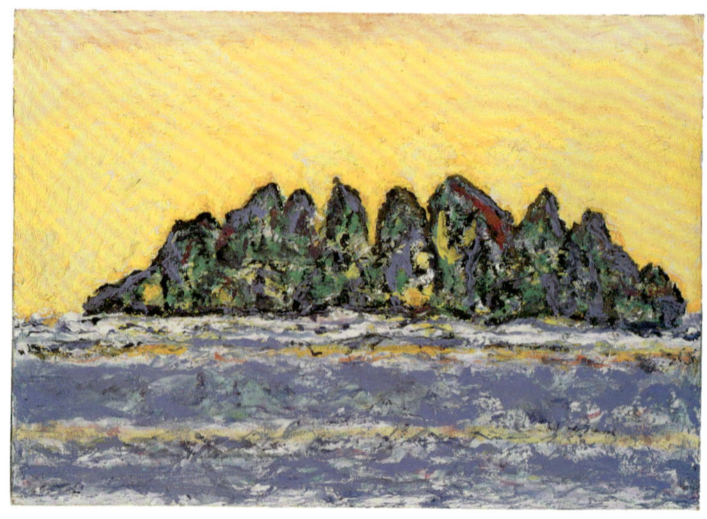

Untitled

1. Baldwin, 88.

2. *Abstraction (Still Life with Idol)* is not in the Wein exhibition at Boston University; instead it is included in the Delaney retrospective held simultaneously at the Philadelphia Museum of Art.

3. Bearden and Henderson, 283.

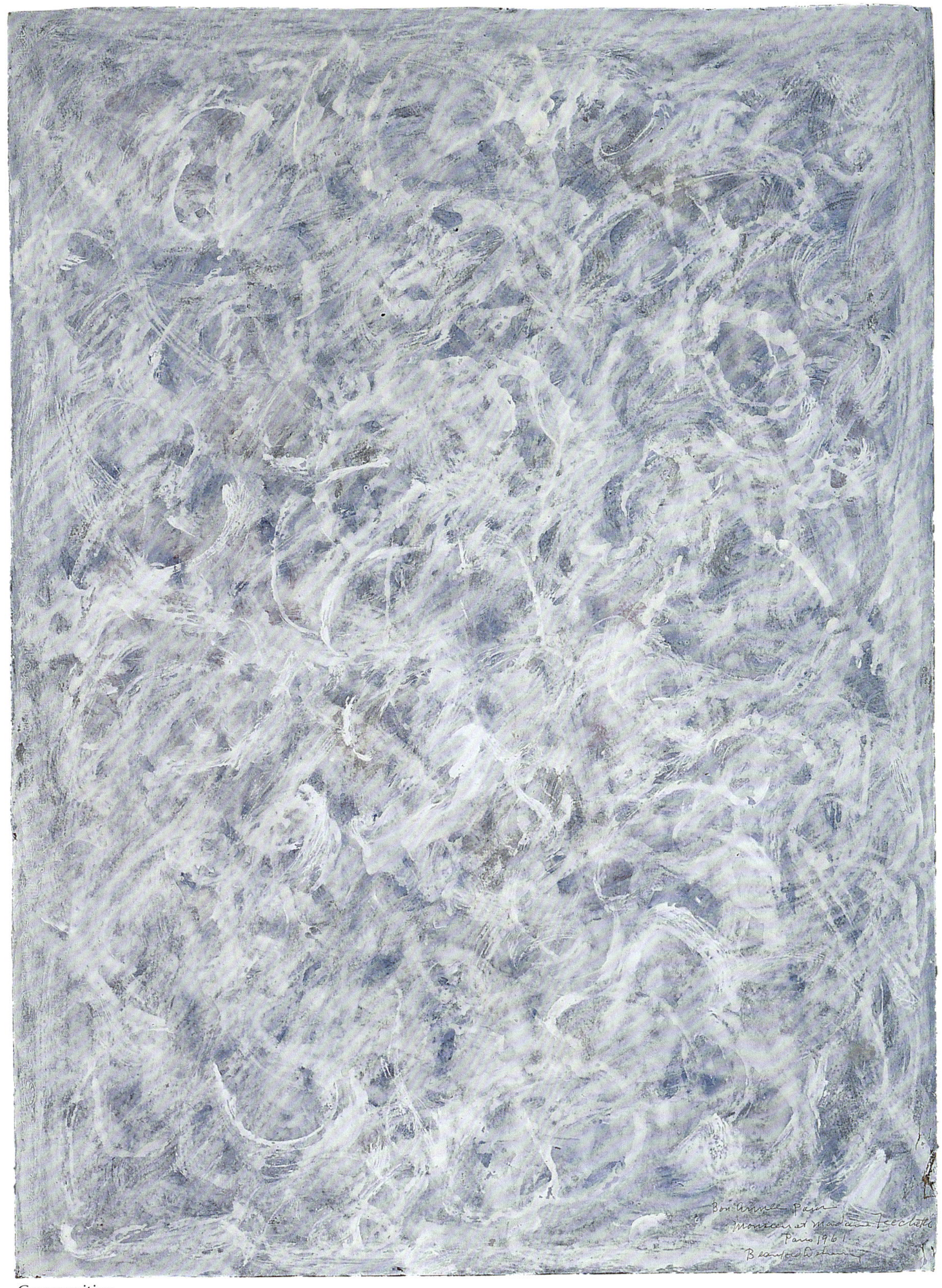

Composition

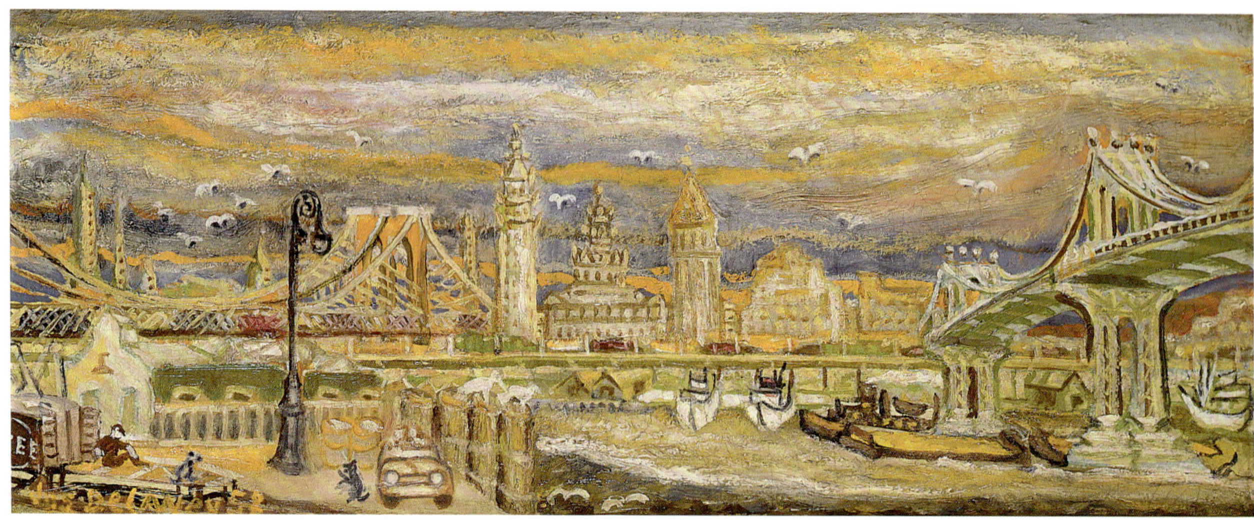
New York City View with Bridge

JOSEPH DELANEY • (1904–1991)

New York City View with Bridge, 1958

Oil on canvas, 12 x 29½ in. (30.5 x 74.9 cm)

Dance Rehearsal, n.d.

Ink wash on paper, 10¼ x 16½ in. (26.1 x 41.9 cm)

Joseph Delaney loved to paint people and the city he lived in, portraying many parts of New York City, including the Waldorf Cafeteria, Greenwich Village, Harlem, and Times Square. Filling numerous sketchbooks with figure studies, Delaney was constantly observing the human form and movement. He painted and sketched men and women, from celebrities to people living on the street, from individual portraits to bustling scenes of city crowds. Indeed, his subject was life itself, as he wrote in a 1968 pamphlet:

> About beauty. . . . Beauty that is pleasant and without question in people and surroundings is conventional. But beauty is not always good to look at. It might . . . [appear in people who] know the side of reality which is suffering. The artist will understand the subject of life in all its expressions because he is always looking restlessly at life.[1]

Born in Knoxville, Tennessee, on 13 September 1904, Delaney was one of ten children born to Reverend Joseph Samuel Delaney and Delia Johnson Delaney. He was the younger brother of artist Beauford Delaney [see entry on Beauford Delaney]. In the mid-1920s, Delaney left Knoxville and traveled through Kentucky and Illinois, where he enlisted for a three-year rotation with the Illinois National Guard. While stationed in Chicago, Delaney met many jazz musicians and painted portraits of Eubie Blake and Mahalia Jackson, among others. Delaney traveled back to Knoxville briefly before relocating to New York City in 1930 to pursue a career in art, as his older brother was doing. Delaney enrolled at the Art Students League, where he met and became friends with Jackson Pollock, of whom he painted a portrait. While at the Art Students League, Delaney studied under Thomas Hart Benton, George Bridgeman, and Alexander Brook. All were influential on Delaney, and Bridgeman, an anatomy instructor, greatly affected Delaney with his interest in the human form. Although Delaney only studied at the Art Students League for a few years, it was central to his experience as an artist.

Like many artists during the Depression, Delaney was employed by the Federal Arts Project (FAP) of the Works Progress Administration (WPA). From 1936–39, Delaney worked on a variety of projects. He painted a WPA mural on Pier 72, New York City, with artists Norman Lewis and Edward Lanning, and made drawings of Paul Revere silver from the Metropolitan Museum of Art for the Index of

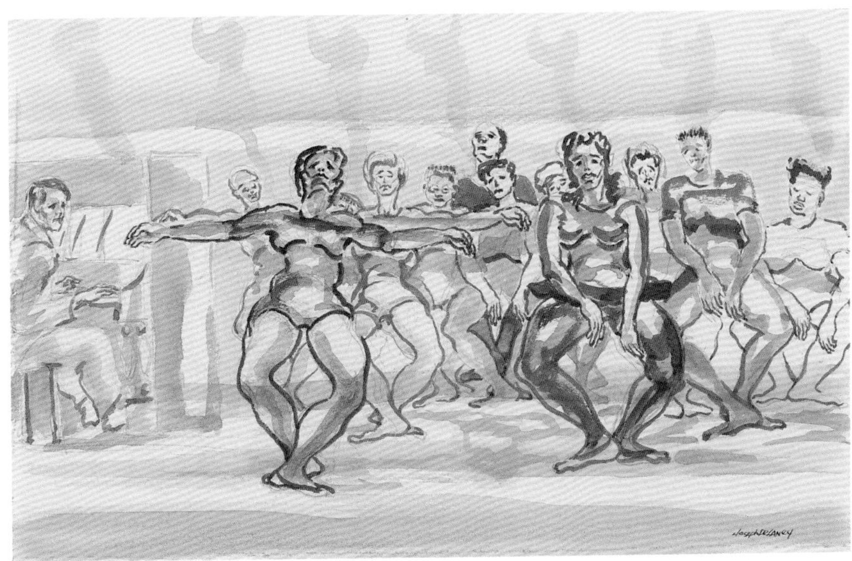

Dance Rehearsal

American Design (a division of the FAP). About this time he became associated with a group of artists working around Fourteenth Street and Union Square.

Organized by Vernon Porter, Juliana Force, and Gertrude Whitney, the Washington Square Outdoor Art Show started in 1931. Delaney was one of the first African American artists, along with Palmer Hayden, to participate in the exhibit, displaying his work and painting portraits in the inaugural year of the outdoor show. In the late 1960s Delaney reflected on his experiences with the Washington Square Outdoor Art Show; in a pamphlet he wrote:

> I really want to talk about selling paintings and doing portraits on the sidewalk from the experience of one who had for 39 years been doing so in Washington Square Park, in Brooklyn's Prospect Park, in White Plains's Germantown, two Worlds' Fairs, museums and gallery shows. Of all the exhibitions, no show is more intimate and free and sensitive as the Washington Square Outdoor Art Exhibit.[2]

Delaney's 1958 oil painting, *New York City View with Bridge*, demonstrates his keen interest in depicting New York City in various views. Using expressionistic lines and vivid colors, Delaney painted the bridges and skyline of New York City, including people, boats, and the ongoing city life in the foreground. His simultaneous fascination with the human form can be seen in his numerous sketchbooks, drawings, and portraits. His undated sketch, *Dance Rehearsal*, depicts dancers in various positions at rehearsal. Using ink wash on paper, Delaney captures the fluidity and grace of both the human form and the dancers' movements.

Throughout his career, Delaney was honored with many awards and exhibitions, including a Julius Rosenwald Fund fellowship in 1942. He won first prize for his 1944 painting *East River* (Clark-Atlanta University Collection) at the 1946 Atlanta University Exhibition. Delaney continued to paint figuratively throughout his life, even during the height of Abstract Expressionism in the 1950s. In 1986 Delaney returned to Knoxville for his last major exhibition, titled *Homecoming '86*. He was also artist-in-residence at the University of Tennessee from 1985 until his death on 24 November 1991. M.R.

BIBLIOGRAPHY

Bearden, Romare and Harry Henderson. "Joseph Delaney," in *A History of African-American Artists from 1792 to the Present*. New York: Pantheon Books, 1993.

Delaney, Joseph. Interview with Greta Berman, 20 October 1981, in *Joseph Delaney Parades: Paintings and Drawings of New York City Crowd Scenes*. exh. cat. New York: Henry Street Settlement, Louis Abrons Arts for Living Center, 1982.

Joseph Delaney Papers, Archives of American Art, Smithsonian Institution, Roll 82.

Workman, Robert G. "Joseph Delaney," in Patricia Hills, *Social Concern and Urban Realism: American Painting of the 1930s*. exh. cat. Boston: Boston University Art Gallery, 1983.

1. Joseph Delaney, "Thirty-Six Years Exhibiting in Washington Square Outdoor Art Shows," 27 March 1968 in *Joseph Delaney Papers*, n.p.
2. Ibid., n.p.

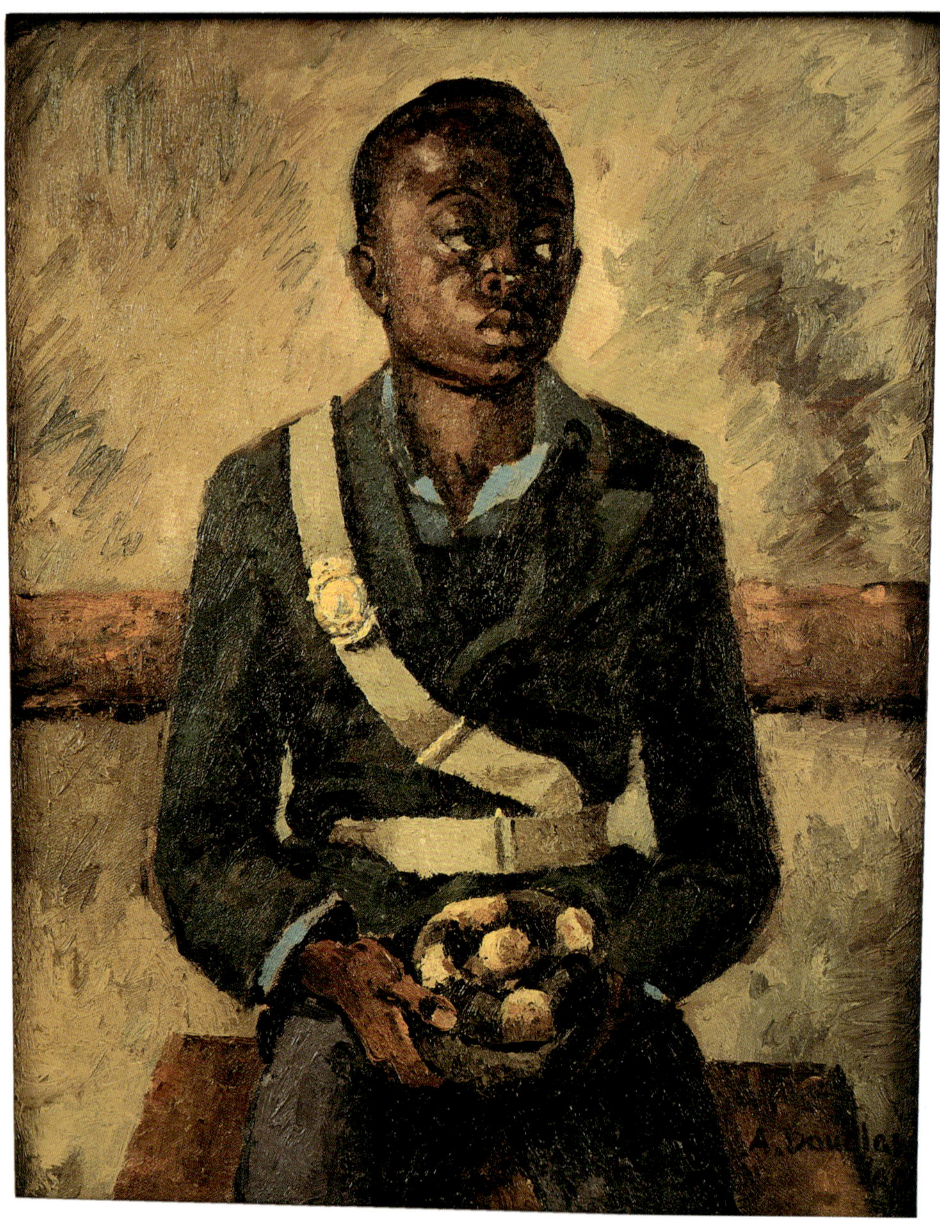

AARON DOUGLAS • (1899–1979)

Untitled (Portrait of a Boy), 1940

Oil on canvas, 19¼ x 15½ in. (48.9 x 39.4 cm)

Born in Topeka, Kansas, on 26 May 1899, Aaron Douglas was one of the first African American artists in the United States to explore modernism and incorporate African art motifs into his own work. His father, Aaron Douglas, Sr., was a baker, originally from Tennessee, and his mother, Elizabeth Douglas, born in Alabama, was a homemaker. Douglas grew up in a politically active, cohesive, and highly literate community that included organizations such as the Black Topeka Federation. After graduating from high school, Douglas enrolled at the University of Nebraska, Lincoln, where he majored in art, receiving his B.F.A. in 1922. In 1926 Douglas married his high school sweetheart, Alta Mae Sawyer.

After a short stint teaching art in Lincoln, Nebraska,

Douglas moved to New York. In 1925 he arrived in Harlem where he quickly became friends with notable intellectuals and artists of the Harlem Renaissance, including W.E.B. Du Bois, Alain Locke, Countee Cullen, and Langston Hughes, as well as patron Albert C. Barnes. Soon after his arrival, Douglas was commissioned by the editors to provide illustrations for two of the most significant black periodicals of the time: W.E.B. Du Bois's *Crisis* magazine, the journal of the National Association for the Advancement of Colored People (NAACP), and Charles S. Johnson's *Opportunity* magazine, the journal of the Urban League. Douglas also contributed illustrations to the radical magazine *Fire!!*, of which there was only one issue, as well as to many books by his peers, including James Weldon Johnson's 1927 *God's Trombones*.

Through Charles S. Johnson, Douglas met German artist Winold Reiss, with whom he worked from 1924–27. In 1925 Alain Locke commissioned Douglas to illustrate the anthology of essays, poems, and short stories, *The New Negro*. Douglas was recognized early on for his artistic talent, and received a Barnes Foundation Fellowship in 1928–29. In 1931 he traveled to Paris where he studied at the Académie Scandinave and met African American artist Henry Ossawa Tanner.

During the Depression Douglas worked for the Public Works of Art Project and completed his 1934 series *Aspects of Negro Life* for the 135th Street branch of the New York Public Library. Later he worked on the Federal Art Project (FAP) of the Works Progress Administration (WPA). In 1935 Douglas became the first president of the Harlem Artists Guild. He was also on the executive committee for the American Artists Congress (AAC) and presented a paper, "The Negro in American Culture," when the AAC convened in New York City in February 1936.

Painter, muralist, and illustrator, Douglas was also well-known as an educator. In 1937 he won a Julius Rosenwald Fund fellowship, which he used to travel to the South to visit a variety of well-known black educational institutions, including Tuskegee Institute and Dillard University. Also in 1937, Douglas founded and chaired the Art Department at Fisk University in Nashville, Tennessee, until his retirement in 1966. In 1938, with his second Rosenwald fellowship, he traveled to Haiti and the Dominican Republic, where he completed a series of island watercolors. In addition to teaching at Fisk University, Douglas returned to school to complete his M.A. from Columbia University Teachers College in New York in 1944. In 1951 he won a Carnegie Grant-in-Aid for the Improvement of Teaching Project. Douglas received an honorary doctorate from Fisk University in 1973.

Douglas's art, as seen in his murals and illustrations, melds Egyptian art, Cubism, African art, and Art Deco into a distinctive style recognizable by its stylized human figures, flat shapes, solid colors, and superimposed concentric circles and chevrons. Though best known for his magazine illustrations and large-scale murals in this style, Douglas also dedicated much of his career to painting portraits of African Americans, as exemplified in the sensitive portrayal of an African American boy in his 1940 oil painting, *Untitled (Portrait of a Boy)*. Rendered in a naturalistic style, the intimate and detailed portrait of the young boy demonstrates the influence of Douglas's teacher and mentor Winold Reiss, who was also known for his equally sensitive depictions of African Americans.

An excerpt from a letter he wrote to Langston Hughes in 1925 best expresses Douglas's own artistic goals and demonstrates how he has come to be regarded as one of the fathers of African American art. In the letter Douglas wrote:

> Your problem, Langston, my problem, no our problem is to conceive, develop, establish an art era. Not white art painted black. . . . Let's bare our arms and plunge them deep through laughter, through pain, through sorrow, through hope, through disappointment, into the very depths of the souls of our people and drag forth material crude, rough, neglected. Then let's sing it, dance it, write it, paint it. Let's do the impossible. Let's create something transcendently material, mystically objective. Earthy. Spiritually earthy. Dynamic.[1]

Douglas died 2 February 1979 in Nashville, Tennessee, leaving behind a diverse body of work ranging from intimate portraits to vibrant magazine illustrations, to large-scale politically charged murals that have inspired many generations of African American artists. M.R.

BIBLIOGRAPHY

Bearden, Romare and Harry Henderson. "Aaron Douglas," in *A History of African-American Artists from 1792 to the Present*. New York: Pantheon Books, 1993.

Kirschke, Amy Helene. *Aaron Douglas: Art, Race and the Harlem Renaissance*. Jackson: University Press of Mississippi, 1995.

1. Letter from Aaron Douglas to Langston Hughes, 21 December 1925, James Weldon Johnson Memorial Collection of Negro Arts and Letters, Beinecke Rare Book and Manuscript Library, Yale University. Quoted in Kirschke, 78–9.

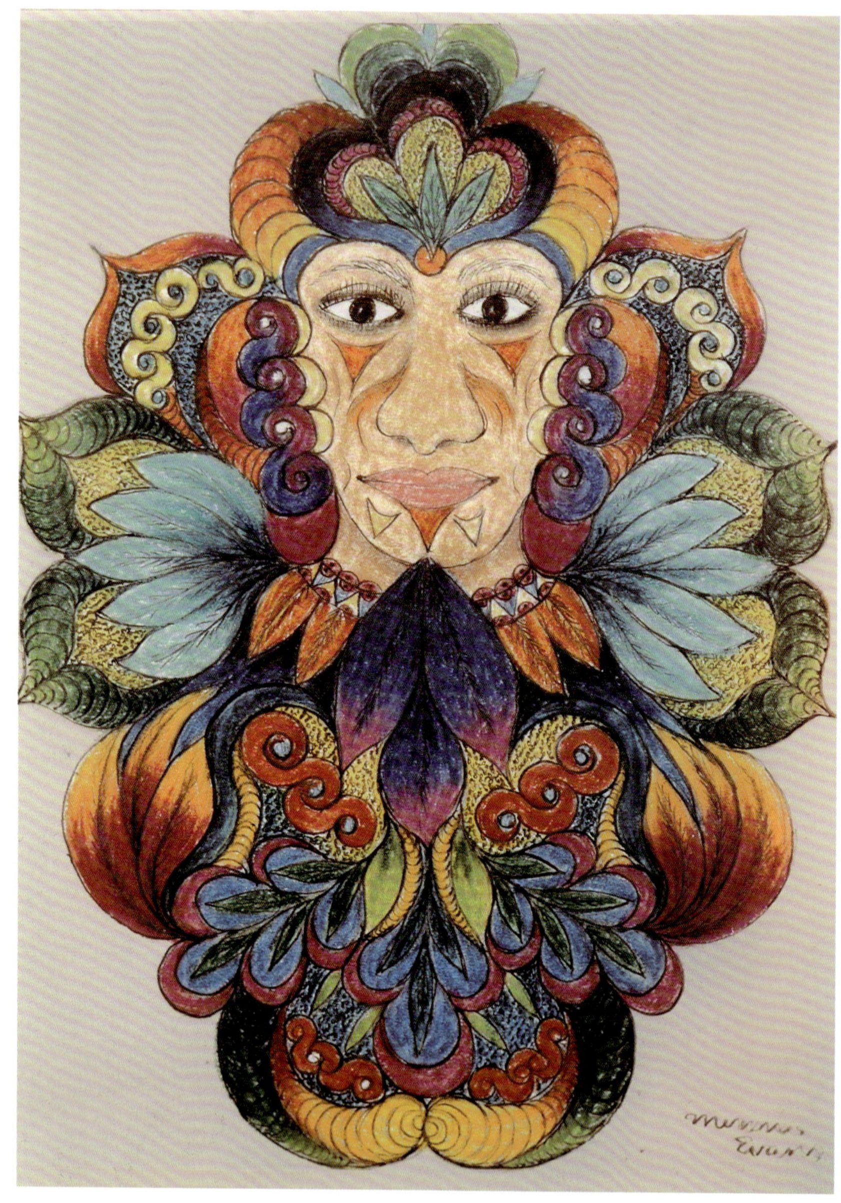

MINNIE EVANS • (1892–1987)

Untitled (Woman's Head with Flowers), 1955

Crayon and pencil on paper, 11½ x 9 in. (29.2 x 22.9 cm)

A descendant of Caribbean slaves, self-taught artist Minnie Eva Jones Evans was born on 12 December 1892 in Long Creek, Pender County, North Carolina. As Evans's mother Ella was only thirteen when she was born, they went to live with her grandmother in Wilmington, North Carolina. She attended school up to the sixth grade and then went to work at various jobs, including hawking shellfish. In 1908, at the age of sixteen, she met and married Julius Caesar Evans, with whom she had three sons. In 1916 Evans worked as a domestic on the Pembroke Park Estate at Wrightsville Beach, North Carolina. A devout Baptist, she also regularly attended services at the nearby

St. Matthew's African Methodist Episcopal Church. In 1948 she moved to another property owned by the Pembroke Family, Airlie Gardens, where she worked as a gatekeeper until the mid-1970s, when she retired.

From a young age, Evans had vivid dreams and visions, but it was on Good Friday, 1935, that Evans heard a voice tell her that she should draw. After this epiphanic moment, her career as an artist began. The Good Friday vision led to her first two drawings, abstract landscapes rendered in ink on paper, titled *My Very First*, and *My Very Second*, both of which are in the collection of the Whitney Museum of American Art. Evans would go on to create over 1,000 works, ranging from small wax crayon drawings to large multimedia works and collages.

Evans came to national recognition with the assistance of photographer Nina Howell Starr. Starr first met Evans in 1962, while a graduate student in photography at the University of Florida. Struck by the originality and beauty of her work, Starr began to promote Evans and arranged for her first solo exhibition in 1966 at the Church of the Epiphany, New York. While in New York Evans visited the Metropolitan Museum of Art, where she encountered for the first time artworks from all over the world, many of which would influence her later work. After this visit, she increased the size and scale of her drawings and began incorporating collage into her drawings and paintings. A *Newsweek* article titled "Beautiful Dreamer" (4 August 1969) highlighted her talent and brought her further national attention.

The hybrid creatures, fantastic forms, biblical imagery, and bright colors that fill Evans's pictures do not easily lend themselves to interpretation. Even she admitted to the unique complexity of her visual representations. She described her own response to her work: "When I get through with them I have to look at them like somebody else. . . . They are just as strange to me as they are to anybody else."[1]

Untitled (Woman's Head with Flowers) of 1955 is characteristic of Evans's style. Lush floral adornments frame a frontal face with kaleidoscopic symmetry. Though her dreams serve as the primary sources of her drawings, her surroundings and other works of art have also influenced her imagery. Clearly her experience of working at Airlie Gardens informed many of the botanical forms present in her works. Her images also incorporate visual and thematic elements from Caribbean, East Indian, Chinese, and Western cultures.

Minnie Evans received many honors and recognitions, both throughout her lifetime and after. In 1969 she was honored at a luncheon by Links, a national organization of African American women in Wilmington, North Carolina. She had her first retrospective in 1975 at the Whitney Museum of American Art, and has had many solo exhibitions since then. Evans retired from working at Airlie Gardens in 1974 at the age of 82. After her mother died at 102 in 1981, Evans moved into a nursing home where she continued to draw and paint until her death on 16 December 1987. In 1994, the mayor of Greenville, North Carolina, declared May 14th "Minnie Evans Day," celebrating her fascinating life and work with an exhibition and festivities.

M.R.

BIBLIOGRAPHY

Evans, Minnie. *Minnie Evans: Artist.* exh. cat. Edited by Charles M. Lovell and Erwin Hester. Greenville, North Carolina: Wellington B. Gray Gallery, East Carolina University, 1993.

Farrington, Lisa E. *Creating Their Own Image: The History of African-American Women Artists*. Oxford: Oxford University Press, 2005.

Kahan, Mitchell D. *Heavenly Visions: The Art of Minnie Evans*. exh. cat. Raleigh, North Carolina: North Carolina Museum of Art, 1986.

Lyons, Mary E. *Painting Dreams: Minnie Evans, Visionary Artist*. Boston: Houghton Mifflin, 1996.

1. Quoted in Lyons, 39.

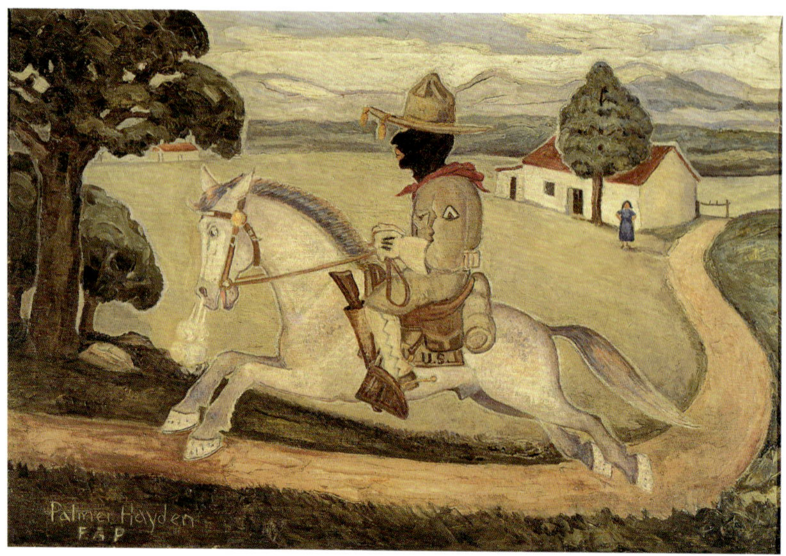

10th Cavalry Trooper

PALMER HAYDEN • (1890–1973)

10th Cavalry Trooper, 1939

Oil on canvas, 20 x 30½ in. (50.8 x 77.5 cm)

The Theatre, 1950

Oil on canvas, 20 x 26 in. (50.8 x 66.1 cm)

Palmer C. Hayden holds a special niche in the history of African American art. While some consider his art to be "folkloric" or "naïve" in both subject matter and paint application, others point to his technical abilities in structuring his compositions, his willingness to research the themes he paints, and his record for accruing prizes and gold medals at exhibitions. In fact, he admitted that during the 1930s, while doing scenes of New York harbor for the Federal Art Project (FAP), he consciously decided "to do folk paintings. Negro paintings of folk life, just as I remembered out of my experiences as a child and growing up in Virginia."[1]

Hayden was born Peyton Cole Hedgeman, the fifth of ten children, and raised in Widewater, Virginia, on the Potomac near Washington, D.C. His father, James Hedgeman, worked on the waterfront; his mother was Nancy Belle Cole, whom Hayden remembers as singing spirituals at home. At the age of sixteen he left home to live with an aunt in Washington, D.C., where he tried to find work. Rebuffed because of his race by a commercial artist, whom he had hoped to assist, he became a drugstore delivery boy. For the next five years he was employed as a circus roustabout, a fisherman, and a sand hog, working from Chesapeake Bay to Boston. In 1911 he joined the Army, which promised in its posters that he would "See the World." Needing a recommendation (required of African Americans), he requested one from his New York landlord, who misidentified him as "Palmer C. Hayden," hence his name change. He stayed in the Army for nine years, serving in the Philippines and later, during World War I, in a Cavalry unit at West Point, New York.

During all these early working years, he continued to draw. From the beginning of grade school, Hayden received praise from his teachers for his drawing talents. As a roustabout he found time to make drawings of circus people, and he drew horses and the countryside at West Point. His commanding officers, recognizing his abilities, set him to work drawing maps.

Leaving the Army in 1920, he moved to New York with plans to become a commercial artist. That summer he enrolled in a six-week class in drawing and painting at Columbia University, where he met other art students. It was the art environment that encouraged and nurtured him: "You see what the others are doing and all that helps you more than what the instructor tells you."[2] He later acknowledged that he thought many artists suffered from

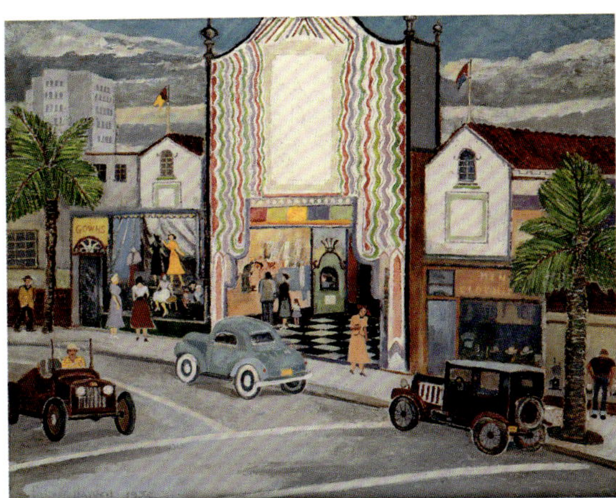

The Theatre

an academic training. He got a job in the post office to support himself, then moved to Greenwich Village, where he painted at night. He became friends with another African American artist from Virginia, Cloyd Boykin, who worked as a janitor. Boykin was later the inspiration for one of Hayden's most famous paintings, *The Janitor Who Paints*, 1931 (Smithsonian American Art Museum).

After five years Hayden lost his post office job, because he took off too many days to paint. In the Village, he met and worked at handyman jobs for a wealthy woman, Alice M. Dike, who encouraged his career in art. After he won a $400 prize from the Harmon Foundation, she gave him an additional $3,000 for the purpose of traveling to Europe. He sailed in 1927 for Paris, where he met the older African American artists, Henry Ossawa Tanner and Laura Wheeler Waring, and the philosopher and art writer Alain Locke. He became part of the expatriate group of artists and writers that frequented the cafés, including Augusta Savage, Aaron Douglas, Hale Woodruff, Eric Walrond, and Countee Cullen. Instead of enrolling in one of the art schools, he took occasional private lessons with Clivette Lefevre, one of the instructors at the Ecole des Beaux-Arts, and produced a number of Paris landscapes, Brittany coast seascapes, and genre scenes of the Americans in Paris. With free rent, offered to him by his French tutor, and by occasional sales of his paintings through the Harmon Foundation, he managed to stay in Paris until 1932.[3]

Back in New York in the midst of the Depression, he got a job as an art handler at the Harmon Foundation and continued to paint. At the outdoor art shows held at Washington Square in Greenwich Village he met William H. Johnson and Beauford and Joseph Delaney. He eventually joined the easel section of the FAP and painted waterfront scenes. He left the FAP in 1940, married Miriam Hoffman, a schoolteacher, and embarked on an ambitious project to paint scenes based on the life of John Henry, known through the famous ballad as "the steel-driving man." Sarah Lawrence College exhibited the fourteen paintings in the series, which were also shown at the Argent Galleries in New York in 1947. By this time he had given up landscapes, and abstraction had no appeal for him. He wanted only to paint pictures that told stories and that drew on his memories of his youth. He recalled: "I paint what us Negroes, colored people, us Americans know. We're a brand-new race, raised and manufactured in the United States. I do like to paint what they did."[4]

The two paintings in the Wein collection are painted in Hayden's "folk" style with subjects drawn from his memories. Although Hayden would have been well aware of the anatomical proportions and movement of horses from his years at West Point, his painting *10th Cavalry Trooper* presents an idealized scene of an African American army private riding through the countryside on a hobbyhorse-like steed. The cavalryman keeps his eyes focused on the road ahead, while a country woman, arms akimbo, keeps watch on him in the distance. For *The Theatre* Hayden painted a street scene that could be a typical small Florida town, with its palm trees, Art Deco movie theater, and automobiles. He orchestrates the colors to give sparkle to this scene of figures strolling along the sidewalks, stopping to admire the mannequins in a ladies shop, or buying tickets to a movie. It suggests a summer day when time stands still and small pleasures are available to everyone.

Hayden died at the Veterans Administration Hospital in New York on 18 February 1973. At the time he had been working on a series of paintings of African American soldiers commissioned by the New York Creative Arts Public Service Program. A major retrospective of his work, organized by Samella Lewis for the Museum of African American Art in Los Angeles, was mounted in 1988. P.H.

BIBLIOGRAPHY

Bearden, Romare and Harry Henderson. "Palmer C. Hayden," in *A History of African-American Artists from 1792 to the Present*. New York: Pantheon Books, 1993.

Hayden, Palmer. Interview with James Adams, Camille Billops, and James V. Hatch, 14 May 1972, in *Artist and Influence* 13 (1994): 91–105.

Leininger-Miller, Theresa. *New Negro Artists in Paris: African American Painters and Sculptors in the City of Light, 1922–1934*. New Brunswick, New Jersey: Rutgers University Press, 2001.

Museum of African American Art, Los Angeles. *Echoes of Our Past: The Narrative Artistry of Palmer C. Hayden*, exh. cat. Los Angeles: Museum of African American Art, 1988.

1. Quoted in Hayden, 103.
2. Quoted in Bearden and Henderson, 159.
3. For Hayden's Paris years see Leininger-Miller, 66–104.
4. Quoted in Bearden and Henderson, 166.

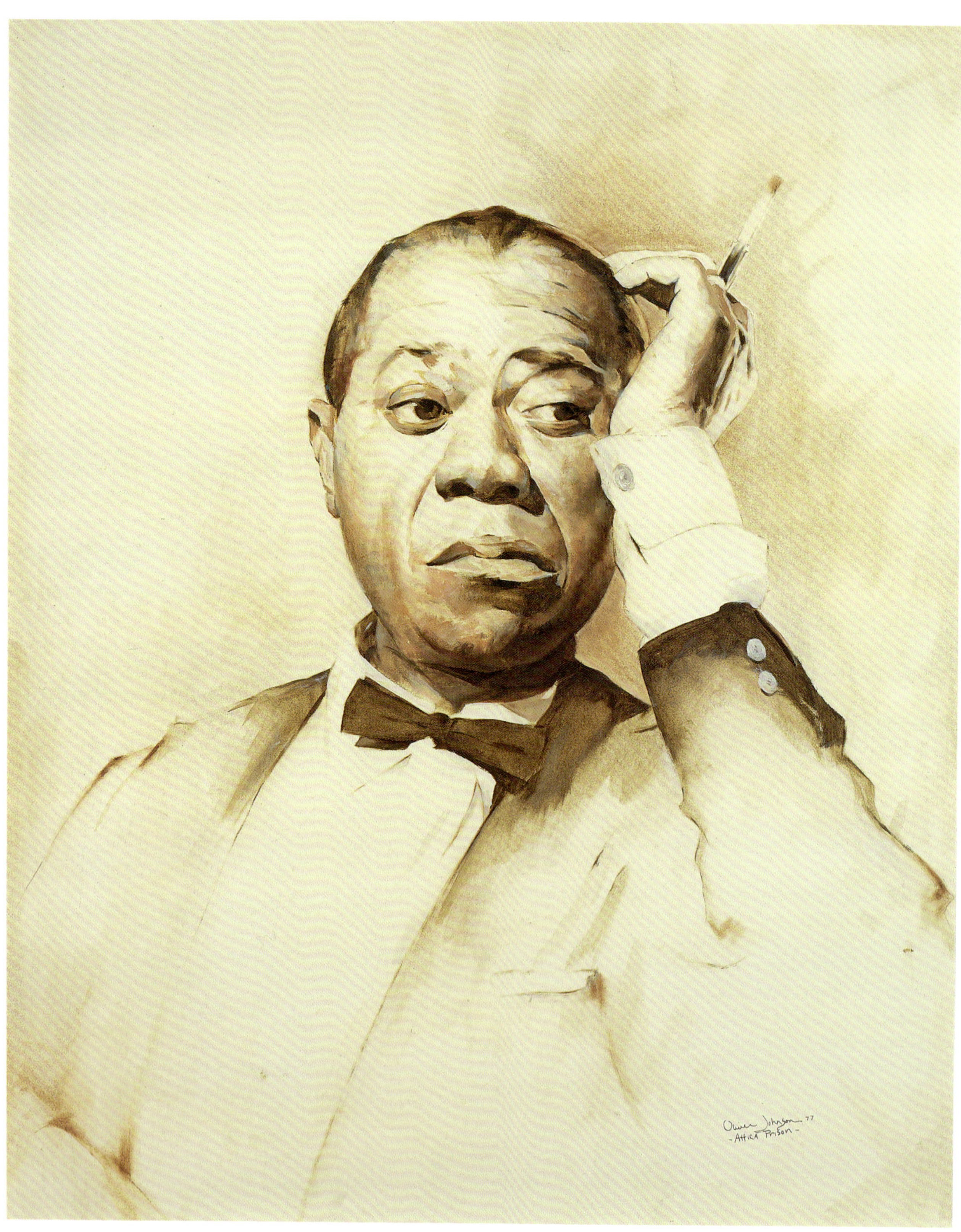
Oliver Johnson 77
-Attica Prison-

OLIVER JOHNSON • (born 1948)

Louis Armstrong, 1977

Oil on paper, 27 x 22 in. (68.6 x 55.9 cm)

Self-taught artist Oliver Johnson was born on 13 December 1948 in Jacksonville, Florida. He had a turbulent youth, moving with his mother all along the east coast, including Baltimore, New York, and Maine. As a young man, he spent time in reform schools and prisons in New York State, including Rikers Island, Sing Sing, Auburn, and Attica. Johnson has commented on his experiences in prison: "I first went to Sing Sing. It was really good. It was the first time that I met a whole crew of artists. We had a whole floor. And in Auburn, there was also an art program. Money received from work we sold went into buying special art materials like big tubes of paint."[1]

During his incarcerations Johnson drew and painted, often using books or magazines on art from the prison library as sources of inspiration. Some of the works that affected him most deeply were reproductions of a painting of jazz singer Nina Simone and Salvador Dalí's 1954 painting *Crucifixion*, which he saw in the adult school at Rikers.[2] Often he would sell his drawings to his fellow inmates for packs of cigarettes. While imprisoned at Auburn, Johnson was encouraged to paint by his fellow inmates; he even conducted art classes for the other prisoners.

Johnson painted this moving portrait of jazz musician Louis Armstrong in 1977 while imprisoned at Attica Correctional Facility. Although painted from a photograph of Armstrong, Johnson modified the image to create his own individual interpretation. His delicate use of light and expert modeling of Armstrong's features contribute to the intimacy of the portrait. Proud of his work, Johnson signed and labeled the painting "Attica Prison, 1977," marking the moment when he realized he wanted to make a change in his life. At that moment, Johnson recently recalled, "I felt things were happening and wanted to start to dictate my whereabouts. . . . After the Louis Armstrong piece I knew I had to come home, to change, and I did."[3]

Johnson's talent as an artist has not gone unrecognized. In 1977 a New York television station reported on a group show at the Bedford Stuyvesant Restoration Art and Cultural Center in Brooklyn, which highlighted Johnson's work. The program caught the eye of gallery director Félicie Balay and her husband Roland Balay, the former president of Knoedler Gallery in New York. Recognizing Johnson's talent, they arranged for his first exhibition at the Wildenstein Gallery in New York City in 1979. Johnson's works are in the collections of Malcolm Forbes, the late Nelson Rockefeller, Fred Woolworth, and Bill Cosby, who also included some of Johnson's paintings on the set of the television series *The Cosby Show*.

An excellent draftsman, Johnson is well-known for his naturalistic portraits in many media, including oil, watercolor, pastels, charcoal drawings, and etchings. He also has done many still-lifes as well as a series on cats. Reflecting on his life in prison, Johnson has described it as a step in his development as an artist, stating: "It was my good fortune to be able to go to prison. Without it I never would have been able to be a painter—there was no one to support me."[4] Johnson continues to exhibit widely and is currently represented by Gallery Felicie in New York. His most recent series is on jazz.

M.R.

BIBLIOGRAPHY

Artist Website: www.galleryfelicie.com/oliverbio.asp (2 August 2005).

Lipson, Karen. "From Attica to Art Gallery," *Newsday*, 2 August 1985.

Unsigned. "A Lot of Struggle," *ARTnews* 78 (September 1979).[5]

Wildenstein Gallery. *Oliver Johnson: Paintings, Pastels, Drawings*. exh. brochure. New York: Wildenstein, 1979.

1. Quoted in Shepard, Joan, "Prison Break Brought Out Young Artist's 'Great Talent,'" *Daily News*, 4 August 1985.
2. Oliver Johnson, telephone interview with Melissa Renn, 26 July 2005.
3. Ibid.
4. Quoted in Lipson.
5. All clippings and articles provided by Félicie Balay.

WILLIAM H. JOHNSON • (1901–1970)

Evisa, 1929

Oil on canvas, 31¾ x 25½ in. (80.7 x 64.8 cm)

Born in Florence, South Carolina, on 18 March 1901, William Henry Johnson was the first son of Alice Smoot Johnson, whose ancestors were both African American and Sioux, and Henry Johnson, who worked as a fireman for the railroad. Johnson attended segregated schools in Florence and worked at the local YMCA and the Atlantic Coast Line Railroad Company. Like countless others who were part of the Great Migration, he arrived in New York in 1918. He lodged with his uncle, Willie Smoot, and his wife, and worked as a hotel porter, short-order cook, and stevedore, loading ships for the war effort. In three years he had saved enough money, after sending home a considerable part of it to his parents and siblings, to enroll at the National Academy of Design (NAD).

In Johnson's second year, painter Charles Webster Hawthorne joined the faculty and took an interest in the talented, somewhat older student. In his teaching Hawthorne stressed color over drawing, and expressive spontaneity in the handling of the brush.[1] Hawthorne instructed his students: "Anything under the sun is beautiful if you have the vision—it is the seeing of the thing that makes it so. . . . The painter . . . must show people more than they already see. . . . Here is where art comes in."[2] For three years, from 1924–26, Johnson also attended Hawthorne's Cape Cod School of Art, earning his tuition, room, and board by doing handyman jobs for Hawthorne. After Johnson's fifth year at the NAD, Hawthorne helped him raise $1,000 toward financing a study trip to Paris. Johnson spent a good part of the fall of 1926 working as a studio assistant for New York painter George B. Luks, who contributed $600 toward the travel fund.

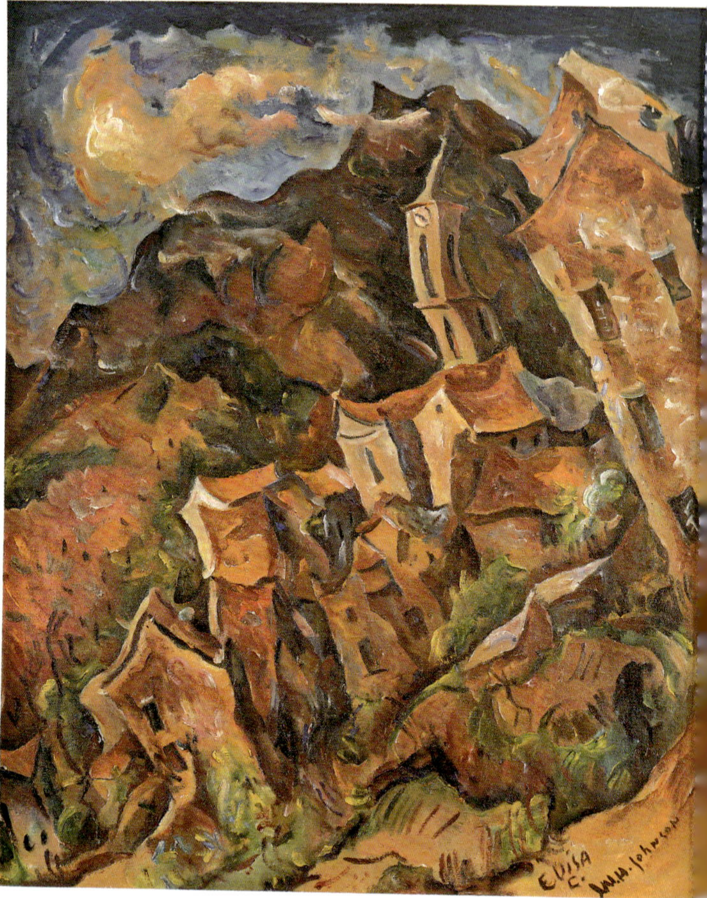

Johnson arrived in Paris in November 1926, rented Whistler's former studio at 86 rue Notre-Dame-des-Champs, met Henry Ossawa Tanner, and began to absorb influences from artists whose work he admired. He was attracted to Gauguin's images of Tahitians and adopted the term "primitive" for himself, as Gauguin had done. Bearden and Henderson suggest that "Johnson used the word *primitive* to mean a sensitive man whose inner life lay outside a culture that imposed on him strict requirements on how he should behave and even paint."[3] A large Soutine exhibition held in Paris in 1927 introduced Johnson to expressionist portraiture and landscape, and he moved to the southern French village of Cagnes-sur-Mer. Applying Hawthorne's precepts and using Soutine's art as a guide, he painted landscapes with tilted buildings and heaving masses of trees. It was during this time that he painted *Evisa*, which represents a village in Corsica, France, painted in the energetic, painterly style he was then adopting. He had two solo exhibitions in France, and set his sights on becoming a successful painter like Tanner.

In November 1929 Johnson returned to New York and received the Fine Arts Award from the Harmon Foundation, and a $400 cash award as a Harmon Gold Medal recipient. He also showed in the Harmon exhibitions of 1928, 1929, 1930, 1931, and 1933. He took his paintings to Florence, South Carolina, in early 1930, where they were shown for one day at the YMCA. Harassed by the Florence police, arrested, and briefly jailed on trumped-up charges, he left embittered and returned to Europe in

May 1950 having spent barely six months in the States.

In late May or early June of 1930, he married Danish weaver and ceramicist Holcha Krake, fifteen years his senior, whom he had met the previous year when she, her sister, and her sister's husband, German sculptor Christoph Voll, were touring France. After their marriage the couple lived close to her family in Kerteminde, a Danish fishing village. Krake's research into craft folk traditions of weaving, dyeing, and pottery took them on extended trips, including to Tunisian Arab villages. Johnson enjoyed painting the Arabs as well as Danish fishermen, and referred to both as "primitive," meaning they were untouched by European culture. In Europe Johnson and Krake had many exhibitions together.

On a subsequent trip to Oslo, Johnson met Edvard Munch and Pola Gauguin, the son of Paul Gauguin. With growing fascism in Europe, the deepening Depression, and few sales, Johnson and Krake made the decision to return to the United States. They sailed for New York in November 1938. They moved into a cold-water flat on West 15th Street but had no prospects for jobs. Finally, at the end of March 1939, Johnson got a job teaching at the Harlem Community Art Center, funded by the Works Progress Administration (WPA). In August of that year he transferred to a division of the Federal Art Project (FAP) and painted murals and made prints until January 1943. He then got a job at a defense factory.

From 1938–44 he turned toward figurative art, using a "folk-like" style of simplified forms, bold color, and flat patterning, and subjects of urban African American couples dancing, farmers and mules, and biblical scenes. Richard J. Powell suggests several reasons for these changes: first, as a weaver, his wife was long interested in folk culture as a source for her own art. Secondly, at the Harlem Community Art Center he met fellow artists and models who would have had a positive response to his African American subjects, and FAP policy across the country encouraged artists to paint the regional diversity of America. Powell also notes that Johnson's friend, John Graham, might have influenced him, since Graham had theorized about "Negro Art," which, he held, included the "drama of stripes."[4] Johnson's works at this time are like crazy-quilts of stripes—which also recall the pieced freehand quilt work of American Southerners as well as African textiles. *Breakdown with Flat Tire*, c. 1940–41 (Smithsonian American Art Museum) is an example of his new style. During the early 1940s, and perhaps influenced by Jacob Lawrence's art, Johnson also embarked on a series of paintings that focused on the history of African Americans in the United States, including Nat Turner, Frederick Douglass, and John Brown.

Johnson's life did not end well. In January 1944 Krake died of breast cancer. Johnson's mental health was also deteriorating because of a syphilitic infection contracted years earlier. His behavior became irrational and even delusional. In 1946 he sailed for Denmark with all of his and Krake's worldly possessions and sought out Krake's relatives. In Oslo he became homeless and confused and was rescued by the Traveler's Aid Society, which returned him to New York. He entered a state hospital and spent the remainder of his life—twenty-three years—in a mental condition of increasing dementia. His possessions, including over 1,100 artworks, were secured by Mary Brady of the Harmon Foundation and eventually the majority of them were turned over to the Smithsonian American Art Museum. The museum held the first retrospective of his work in 1971.

P.H.

BIBLIOGRAPHY

Bearden, Romare and Harry Henderson. "W. H. Johnson," in *A History of African-American Artists from 1792 to the Present*. New York: Pantheon Books, 1993.

Powell, Richard J. *Homecoming: The Art and Life of William H. Johnson*. Washington, D.C.: National Museum of American Art, Smithsonian Institution, 1991.

1. On Hawthorne's influence, see Powell, 12–14.

2. *Hawthorne on Painting: From Students' Notes Collected by Mrs. Charles W. Hawthorne* (New York: Dover Publications, 1960), 17, as quoted in Bearden and Henderson, 186.

3. Bearden and Henderson, 187.

4. See Powell, 125–55.

LOÏS MAILOU JONES • (1905–1998)

Haitian Market, 1961

Oil on canvas, 38½ x 18½ in. (97.8 x 46.9 cm)

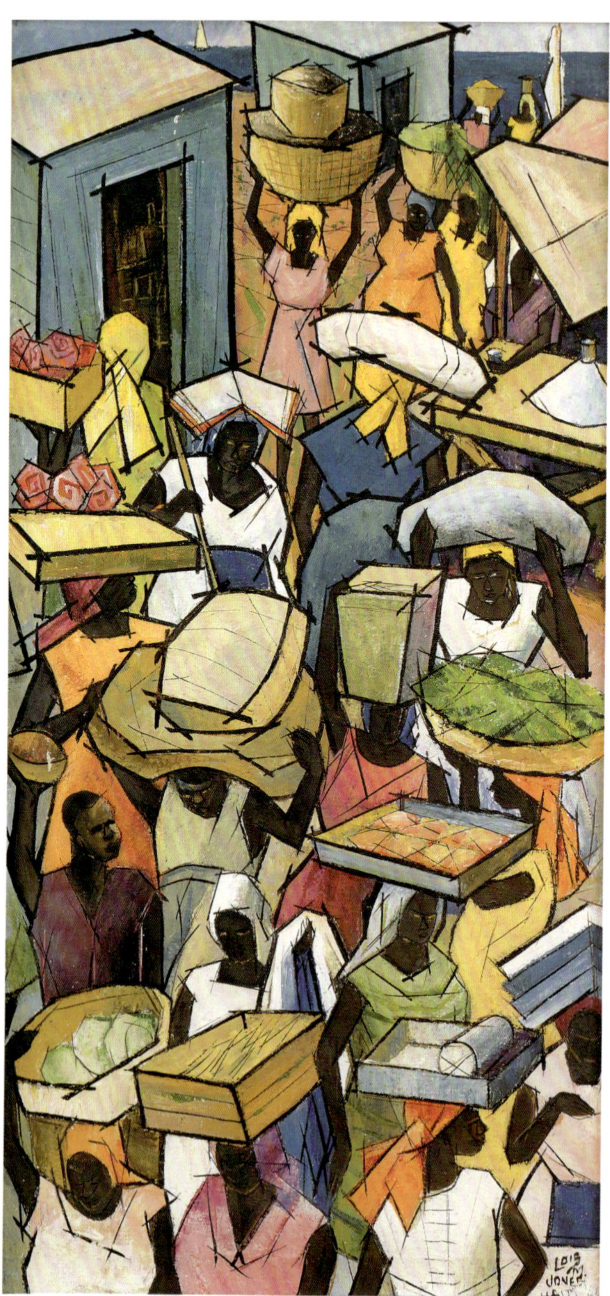

Throughout her career, Loïs Mailou Jones worked in many different painting styles, ranging from Impressionism and Cubism to academic realism and portraiture, to a contemporary synthesis of African, Caribbean, American, and African American iconographic design and thematic elements. In addition to her work as a painter, Jones also designed textiles, illustrated books and periodicals, and taught art at Howard University for forty-seven years. Her students include Hiawatha Brown, Elizabeth Catlett, David C. Driskell, Robert Freeman, Martha Jackson-Jarvis, Gwendolyn Knight Lawrence, Mary Lovelace O'Neill, Malkia Roberts, and Peter Robinson.

Loïs Mailou Jones was born in Boston, Massachusetts, on 3 November 1905 to Thomas Vreeland Jones and Carolyn Dorinda Adams. Her family spent summers at Martha's Vineyard, where Jones would meet many of her mentors, including sculptor Meta Vaux Warrick Fuller and writer Dorothy West. She attended the Boston High School of Practical Arts, then enrolled at the School of the Museum of Fine Arts, Boston. During her senior year, she won the Nathaniel Thayer Prize for excellence in design. In 1926 she also studied at the Boston Normal Art School (now Massachusetts College of Art). In 1927, after receiving her certificate and graduating with honors from the Museum School, she began graduate work at the Designers Art School of Boston.

In 1927, while attending the "Forum," a gathering for young African Americans in Boston, Jones heard a speech by Charlotte Hawkins Brown, founder and director of the Palmer Memorial Institute in Sedalia, North Carolina. Brown was searching for someone to teach art at the black preparatory school and hired Jones to establish its art department. Her work as both a teacher and an exhibition coordinator at the Palmer Memorial Institute caught the attention of Howard University art professor James Herring when he visited in 1930. Shortly after, Herring hired her to teach at Howard, where she remained until her retirement in 1977.

An active member of the New Negro movement, Jones participated in many Harmon Foundation exhibitions; in 1930, her charcoal drawing of one of her students from Palmer Memorial Institute won honorable mention. In 1937–38, she traveled to Europe with the assistance of a General Education Board Fellowship to study at the Académie Julian in Paris. There, Jones met artist Céline Tabary and Symbolist painter Émile Bernard. She participated in the French movement parallel to the Harlem Renaissance, Négritude. Jones's work from this period ranges from Impressionist and Cubist-influenced still-lifes to *plein air* landscapes, to works that incorporate African art and culture.

Jones also worked as an illustrator for the Associated Publishers of Washington, D.C., founded by Carter G. Woodson, a colleague at Howard University. Woodson published black literature as well as the periodicals *Journal of Negro History* and *Negro History Bulletin*, and initiated National Negro History Week (now Black History Month). Jones illustrated *The Picture Poetry Book* (1936) and *African Heroes and Heroines* (1939), and provided illustrations for the *Negro History Bulletin*.

Despite her successes, Jones faced many challenges as an African American artist. In her early career, many museums still did not accept or display works by African American artists. In 1941, for example, Jones submitted a painting to the Corcoran Gallery of Art in Washington, D.C., for a competition. She had her friend Céline Tabary deliver the painting so that it would be accepted. Jones's painting ended up winning the prestigious Robert Woods Bliss Prize for Landscape, from the Society of Washington Artists. Her ethnicity remained unknown to the judges, and, fearing it might be revoked, Jones had the award mailed to her rather than receiving it in person.

Jones's talent and persistence as an artist led to many exhibitions, including an early solo exhibition at the Robert C. Vose Gallery in Boston in 1939, a retrospective at Howard University in 1972, and a solo exhibition at the Museum of Fine Arts, Boston, in 1973. In France in 1952, Jones published *Peintures, 1937–1951*, which was one of the earliest monographs on an African American artist.

Jones's marriage in 1953 to Haitian artist Louis Vergniaud Pierre-Noël greatly influenced her life and art. They traveled frequently to Haiti, making it their second home. Jones's 1961 painting *Haitian Market* shows her synthesis of European, African, and Caribbean design. Like many of her paintings of Haiti, this work depicts the market in a Postimpressionistic and Cubist-influenced style that employs multiple viewing perspectives with bold colors and a strong sense of design and texture. Haiti was a significant subject for Jones, as she described in an interview:

> For me Haiti is Africa, for it marvelously expressed the roots, links, and ties to mother Africa. I feel that Haiti, black America, and Africa are one. We must share our collective inspiration, heritage, and strength to achieve universal significance. To that end I have dedicated my life and my career.[1]

Jones would travel to Haiti regularly until 1986, when political strife in Haiti postponed her visits until 1989.

Jones continued to travel to Africa, Haiti, and Paris until the end of her life. In 1970 she visited eleven African countries with a grant from Howard University to research, document, and photograph art for Howard. Her 1971 painting *Magic of Nigeria* (Collection of Dr. Tritobia Hayes Benjamin) was displayed at the Second World Black and African Festival of Arts and Culture (FESTAC) in Nigeria in 1977. In 1990 Jones held a solo retrospective exhibition, *The World of Loïs Mailou Jones,* at the Meridian International Center. On her eighty-fourth birthday, Jones suffered from a massive heart attack; she died nine years later in 1998.

Loïs Mailou Jones's impressive achievements as both an African American and woman artist can be seen in her many honors and exhibitions, as well as in the careers of her students. Jones was one of ten African American artists honored by President Jimmy Carter at the White House for Outstanding Achievements in the Arts in 1980, and in 1984, July 19th was declared "Loïs Jones Day" in Washington, D.C. In 1986 she was honored by the Women's Caucus for Art with an Outstanding Achievement Award in the Visual Arts, and in 1996 she was named Artist of the Year by the Studio Museum of Harlem, an honor undoubtedly deserved for an artist who opened doors for successive generations of both African American and women artists.

M.R.

BIBLIOGRAPHY

Bearden, Romare and Harry Henderson. "Loïs Mailou Jones," in *A History of African-American Artists from 1792 to the Present*. New York: Pantheon Books, 1993.

Benjamin, Tritobia H. *The Life and Art of Loïs Mailou Jones*. San Francisco: Pomegranate, 1994.

Farrington, Lisa E. *Creating Their Own Image: The History of African-American Women Artists*. Oxford: Oxford University Press, 2005.

Gillespie, Fern. "The Life and Legacy of Loïs Mailou Jones," *Howard Magazine* (Winter 1999): 8–19.

1. Quoted in Gillespie, 13.

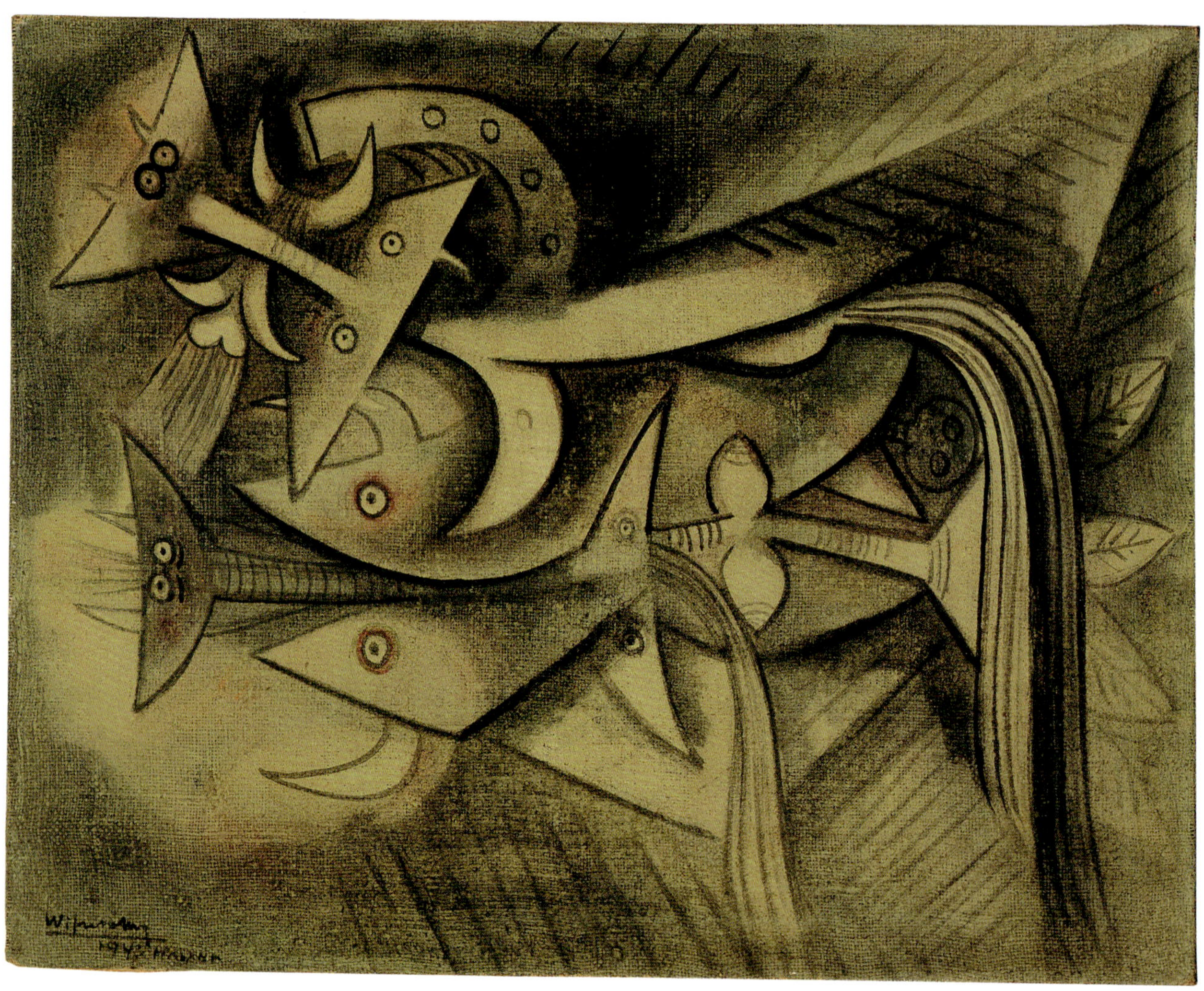

WIFREDO LAM • (1902–1982)

Untitled, 1943

Oil on burlap, 24 x 31 in. (60.9 x 78.7 cm)

Wifredo Oscar de la Concepción Lam y Castilla was born 2 December 1902 and raised in Sagua la Grande, Cuba, where he was exposed at an early age to a variety of religions and cultures. Lam's father, Lam Yam, was a Chinese immigrant who practiced ancestor worship, and Lam's mother, Ana Serafina, practiced traditional Afro-Cuban beliefs. Raised Roman Catholic, Lam learned about the Afro-Cuban religion of Santería from his godmother and spiritual guide, Mantonica Wilson.

In 1916 Lam moved to Havana, where he studied fine arts at the Academia de San Alejandro from 1918–22. In 1923 he left for Spain and worked with academic painter Fernández Alvarez Sotomayor, taking classes at the Academia Libre. In 1929 Lam married Eva Piriz, with whom he had one son; both mother and son died of tuberculosis in 1931. A politically active member of the Spanish Republican Party, Lam fought against the Fascists in the Spanish Civil War (1936–39) and created political works, including propaganda posters.

In 1938 Lam left Spain and moved to Paris, where he was introduced to Pablo Picasso through Catalonian sculptor Manolo Hughé. He also met Henri Matisse, as well as André Breton, leader of the Surrealist movement. Lam became an active member in both Cubist and Surrealist circles. In 1940, when France capitulated to the Nazis, he moved to Marseilles, which was a refuge for anti-fascist intellectuals. In Marseilles he illustrated André Breton's Surrealist book *Fata Morgana* (1940). As the war intensified, Lam and other surrealists left Marseilles for the Caribbean, where, on the island of Martinique, he met Aimé Césaire, a leading poet of the Négritude movement, who became Lam's friend and collaborator.

In 1942 Lam returned to his homeland of Cuba for the first time in nearly twenty years. His rediscovery of Afro-Cuban culture transformed his life and art. His 1943 *Untitled* oil painting superbly demonstrates his signature style, one that synthesizes Cubism and Surrealism with Afro-Cuban culture. The hybrid human, animal, and vegetal forms that appear in Lam's work range from deities to symbols of Cuban nationalism, to creatures offered as sacrifices in Santería rituals. His recurring bird- and bat-like hybrid forms have an origin in one of Lam's earliest memories. He recalled to one biographer seeing a bat hanging over his head when he was five years old:

> For me this animal had two heads. . . . In that little space I felt for the first time the fear of being no more than a thing among other things, a mute presence with regard to nameless objects. This happened in 1907. It was then I first experienced the feeling of the passing of the days, of a linkage in memory and of a time which stops for no one. In that room, with the open wardrobe revealing—like a decapitated figure—my father's clothes, the looking-glass reflected the magic of moving images, my own image and that of the awakened bat, awkwardly flying in pursuit of its own shadow. . . . From that morning in 1907, from the presence of that demented bird, dates the first moment of my consciousness of *being there*.[1]

This dreamlike memory marks his first moment of self-awareness, signaled by the appearance of the bat-like creature. As the passage suggests, this incident greatly affected Lam, and became an underlying motif in many of his artworks.

In 1944 Lam met and married German chemist Helena Holzer, with whom he traveled to Haiti. In Haiti, Lam, joined by Breton, attended voodoo rituals that influenced the imagery of Lam's art. In the 1940s Lam received recognition in Cuba and worldwide, including a series of shows at the Pierre Matisse Gallery in New York and a 1945 exhibition organized by Pierre Loeb in Paris. In 1950 Lam and Holzer divorced and in 1952 he returned permanently to Paris, although he continued to visit Cuba and New York regularly. In 1959 he married artist Lou Laurin, with whom he had three children.

Although Lam received many honors and exhibitions throughout his life, a renewed interest in his work over the last twenty years invites a reconsideration of modernism that includes Lam as a central figure. A pivotal player in both Cubism and the Surrealist movement, Lam went beyond both to create a unique style that incorporated his own Afro-Cuban culture. He died in Paris on 11 September 1982.

M.R.

BIBLIOGRAPHY

Fouchet, Max-Pol. *Wifredo Lam*. New York: Rizzoli, 1976.

Sims, Lowery Stokes. *Wifredo Lam and the International Avant-Garde, 1923–1982.* Austin, Texas: University of Texas Press, 2002.

Studio Museum in Harlem. *Wifredo Lam and His Contemporaries, 1938–1952.* exh. cat. New York: Studio Museum in Harlem, 1992. Maria R. Balderrama, ed., with essays by Giulio V. Blanc, Julia P. Herzberg, and Lowery Stokes Sims; foreword by Kinshasha Holman Conwill; introduction by Jacques Leenhardt.

1. Quoted in Fouchet, 41–44.

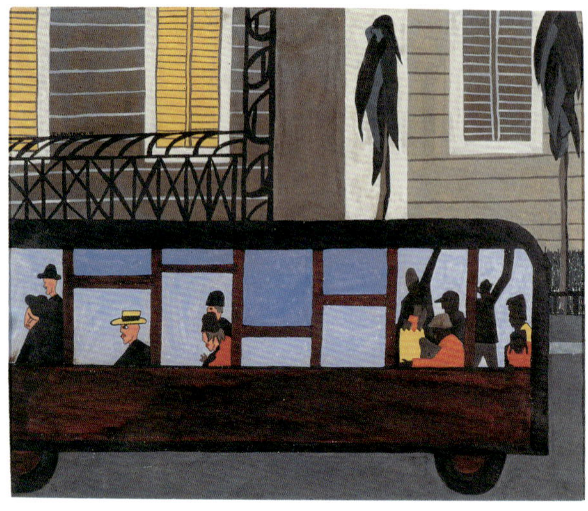

Bus

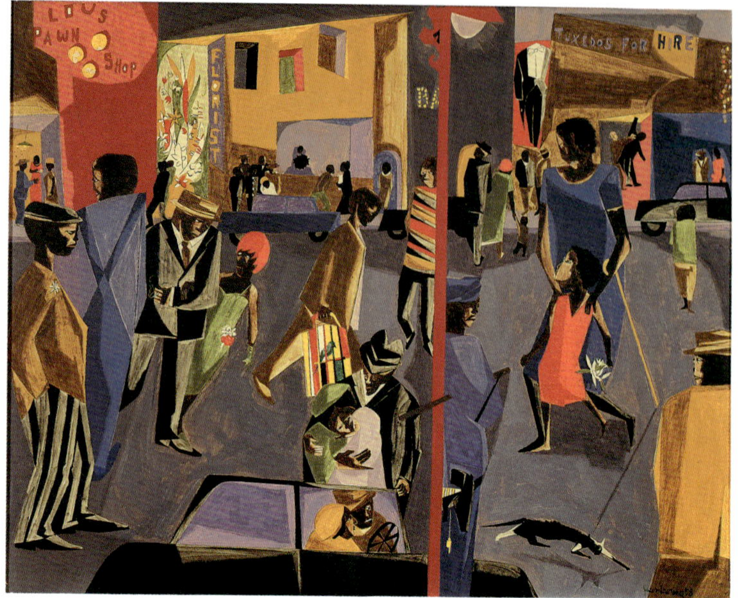

Fulton and Nostrand

JACOB LAWRENCE • (1917–2000)

Bus, 1941

Gouache on paper, 17 x 22 in. (43.2 x 55.9 cm)

Fulton and Nostrand, 1958

Egg tempera on hardboard, 24 x 30 in. (60.9 x 76.2 cm)

Born in Atlantic City, New Jersey, on 7 September 1917, Jacob Lawrence was the first son of Jacob and Rosa Lee Lawrence. After moving to Easton, Pennsylvania, his parents separated. Leaving her children in foster homes, Rosa left to find work in New York. In 1930 she brought them to Harlem.

Early in the 1930s Lawrence went to the after-school program at Utopia House and was encouraged by Charles Alston, a young art instructor from Columbia University. Later Lawrence enrolled in art classes at the 135th Street Public Library with Alston as instructor. With the encouragement of Augusta Savage, he enrolled at the Harlem Art Workshop, where he met his future wife, Gwendolyn Knight. From 1936–38 he received a scholarship to study at the American Artists School. Late in 1938, after reaching the eligible age of twenty-one, he joined the Federal Art Project (FAP) of the Works Progress Administration (WPA), serving in the easel division for about eighteen months.

It was during the 1930s that Lawrence developed his mature signature style—a reductive figurative modernism uniquely wedded to socially concerned subject matter. It was an expressive Cubism characterized by simplified shapes and a limited palette of flat, pure color. His subjects throughout his career came from his community—everyday people living and working in Harlem or other urban centers—and from African American history. For his history paintings he worked in the series format, painting scenes based on his library research at the Schomburg Library in Harlem: *Toussaint L'Ouverture* (1937), *Frederick Douglass* (1938–39), *Harriet Tubman* (1939–40), *Migration* (1940–41), and *John Brown* (1941–42). For these series he received fellowships from the Julius Rosenwald Fund. His *Migration* series of 60 paintings gave pictorial form to the movement of African Americans from the South to northern and western cities beginning in World War I. Edith Halpert, director of the Downtown Gallery, arranged for *Fortune* magazine to publish twenty-six of the images in its November 1941 issue. With the check from *Fortune* in hand, that summer Lawrence married Knight and the two traveled to New Orleans for their honeymoon. They stayed until the late winter when they briefly visited relatives in Virginia before returning to New York.

During World War II Lawrence was inducted into the U.S. Coast Guard, first serving on a weather patrol boat and later on the troop carrier *USS General Richardson* before his discharge in December 1945. His commanding officer, recognizing his talent, urged him to paint. While still in the service, in 1943, he became the first African American artist to have a solo exhibition of his paintings at the Museum of Modern Art in New York. Following the war he taught briefly at Black Mountain College with Josef Albers. A commission from *Fortune* to paint scenes of the condition of southern African Americans in the post–World War II years took him back to the South in June and July 1947. In 1958 he began teaching at Pratt Institute in Brooklyn. In 1962 he made a brief trip to Nigeria where his work was being exhibited; in 1964 he and his wife returned there and lived for about nine months. From 1966–69 he taught at the New School for Social Research; in the late 1960s he also taught at the Art Students League. During the summers he often taught at the Skowhegan School of Painting and Sculpture in Maine.

During the 1960s Lawrence was deeply affected by the Civil Rights movement and painted works that comment on those years, such as *The Ordeal of Alice*, 1963 (Private Collection), which depicts a young black girl in a white dress being taunted by jeering demons, as African American children were during the years of the desegregation of the public schools.

In 1970 he left his teaching position at Pratt and took a job at the University of Washington. He lived, painted, and taught in Seattle until his death in 2000. He was the recipient of numerous awards and honorary degrees, including election to the American Academy of Arts and Letters in 1983. He received the National Medal of Arts in 1990.

Throughout his career Lawrence always openly acknowledged the influence of the community, which included the families of Harlem, the street corner orators, black nationalists, communists, church preachers, and gospel singers. He has said,

> I'm dealing with struggle throughout my [work]. Sometimes that struggle is apparent, sometimes it is not apparent. I think struggle is a beautiful thing. I think it is what made our country what it is, starting with the revolution. The American people in general have always gone through this. Of course the black people have continued this struggle also. I would like to think of this symbol [of struggle in my work] as being not just a black symbol, but a symbol of our—man's—capacity to endure and to triumph.[1]

Lawrence painted *Bus* in the summer of 1941 when he and Gwendolyn Knight Lawrence visited New Orleans, where he finished the panels of his John Brown epic. It was his first visit to the South and thus the first time he experienced southern Jim Crow. A scene of racial segregation with white riders in the front of the bus while black riders are made to crowd in the rear, *Bus* was published in *Survey Graphic* in November 1942.[2]

In 1958 Lawrence painted *Fulton and Nostrand*, a view of the Bedford-Stuyvesant neighborhood of Brooklyn, where he and Knight then resided. The following year the painting was included in the famous exhibition held at the Pushkin Museum of Fine Arts, *American Sculpture and Painting: American National Exhibition in Moscow*. The show proved controversial, yet it was one of the first instances of cultural exchange with the Soviet Union. Lawrence's painting typifies his street scenes, with its kaleidoscope of flatly colored shapes representing busy pedestrian-filled sidewalks and streets, storefronts, and shop signs.

P.H.

BIBLIOGRAPHY

Nesbett, Peter T., *Jacob Lawrence: The Complete Prints (1963–2000)*. Seattle: University of Washington Press, 2001. Essay by Patricia Hills.

Nesbett, Peter T. and Michelle DuBois, eds. *Jacob Lawrence: Paintings, Drawings, and Murals (1935–1999): A Catalogue Raisonné*. Seattle: University of Washington Press, 2000.

———, eds. *Over the Line: The Art and Life of Jacob Lawrence*. Seattle: University of Washington Press, 2000. Essays by Patricia Hills, Paul J. Karlstrom, Leslie King-Hammond, Lizzetta LeFalle-Collins, Richard J. Powell, Lowery Stokes Sims, Elizabeth Steele, and Elizabeth Hutton Turner.

Wheat, Ellen Harkins. *Jacob Lawrence: American Painter*. exh. cat. Seattle: University of Washington Press in association with the Seattle Art Museum, 1986.

1. Quoted in Nesbett, *Jacob Lawrence: The Complete Prints*, 22.
2. See Patricia Hills, "'In the Heart of the Black Belt': Jacob Lawrence's Commission from *Fortune* to Paint the South," *The International Review of African American Art* 19:1 (2003): 28–36.

HUGHIE LEE-SMITH • (1915–1999)

Man with Balloons, 1960

Oil on canvas, 36¼ x 46 in. (92.1 x 116.8 cm)

The Other Side, 1960s

Oil on canvas, 36 x 48 in. (91.4 x 121.9 cm)

End of Act One, 1987

Oil on canvas, 32 x 34¼ in. (81.3 x 86.9 cm)

We easily recognize the paintings of Hughie Lee-Smith, done from the 1960s through the late 1980s, in terms of subject matter, composition, coloration, and theme. He places usually one, two, or three isolated figures, never more, never touching, in a bleak, surreal landscape with a flat terrain made up of packed dirt, flat sand, stone, or concrete with one or two brick or cracked stone walls serving as either platform or backdrop. He brings in poles, fluttering ribbons, and balloons as frequent props and stages these subjects and motifs with precision, as if calculated to suggest variations on the Golden Section. The palette consists of a harmony of pinks, blues, soft browns, silvery grays, and sometimes blue-greens when he chooses to show a distant sea. The time of day is either dusk or dawn because long shadows extend horizontally from the figures' forms, holding them in place; the figures themselves are modeled with a clear chiaroscuro. The themes suggest existential loneliness and the queasy restlessness of a Beckett play. As David Driskell has observed, "His concern seems not so much the 'real' people whom he depicts with such exactitude and beauty, not the 'romantic' landscapes in which he has set them, as a psychological investigation of the American experience—its loneliness, barrenness and lack of variety."[1] We don't easily forget these paintings.

Shortly after Hughie Lee-Smith was born on 20 September 1915 in Eustis, Florida, to Luther and Alice Williams Smith, his parents separated and he went to live in Atlanta. His mother later brought him to Cleveland where she had family. He recalls drawing at an early age with his mother's encouragement and taking Saturday classes at the Cleveland Museum of Art. Clarence Carter, his teacher there, taught classical drawing including chiaroscuro. As a teenager he also studied at the Cleveland Institute of Art. In 1935 he held a one-year scholarship to the Art School of the Detroit Society of Arts and Crafts. Returning to Cleveland the following year with a scholarship he attended the Cleveland Institute of Art, where his teachers were Carl Gaertner, Henry O. Keller, and Ralph Stoll, all of whom influenced him. Lee-Smith admired Gaertner for "his absolute control of values, his chiaroscuro approach to painting," Keller for "his insistence on solid drawing," and Stoll for his portraiture.[2] He taught art classes in the Art Studio of the Playhouse Settlement House, which included the Karamu Theatre. For the Gilpin Players in residence he designed stage sets and even performed there as a modern dancer with the "Experiential Dancers." From 1938 to 1940, he also was on the print division of the Ohio Federal Art Project.

During the academic year, 1940–41, he went to Orangeburg, North Carolina, to teach at Claflin College. In 1940 he married Mabel Everette (they later divorced); they moved to Detroit and had a daughter, Christina. During World War II he worked at the Ford plant in the aircraft division; in 1944 he joined the U.S. Navy and was fortunate to be assigned to duties as an artist.

Following the war, in 1945, he returned to school, first to the Detroit Society of Arts and Crafts and then to Wayne State University, receiving a B.S. degree in 1953. Also in 1953 he received the Founders prize at the Detroit Institute of Arts and was named Michigan Painter of the Year by the *Detroit News*.[3]

During the 1950s, a decade in which he received numerous prizes, he worked in a social realist style, choosing often to depict African American youth in desolate urban settings, such as *Boy with Tire*, 1952 (Detroit Institute of Arts), *The Walls*, 1952 (Private Collection), and *Piper*, 1953 (Detroit Institute of Arts).[4] His approach to art was published in the 25 May 1945 issue of *New Masses*:

> A definition of the role of a people's art can be arrived at only by means of a socio-historical approach to the question and not through abstract thinking. The road art must travel in a given society is charted by the historical necessities of the times. It is determined by the needs of the people at any given historical period.
>
> We cannot overemphasize this: if art is to survive it

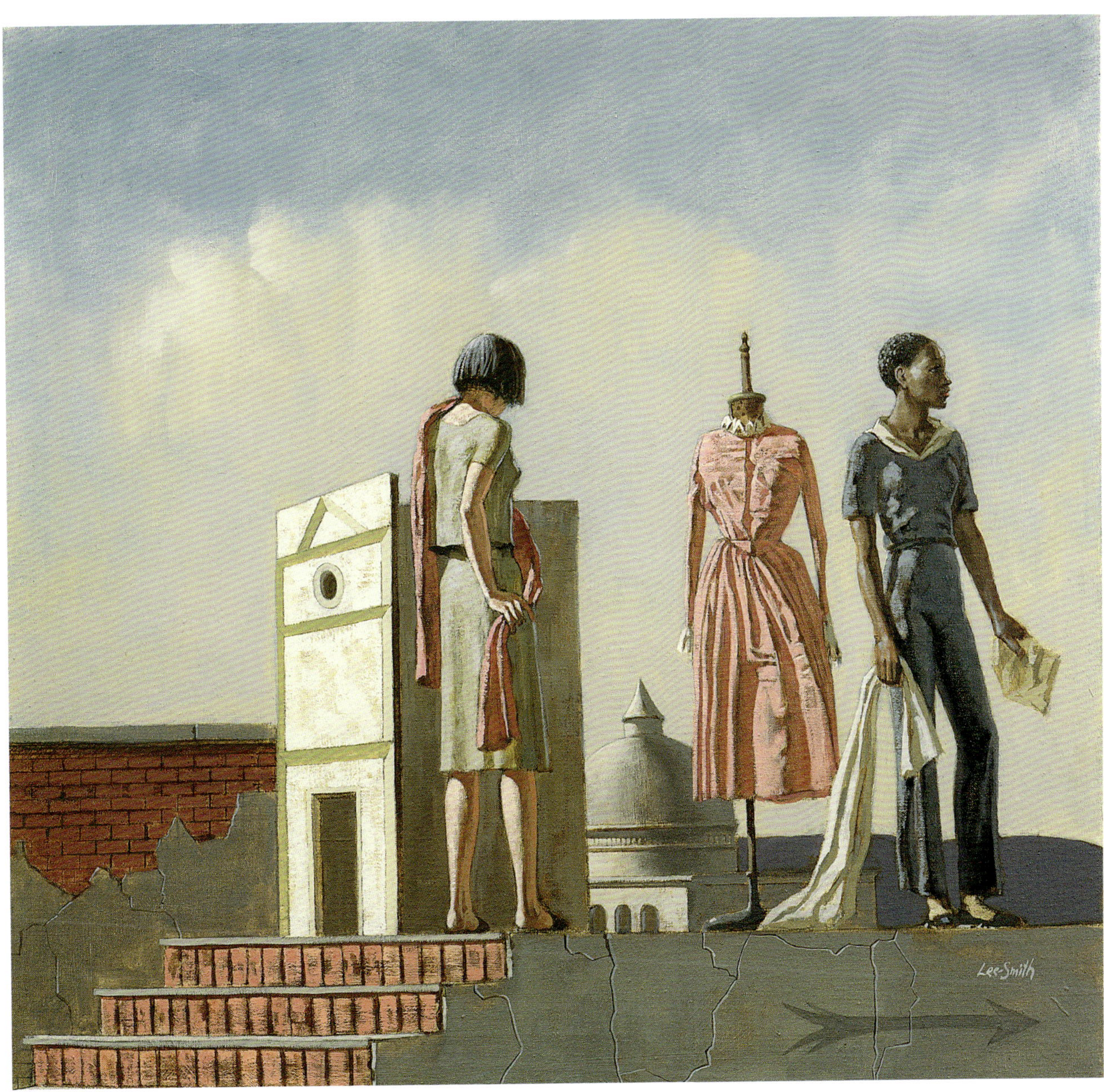

End of Act One

> must express the needs and aspirations of the people and solidify them in the struggle for the achievement of their political, social and economic goals. If art is going to be effective in this social task it must be understood. Form and style must, therefore, meet with the approval of the great majority of people. Unless the artist takes into consideration the art understanding of the common man, I am afraid he is imposing art from above; art that is uncalled for and unwanted.[5]

In 1957 Lee-Smith moved to New York City, and his work gradually evolved. Children disappeared, to be replaced by men and women, black and white, standing in staged scenes not specifically urban, but suggestive of a decaying industrial landscape. Other artists during the late 1950s, such as Philip Evergood and Joseph Hirsch, also moved from a social realism focused on specific issues to more generalized humanist statements, but in the case of Lee-Smith, the alienation that African Americans experienced in a racially divided society was an important factor in generating his imagery. In an interview with Carol Wald in the late 1970s, Lee-Smith spoke of his paintings as part of his inner experiences:

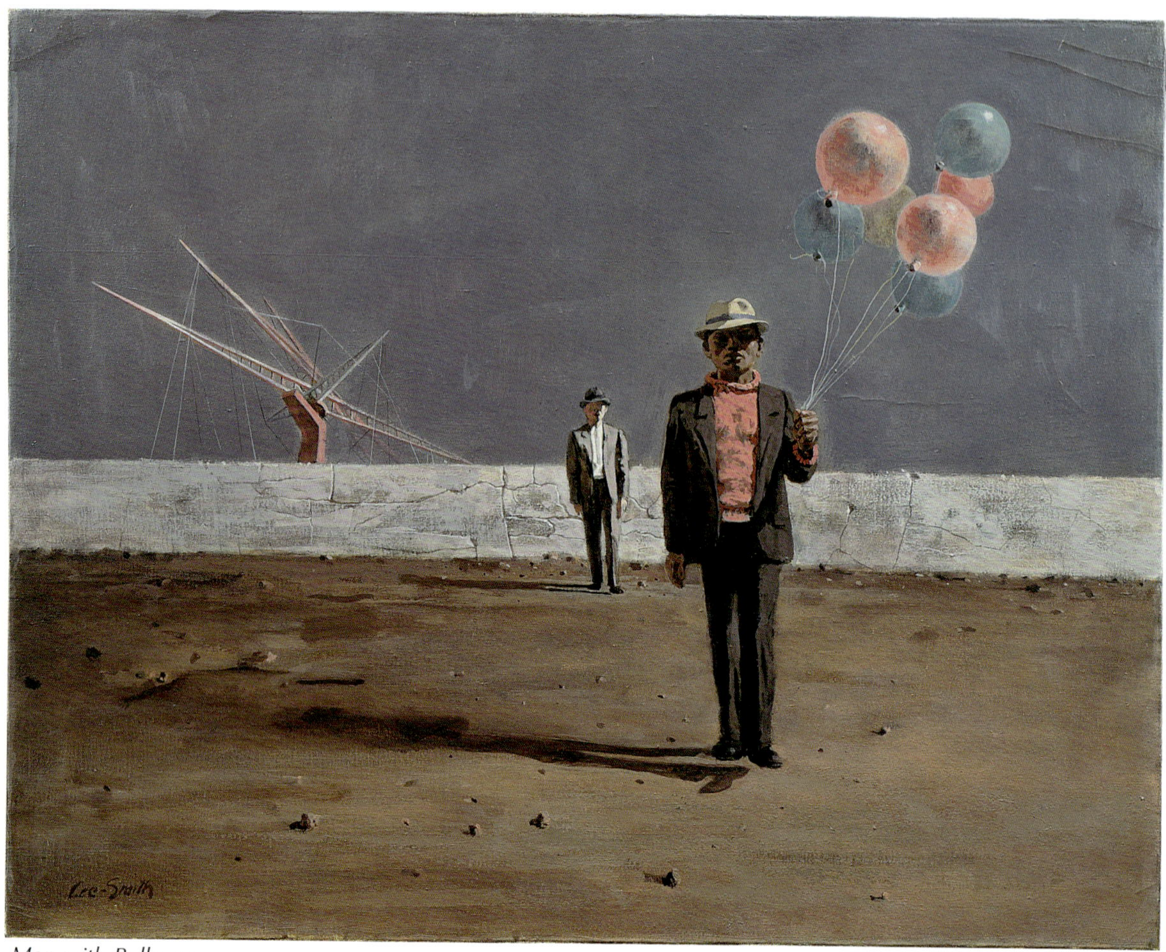

Man with Balloons

> In my case, aloneness, I think, has stemmed from the fact that I'm black. Unconsciously, it has a lot to do with alienation. The condition of the artist is already one of aloneness. Our work depends upon being alone, and we can appreciate the condition of aloneness more than other people. Being one of a group of outcasts in a society makes my sensitivity to the condition of aloneness much sharper than that of the average person. There is an isolation that every sensitive person feels; it is something all creative people recognize. And in all blacks there is awareness of their isolation from the mainstream of society. I felt it much more in my youth. Now I am not so affected by the alienation because I can appreciate my independence as a human being.[6]

Indeed, the paintings in the Wein collection suggest that his concerns with racial difference played a role in the symbolic thematics of his paintings. In *Man with Balloons* a white man stands at the dead center of the composition, facing both the viewer and the back of the black man who stands right of center and holds several pink and blue balloons. Whether the white man watches the black man with suspicion or benevolence is less relevant than that the former, because of his central placement, controls the situation. In *End of Act One* two women, one light in complexion, the other dark, stand on a stage with a mannequin. The darker woman, holding what seems to be a script, looks off stage to the right; the lighter woman waits in the wings to join her sister player. Only the headless mannequin faces us—a cipher as to her race. In *The Other Side* an older white man with dark glasses and arms tucked behind him waits for the viewer to come to "the other side"—toward an unwelcoming landscape of cracked walls and stone steps where we can easily lose our footing. The meanings of all three paintings are not explicit; through their symbolism, they invite the viewer to puzzle out what dreamscapes become when they veer toward the nightmare reality of exclusion and alienation.

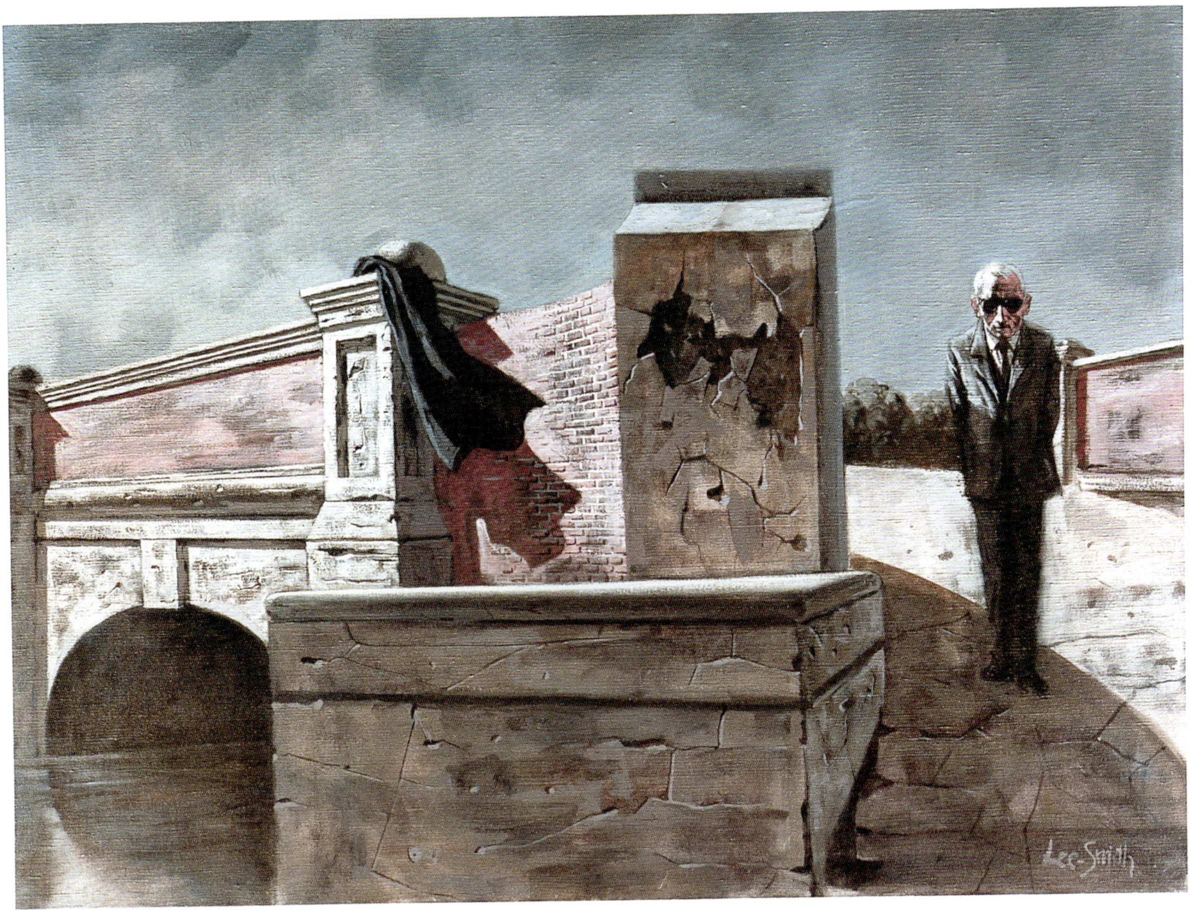

The Other Side

Throughout the 1960s, 1970s, and 1980s, Lee-Smith continued to teach, receive commissions, and paint his memorable paintings. During 1969 to 1971 he was at Howard University and encouraged his African American students who were caught up in the protests and the Black Arts movement of the times. From 1972–92 he taught at the Art Students League in New York. Shortly after he married Patricia Ferry, a former student, in 1978, he moved to Princeton, where he had also taught. In 1963 he was elected to the National Academy of Design as an associate academician, then as a full academician in 1967, the first African American to be so honored since Henry Ossawa Tanner in 1927. In 1973 the Studio Museum in Harlem held an exhibition of his work. In 1988 he designed a mosaic mural for the Prudential Life Insurance building in Washington, D.C., and painted a large mural for the New Jersey Commerce building in Trenton. In 1988–89 a retrospective exhibition was held of his work at the New Jersey State Museum; this exhibition traveled to Chicago. He died on 23 February 1999 in Albuquerque, New Mexico.

P.H.

BIBLIOGRAPHY

Bearden, Romare and Harry Henderson. "Hughie Lee-Smith," in *A History of African-American Artists from 1792 to the Present*. New York: Pantheon Books, 1993.

Kenkeleba Gallery. *Three Masters: Eldzier Cortor, Hughie Lee-Smith, Archibald John Motley, Jr.* exh. cat. New York: Kenkeleba Gallery, 1988.

New Jersey State Museum. *Hughie Lee-Smith: Retrospective Exhibition*. exh. cat. Trenton: New Jersey State Museum, 1988.

1. David C. Driskell, "Hughie Lee-Smith: Master of a Fine Tradition in American Painting," in *Three Masters: Eldzier Cortor, Hughie Lee-Smith, Archibald John Motley, Jr.* (New York: Kenkeleba Gallery, 1988), 38.
2. Quoted in Bearden and Henderson, 329.
3. *Who's Who in America* 40th Edition, Vol. 2 (Chicago: Marquis Who's Who, Inc., 1978–79), 1920.
4. *Boy with Tire*, *The Walls*, and *The Piper* are reproduced in New Jersey State Museum, 12, 16, and 23.
5. Quoted in Lowery S. Sims, "Hughie Lee-Smith: Romantic Realist or Poetic Alchemist?" in New Jersey State Museum, 4.
6. Quoted in Bearden and Henderson, 333, from quotation in Carol Wald, "The Metaphysical World of Hughie Lee-Smith," *American Artist* 43 (October 1978): 101.

NORMAN LEWIS • (1909–1979)

Shopping, 1941
Oil on canvas, 36 x 24 in. (91.4 x 60.9 cm)

Harlem Jazz Jamboree, 1943
Oil on canvas, 17 3/4 x 15 1/2 in. (45.1 x 39.4 cm)

Street Musicians, 1945
Oil on canvas, 25 3/4 x 19 1/4 in. (65.4 x 48.9 cm)

Cosmopolitan, 1946
Oil on canvas, 35 x 20 in. (88.9 x 50.8 cm)

Promenade, 1950
Oil on canvas, 39 1/4 x 29 1/4 in. (99.7 x 74.3 cm)

Carneval II, 1962
Oil on canvas, 64 x 52 in. (162.6 x 132.1 cm)

Triumphal, 1972
Oil on canvas, 87 x 73 in. (220.9 x 185.4 cm) [see frontispiece]

The seven Norman W. Lewis paintings in the Wein Collection show aspects of a wide range of styles in which Lewis worked, from his Social Realist paintings of the 1930s to his transitional works of the 1940s, to his Abstract Expressionist paintings of the 1950s, 1960s, and 1970s. Both his works and his experiences as an African American artist demonstrate the possibilities and challenges African American artists faced during the twentieth century, as well as his interest in and struggle with the relationship between figuration and abstraction.

Lewis was born 23 July 1909 in Harlem, New York, to Wilfred and Diana Lewis. His father worked as a foreman on the docks in Brooklyn and his mother, who had formerly owned a bakery in Bermuda, worked as a seamstress, baker, and housekeeper. Raised in Harlem, Lewis attended Public School No. 5 and the New York Vocational High School, where he studied commercial design and drawing.

After graduating from high school, Lewis worked at a variety of jobs before deciding to pursue a career as an artist. In 1933 Lewis began his formal study of art at the Savage Studio of Arts and Crafts. His early work caught the attention of artists Robert and Lydia Minor, who made it possible for him to study with Raphael Soyer at the John Reed Club Art School from 1933–35, where he participated in a group show.

Active in the African American artist community, Lewis was a member of the "306" group, a group of painters, writers, poets, and performing artists who met in the studio of Charles Alston and Henry Bannarn at 306 West 141st Street. In 1935, with Augusta Savage, Aaron Douglas, and other artists, Lewis helped form the Harlem Artists Guild. He also worked with many other artists to create the federally funded Harlem Community Art Center in 1937.

From 1935–37, Lewis was employed by the Federal Art Project (FAP) under the Works Progress Administration (WPA). Under the FAP, he continued his training as an artist and taught art at P.S. 139 in New York City, where he supervised the creation of a student mural. Lewis continued to work in various positions under the FAP, and in 1938 he was sent to Greensboro, North Carolina, to set up an art center. Unable to tolerate the racism in the segregated South, he quickly returned to New York, where, in 1939, he resumed teaching at the Harlem Community Art Center. In 1941, after being declined employment as a

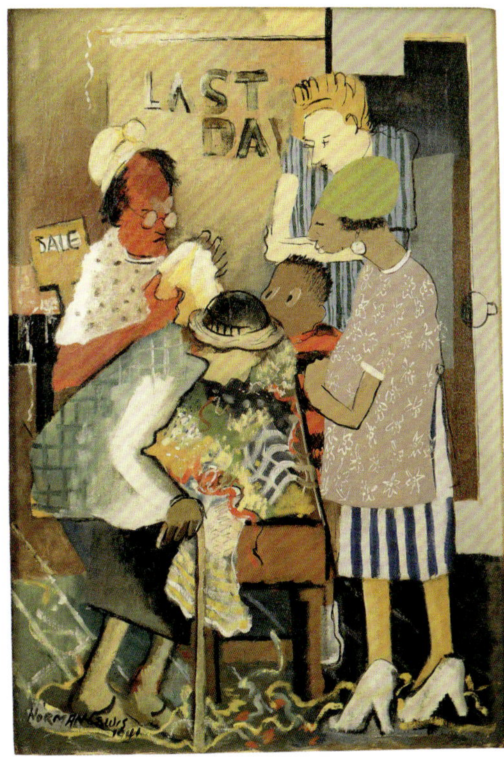

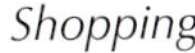
Shopping

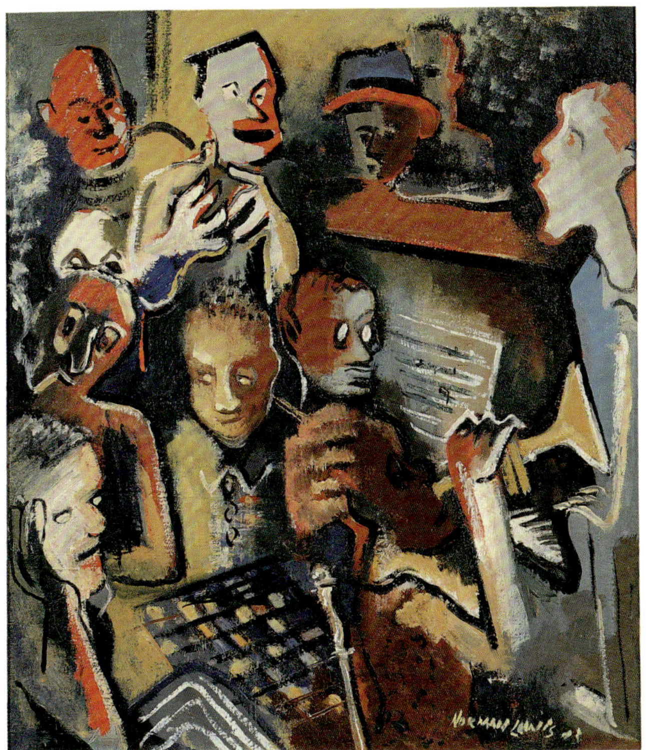
Harlem Jazz Jamboree

camouflage artist during World War II, Lewis relocated to Vancouver, Canada, where he worked at the Kaiser Shipyard. In 1943 he returned to New York, where he taught art at various institutions, including the George Washington Carver School and the Thomas Jefferson School of Social Science.

Lewis's paintings of the 1930s and early 40s demonstrate his leftist political sympathies and a coinciding interest in Social Realism; many of his paintings depict the lives of the poor, the struggling, and the homeless during the Depression. Although his figurative works of this period often depict evictions, bread lines, lynchings, and police brutality, his 1941 *Shopping* offers a slightly more hopeful view of life during the Depression. Rendered in a figurative style, this scene of women shopping in a marketplace shows his interest in modernism in its distorted figures, flat application of colors, and collage-like composition.

Lewis lived and worked in the heart of the jazz world; his 125th Street studio was close to the Apollo Theater and many jazz clubs. Indeed, jazz and music recur throughout Lewis's oeuvre. His 1943 *Harlem Jazz Jamboree* depicts the energy and excitement of the local jazz scene in vibrant colors, wide expressionistic brushstrokes, and abstracted figures.

By 1944, Lewis was investigating new ways of using color, shapes, and figures. Lewis pushes towards greater abstraction in his 1945 *Street Musicians*, which reduces the central figures to geometric forms, bright areas of color, and amorphous shapes against a vivid red background. The flat application of color, abstracted forms, and dynamic use of line in his 1946 *Cosmopolitan* provide an excellent representation of his new direction.

In 1946 Lewis joined the prestigious Marian Willard Gallery in New York, known for showing Abstract Expressionists; he had his first solo exhibition there in 1949. Between 1949 and 1964 he had eight solo exhibitions at the Willard and was widely reviewed in the New York press. In 1949 he exhibited works in the 13th Annual Exhibition of the American Abstract Artists along with Jean Arp, Josef Albers, and Ad Reinhardt. In 1950 Lewis participated in the famous 1950 Studio 35 discussions regarding the Abstract Expressionist movement, and in 1951 he was included in the Museum of Modern Art's *Abstract Painting and Sculpture in America* exhibition. His 1953 painting *Migrating Birds* won the Popularity Prize at the Carnegie International Exhibition, Pittsburgh, in 1955.

Though Lewis's art grew increasingly abstract, as in his 1950 *Promenade* and 1962 *Carneval II*, he did not aban-

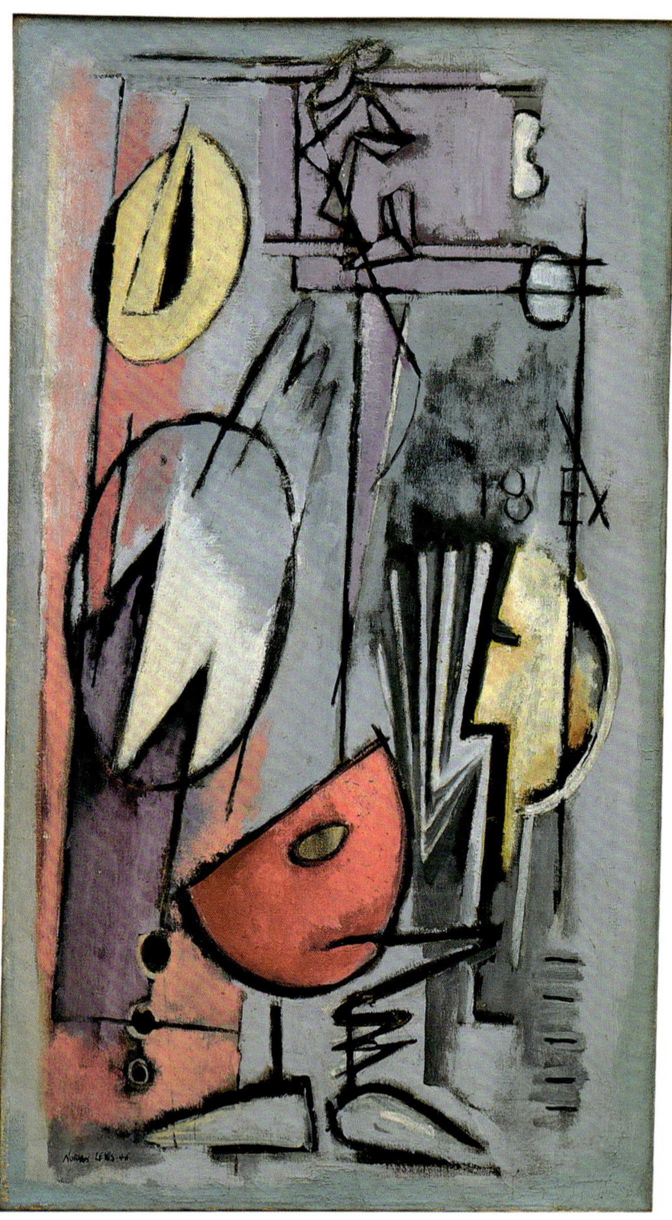

Cosmopolitan

don his leftist political orientation. Even at the Studio 35 sessions, Lewis posed a question regarding the social responsibilities of the artist, to which he received no response.[1] Though initially both *Promenade* and *Carneval II* seem completely abstract, in fact both paintings contain Lewis's signature masses of stylized small figures, which demonstrate his continual interest in representations, whether figurative or abstract, of masses of people. His nuanced abstract paintings have a delicacy that contrasts with the aggressive and thickly painted canvases of other Abstract Expressionist painters, such as Willem De Kooning and Jackson Pollock. *Carneval II*, with its asymmetrical composition and evanescent colors, also anticipates Lewis's later atmospheric abstractions.

Politically active in both the art world and the Civil Rights movement, in 1963 Lewis was a founding member, with Romare Bearden, Hale Woodruff, Charles Alston, and others, of a group that named itself *Spiral*. From 1965–71 Lewis taught at HARYOU-ACT, Inc. (Harlem Youth in Action), an anti-poverty program that encouraged children to stay in school. He also participated in many protests throughout the 1960s. In 1966—along with Alston, Bearden, Jacob Lawrence, Charles White, Woodruff, and others—Lewis withdrew his work from consideration for the First World Festival of Negro Art in Dakar, Senegal, because the U.S. Committee refused to provide the artists with travel honorariums. In 1969 he picketed outside the Metropolitan Museum of Art in protest of the exhibition *Harlem on My Mind* for its failure to include works by many Harlem-based artists and scholars. Lewis was, however, included in the 1969 *Homage to Martin Luther King, Jr.* exhibition held at the Museum of Modern Art, New York, as well as the 1970 exhibition *Black Artists: New York/Boston* at the Museum of Fine Arts, Boston.

Lewis's 1972 *Triumphal* [frontispiece] demonstrates the complexity of interpreting his paintings. Though the title may seem celebratory, Ann Eden Gibson has argued that Lewis's depiction of marchers during the Civil Rights movement "can be read as a bloody confrontation in which it is difficult to tell marchers from their assailants."[2] Others have argued that this painting is much more abstract. Ambiguities are inherent in Lewis's paintings; the juxtaposition of provocative titles with increasingly abstract imagery complicates interpretation. Indeed, Lewis himself stated that he stopped working on a painting when he "arrived at a quality of mystery."[3]

Lewis's association with a wide variety of artistic groups—including the John Reed Club, Harlem Artists Guild, Group "306," Abstract Expressionists, and *Spiral*—places him in a fascinating position within the story of American Modernism, one that questions traditional understandings of both Abstract Expressionism and the role of art and the artist in contemporary society. Perhaps Julian Euell, jazz musician and close friend of Lewis, best describes him:

> When talking to Norman, you had to listen very carefully. It took me awhile to realize that he often talked on several levels at the same time. He could talk about art, bring in music, throw in politics, and finally, introduce the view of the average guy on the street. It was always interesting to watch him pull it all together. Norman was

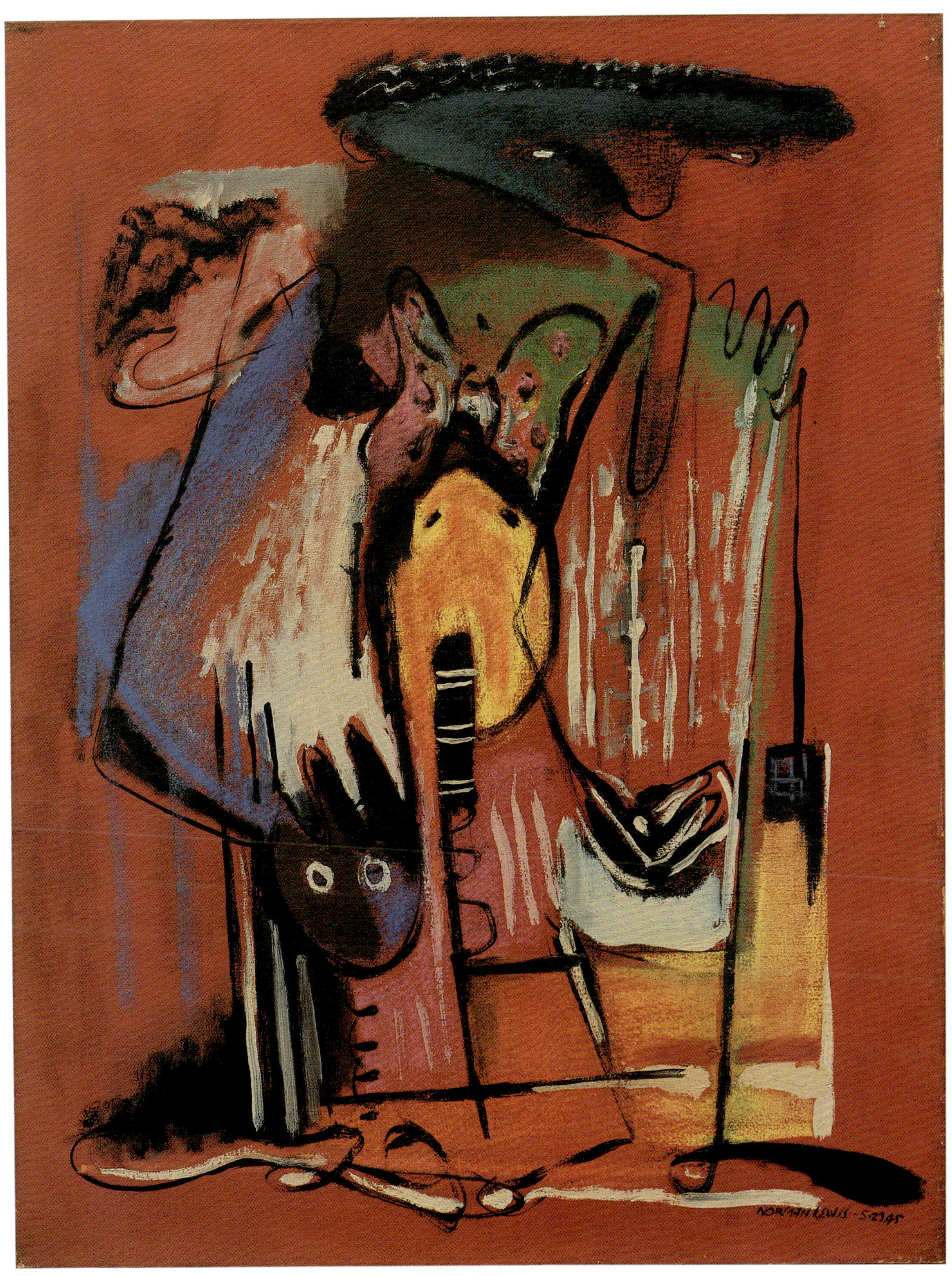

Street Musicians

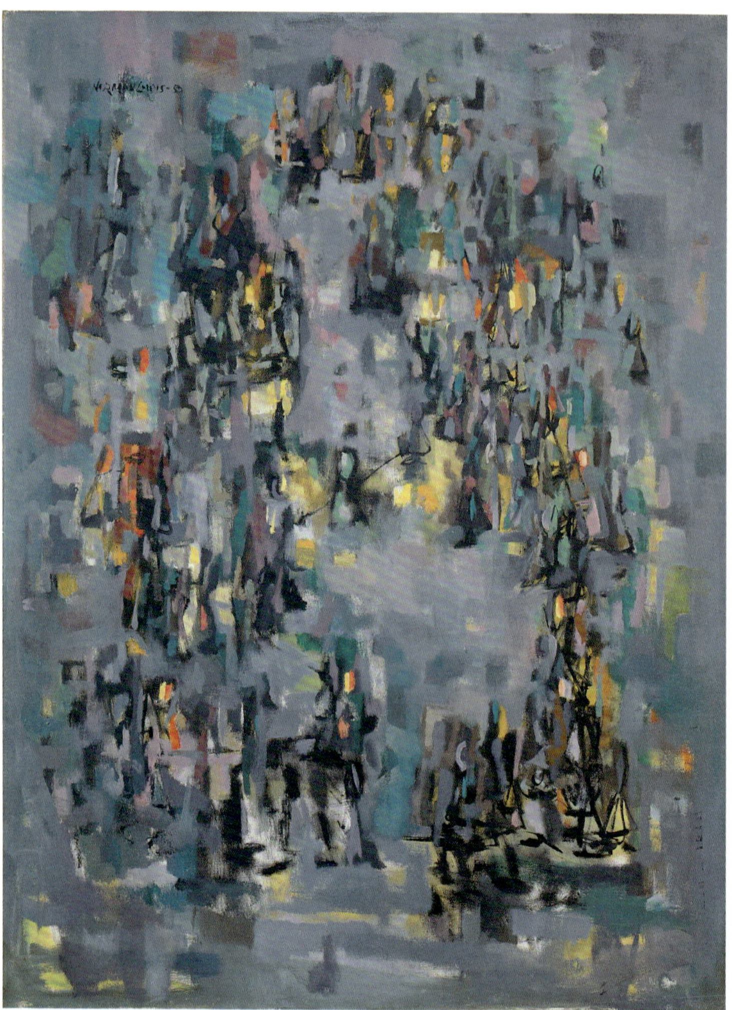

Promenade

a master at working in several idioms at the same time. He had full command of the vernacular of the Harlem community, the art of the "306" Group, and the style and approach of the American Abstract Expressionist artists.[4]

Though widely honored and exhibited during his lifetime—including an Individual Artist's Fellowship from the National Endowment for the Arts, a Guggenheim Fellowship in 1975, and a retrospective exhibition at CUNY in 1976—Norman Lewis has not, until recently, been given adequate historical attention as an Abstract Expressionist artist and a major figure in twentieth-century American art.[5]

M.R.

BIBLIOGRAPHY

Bearden, Romare and Harry Henderson. "Norman Lewis," in *A History of African-American Artists from 1792 to the Present*. New York: Pantheon Books, 1993.

Gibson, Ann. "Recasting the Canon: Norman Lewis and Jackson Pollock," *Artforum International* (March 1992), 66–72.

Kenkeleba Gallery. *Norman Lewis: From the Harlem Renaissance to Abstraction*. exh. cat. New York: Kenkeleba Gallery, 1989. With essays by Ann Gibson and Julian Euell; chronology by Kellie Jones; texts by Norman Lewis.

Studio Museum in Harlem. *Norman Lewis: Black Paintings 1946–1977*. exh. cat. New York: Studio Museum in Harlem, 1998. With essays by Ann Eden Gibson, Jorge Daniel Veneciano, Lowery Stokes Sims and David Craven; introduction by Kinshasha Holman Conwill.

1. Ann Eden Gibson, "Black is a Color: Norman Lewis and Modernism in New York," Studio Museum in Harlem, 36.
2. Ibid., 20.
3. Quoted in Veneciano, 31.
4. Julian Euell, "Thoughts About Norman Lewis," in Kenkeleba, 52.
5. See Ann Eden Gibson's *Abstract Expressionism: Other Politics*. New Haven: Yale University Press, 1997.

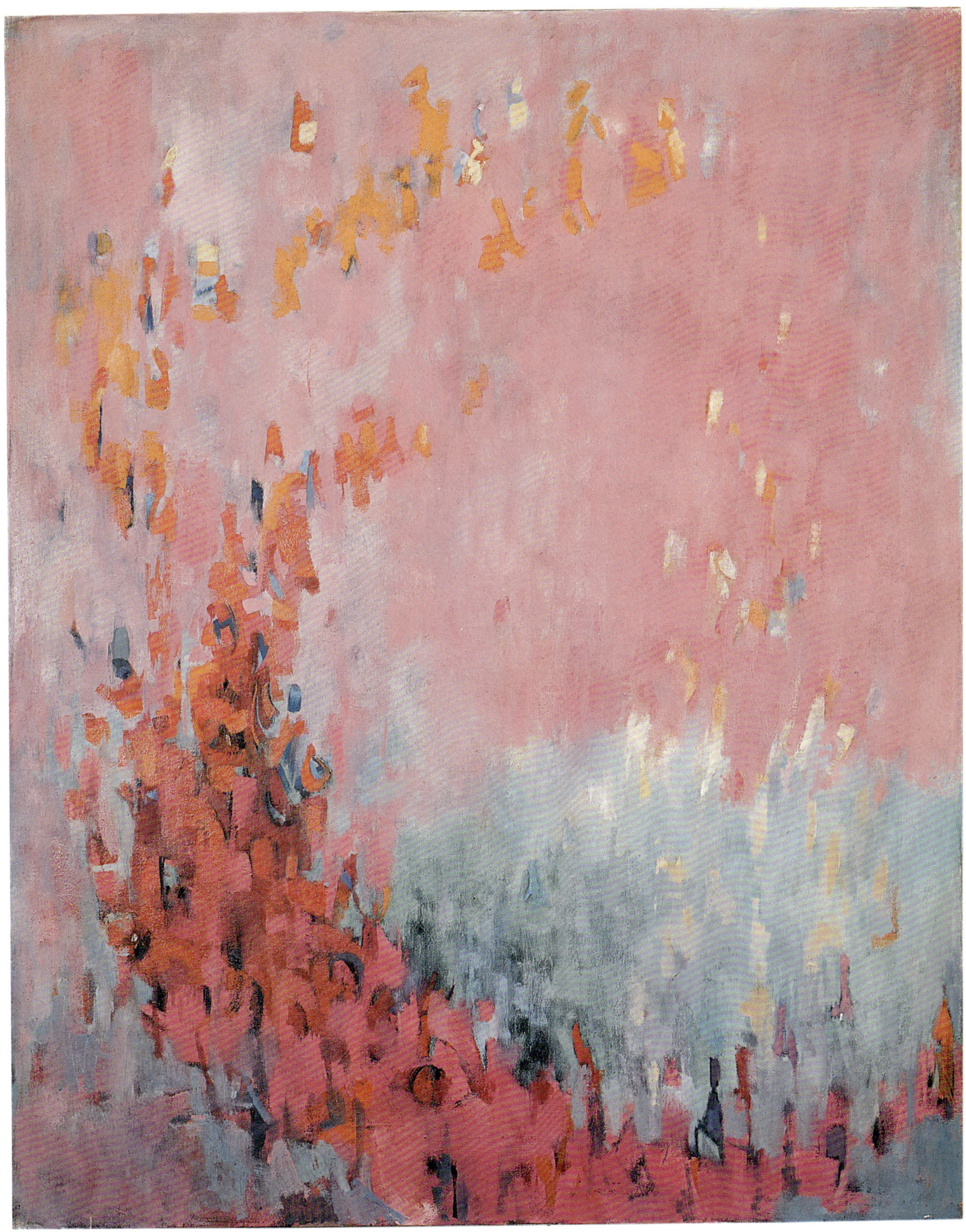

Carneval II

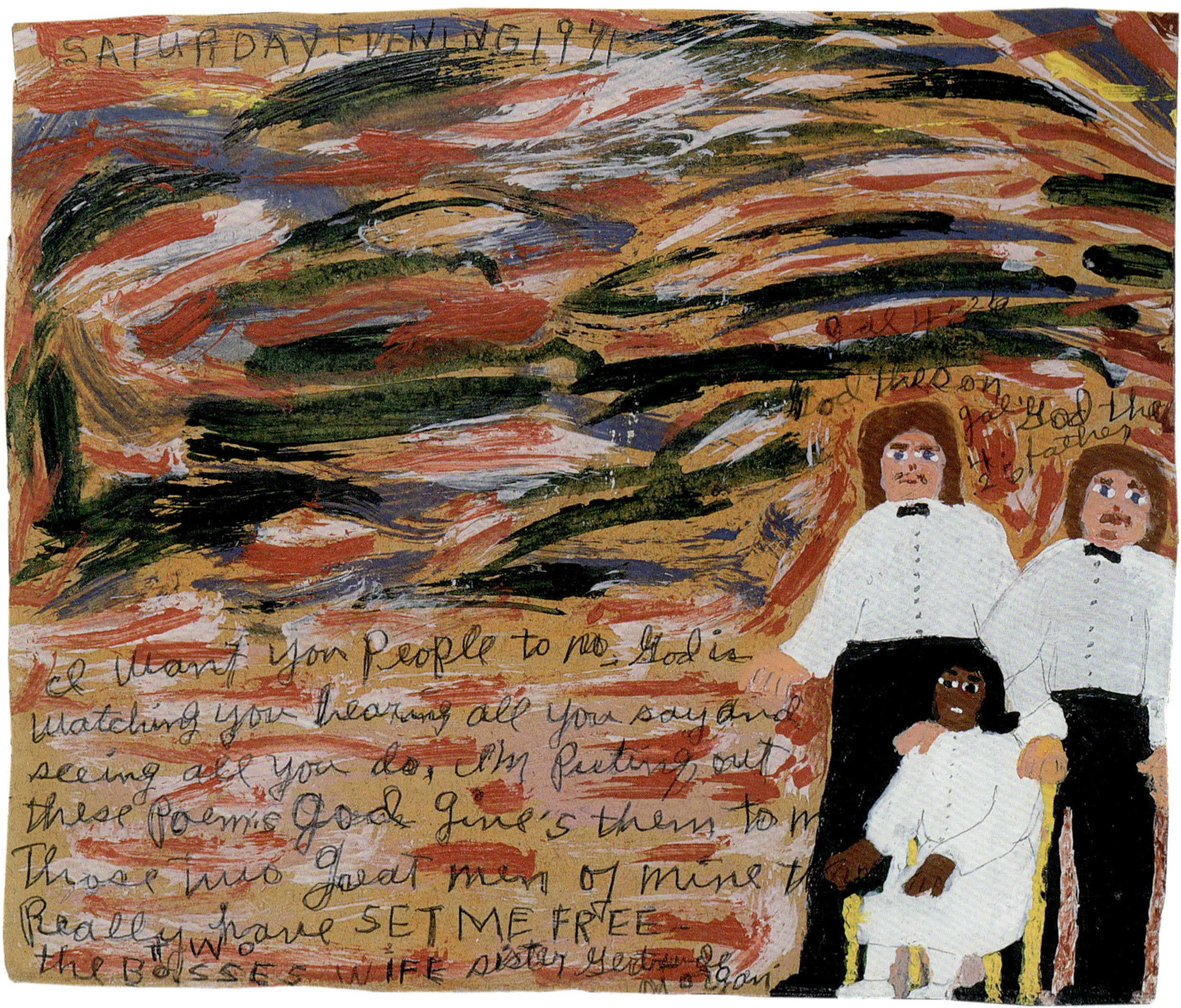

SISTER GERTRUDE MORGAN • (1900–1980)

Saturday Evening 1971, 1971

Acrylic and/or tempera, pencil, and ballpoint ink on paper, 9½ x 11¾ in. (24.1 x 29.9 cm)

Distinguished by their bright colors, expressionistic brushstrokes, and use of many media, Sister Gertrude Morgan's artworks depict biblical subjects, images from the Book of Revelations, angels, demons, apocalyptic visions, and scenes of salvation. Many of her works also incorporate didactic text that ranges from scripture to sermons, to inspired poems.

Poet, preacher, missionary, musician, evangelist, and self-taught artist, Sister Gertrude Morgan (née Gertrude Williams) was born in Lafayette, Alabama, on 7 April 1900. She moved with her family in about 1917 to Columbus, Georgia, where she became an active member of Dr. James Berry Miller's Rose Hill Memorial Baptist Church. On 12 February 1928, Sister Gertrude married Will Morgan, though little is known about the relationship. There was no record of children, and when Sister Gertrude left Columbus for New Orleans, Louisiana, in 1939, it was without her husband.

Throughout her life Sister Gertrude Morgan would have many divine revelations, the first in 1934, in which God instructed her to go and preach to the world. A second revelation followed in 1937. In 1939, she moved to New Orleans where she met Mother Margaret Parker and Sister Cora Williams, with whom she would start an orphanage and day care center. The three women—dressed as street missionaries in black robes with white collars—preached on the streets, in the church, and to inmates in local prisons. Sister Gertrude drew and painted throughout her life, and in 1956 she began to create crayon drawings to help illustrate her sermons. In 1957 she received another revelation in which God told her she was the Bride of Christ, at which point Sister Gertrude changed her dress to white and painted her house, her furniture, and even her Bible white.

Sister Gertrude's visionary art often portrays events from the book of Revelations, scenes that grapple with the presence of evil and sin in the world. She has stated:

> It's sin I been working against, that's why I started the Everlasting Gospel Revelation Mission, to whup up on sin. Satan, he is so mighty. O, he's a mighty demon. It's like he's taken his tail and pulled down a third of the stars of Heaven. That's what he's doing today. Got his old talking tongue, lying tongue, hooked tail!—Amen!—to pull people's minds and health and strength and their ways and actions and their interests—Amen—from God. Let the church say Amen. Satan is always just below your feet, looking for his chance, and you got to say, 'Get back! You low-down crawling devil. Get back! You biting thing!'[1]

A sermon in paint, *Saturday Night 1971* depicts Sister Gertrude in her usual white robe seated in front of two white men denoted as "God the son" and "God the father." The three figures share the scene with prominently placed handwritten text that states: "I want you People to no God is / watching you hearing all you say and / seeing all you do. I'm Putting, out / these Poem's God give's them to me / Those Two Great men of mine that / Really have SET ME FREE. / the TWO BOSSES / wiFE / Sister Gertrude Morgan." Inscribed across a colorful background of energetic brushstrokes, the text becomes powerful and engaging, a visual counterpart to Sister Gertrude's sermons and spiritual presence.

In the early 1960s New Orleans art dealer and entrepreneur E. Lorenz Borenstein came across Sister Gertrude's artwork when she was preaching in the French Quarter. A friendship and business partnership developed; Sister Gertrude displayed her work at his gallery, Associated Artists, and sold her paintings to help support her mission. She would go on to exhibit her work widely, including a booth at George Wein's New Orleans Jazz & Heritage Festival [see page 10]. Throughout the early 1970s Sister Gertrude would sing, conduct prayer services, and sell her art at the festival, labeling her kiosk the "Sister Gertrude Morgan Tabernacle Booth."

Sister Gertrude stopped painting in 1974 when God, in another revelation, instructed her not to make art any longer, though she did one late work in 1979, illustrating her oft-repeated motto, "Jesus is my airplane." She died in July 1980. Her art has been exhibited widely, including a 1973 show at the Museum of American Folk Art with colleagues Bruce Brice and Clementine Hunter, as well as the recent 2004–05 solo exhibition *Tools of Her Ministry: The Art of Sister Gertrude Morgan* at the American Folk Art Museum, New York. M.R.

BIBLIOGRAPHY

Fagaly, William A. "Sister Gertrude Morgan," in *Louisiana Folk Paintings*. exh. cat. New York: The Museum of American Folk Art, 1973.

——. *Tools of Her Ministry: The Art of Sister Gertrude Morgan*. exh. cat. New York: The American Folk Art Museum in association with Rizzoli International Publications, 2004. With essays by Jason Berry and Helen M. Shannon; foreword by Gerard C. Wertkin.

Livingston, Jane and John Beardsley. *Black Folk Art in America: 1930–1980*. Jackson: University Press of Mississippi, 1982.

Moses, Kathy. *Outsider Art of the South*. Pennsylvania: Schiffer Publishing, Ltd., 1999.

1. Guy Mendes, "The Gospel According to Sister Gertrude Morgan," unpublished manuscript, Versailles, Kentucky, 1974, 3–4; quoted in Livingston, 100–01.

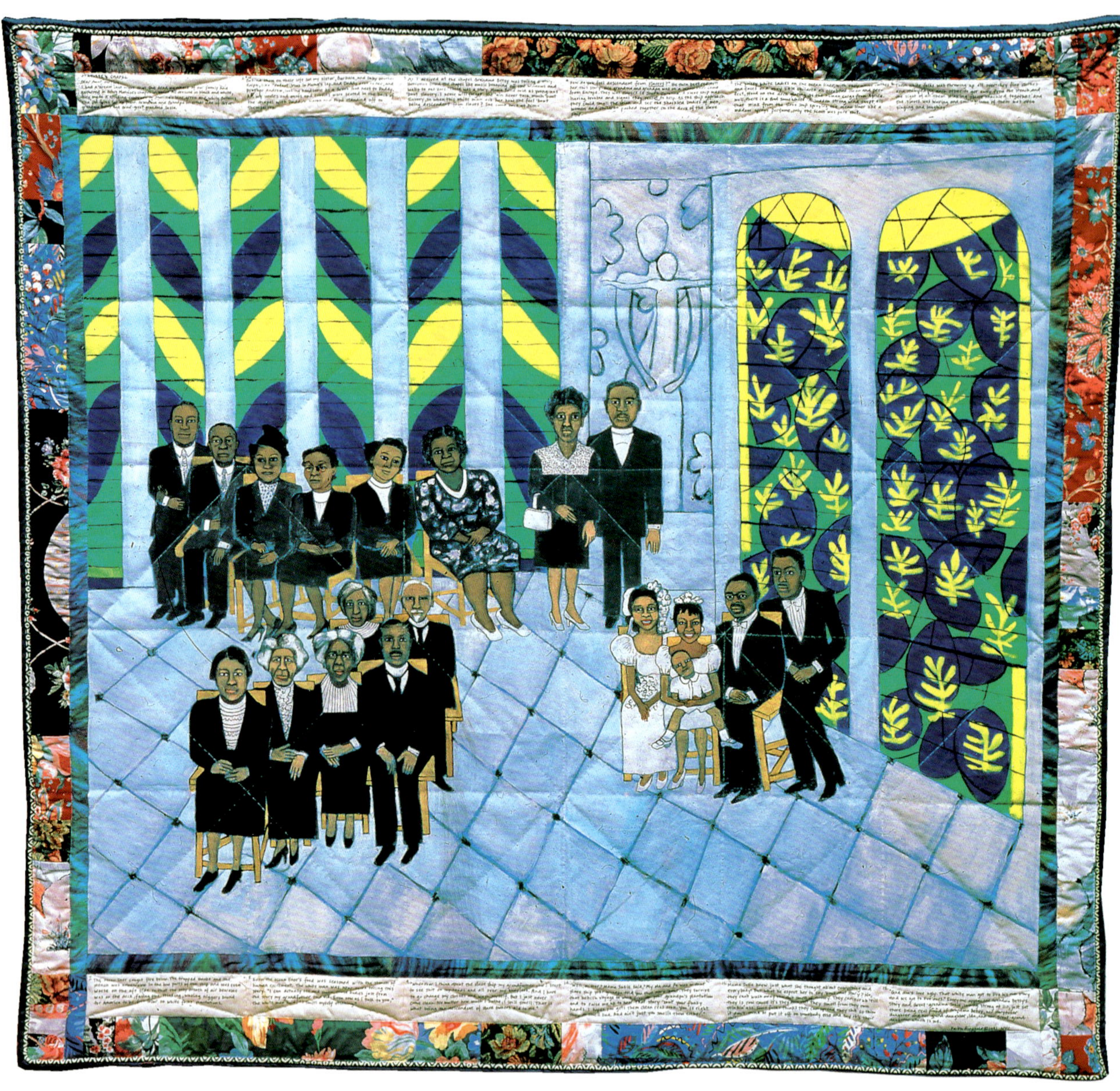

FAITH RINGGOLD • (born 1930)

Matisse's Chapel: The French Collection Part 1: #6, 1991

Acrylic on canvas; printed, tie-dyed, and pieced fabric, 74 x 79½ in. (187.9 x 201.9 cm)

Born 8 October 1930 to Andrew Louis Jones, Sr., and Willi Posey Jones, Faith Ringgold grew up in a working-class family in Harlem. Her family had moved from Florida to New York in the Great Migration of the 1920s. In her autobiography, *We Flew Over the Bridge*, Ringgold describes her early years and how they shaped and inspired her later in life. As a child, Ringgold had asthma and her mother gave her crayons, coloring books, and bits of fabric in order to keep her occupied without too much physical strain. Ringgold writes how such early activities inspired her to use different media and materials, and also encouraged her to experiment. Her interest in mixed media is clearly seen in her creation of story quilts, such as *Matisse's Chapel* from her French Collection series.

Ringgold began her studies as an artist in 1948 when she entered City College of New York as an art education major and studied with painter Robert Gwathmey. While in school, Ringgold also taught art, first as an elementary school teacher and then at the high school level. After she divorced her first husband, Robert Earl Wallace, in 1956, Ringgold went to Provincetown, Massachusetts, in the summer of 1957 to paint. There she began to develop her early painting style, notable for its flat application of color and repetition of shapes and forms.

In 1961 Ringgold traveled to Europe with her mother and two daughters, Barbara and Michele Wallace, and encountered the works of the "Old Masters." She returned to the United States, and in 1962 she married Burdette Ringgold. She began painting political works in 1963. In the midst of the Civil Rights movement, she decided it was time to tell the story of her own experiences through her series *American People*. An active member in the Black Arts Movement, Ringgold completed her *Black Light* paintings and then the *Flag Series*, which employ flat colors, abstracted figures and provocative text to present political and artistic statements on issues ranging from race and Civil Rights to the Vietnam War. Ringgold's political activism can be seen in her participation in the controversial "People's Flag Show," held at the Judson Memorial Church in 1970, which led to her arrest for the desecration of the American flag, along with Jon Hendricks and Jean Toche. They became known as the "Judson Three." Ringgold was also a major figure in the Women's Movement.

In the 1970s, inspired by Tibetan wall paintings, which she had seen on a 1972 trip to the Netherlands, Ringgold began to create cloth wall paintings called *thangkas*. Interested in both African and African American traditions of art and craft, she also made soft sculptures using fabric, beads and other materials. Begun in the 1980s, Ringgold's story quilts are in fact paintings. Like other feminist artists, she purposely made her work collaborative, rejecting the modern myth of the artist as singular genius. In this process, Ringgold would paint the portraits in acrylic on canvas and her mother, Willi Posey Jones, would piece together the border. For Ringgold, the painted quilt was the perfect medium to connect her experience and identity as an artist to both her mother and her grandmother, who were seamstresses and quilters.

Ringgold confronts the European modernist canon in her French Collection series, which depicts a variety of scenes, many of them set in famous French museums. In this series, fictional expatriate artist-heroine Willia Marie Simone travels to different sites in France, interacting with famous monuments and works of art. Willia Marie is an amalgamation of the artist and her mother, as well as other notable African American women artists such as dancer Josephine Baker and singer Nina Simone. The dense text that borders the central image is a letter from Willia Marie to her Aunt Melissa describing a dream she had in which all the dead members of the Ringgold family had gathered in the chapel in Vence, France. Willia Marie's narrative recounts her Grandma Betsy's experience of slavery. The juxtaposition of Grandma Betsy's horrid description of a slave ship with the positive scene of a family reunion is paralleled in the visual contrast of the stark figures clothed in solemn black and white against the colorful blues and greens of Matisse's chapel in the background.[1]

Faith Ringgold remains active as an artist today, continuing to create story quilts including, most recently, a series titled *Jazz*. She has won awards for her children's books, including *Tar Beach*, which was a Caldecott Honor Book as well as the winner of the Coretta Scott King Award for Illustration. She has been the recipient of more than seventy-five awards, fellowships, citations, and honors, including a Guggenheim Fellowship, two National Endowment for the Arts Awards, and seventeen honorary doctorates, one of which is from her alma mater, City College of New York. Throughout each decade Faith Ringgold has responded to changes in her life, the art world, and society with different artistic creations. Ringgold's story quilts brilliantly combine text, painting, and quilting to tell a powerful story. M.R.

BIBLIOGRAPHY

Artist website: http://www.faithringgold.com (27 July 2005).

Dancing at the Louvre: Faith Ringgold's French Collection and Other Story Quilts. exh. cat. New York: New Museum of Contemporary Art in association with the University of California Press, Berkeley, 1998. With essays by Dan Cameron, Michele Wallace, Patrick Hill, Thalia Gouma-Peterson, Moira Roth, and Ann Gibson; introduction by Richard J. Powell.

Farrington, Lisa E. *Faith Ringgold*. San Francisco: Pomegranate, 2004.

Ringgold, Faith. *We Flew Over the Bridge: The Memoirs of Faith Ringgold*. Boston: Little, Brown, 1995.

Wallace, Michele. "For the Women's House," [1972 interview with Faith Ringgold] in *Invisibility Blues: From Pop to Theory*. New York and London: Verso, 1990.

1. For the full text, see *Dancing at the Louvre*, 135–36.

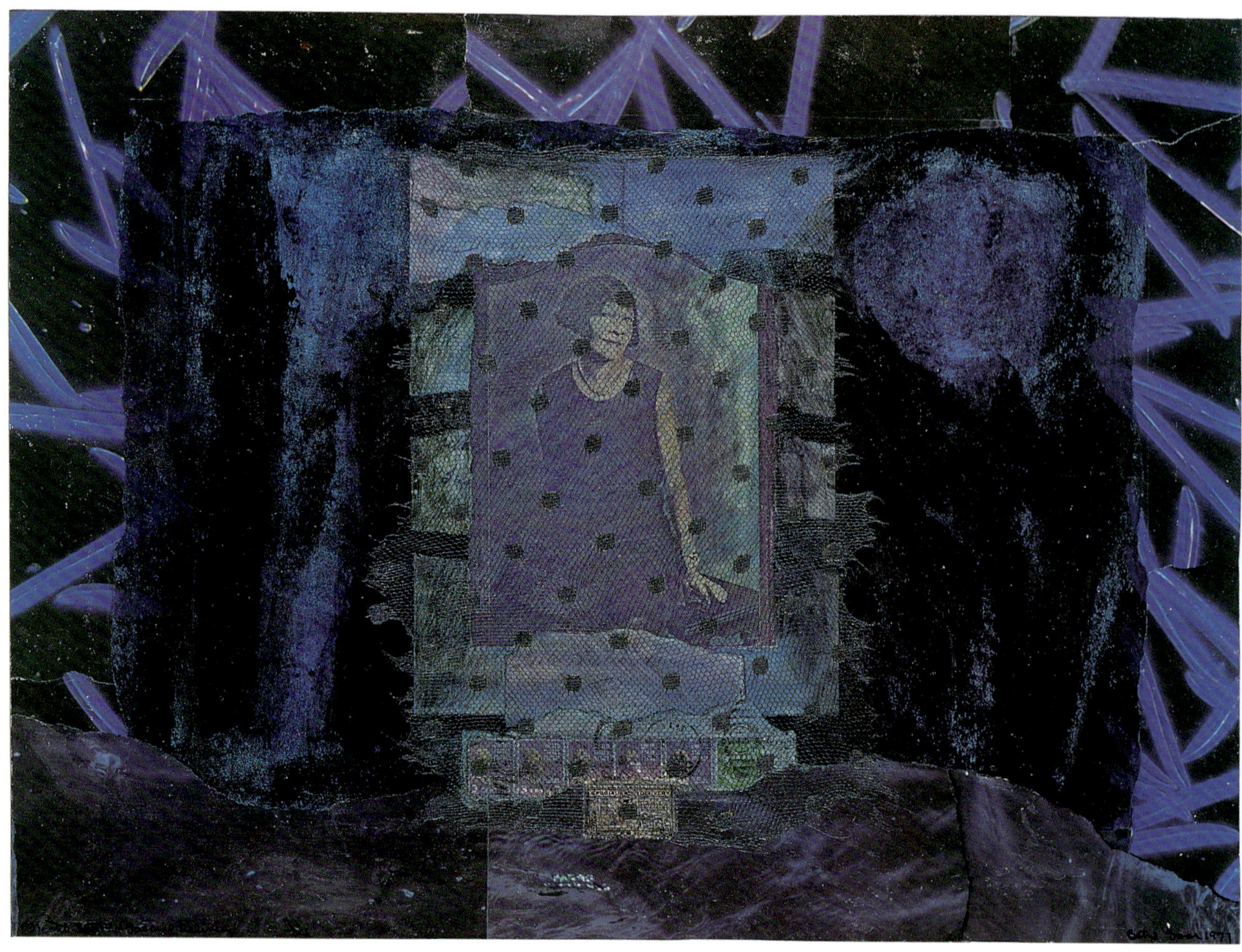

BETYE SAAR • (born 1926)

Night Letter: Special Delivery, 1977

Mixed media collage on paper, 15 x 20¾ in. (38.1 x 52.7 cm)

Assemblage artist Betye Saar works in many media, exploring subjects such as racial stereotypes, African American history, the occult, the importance of ritual, and her personal family history. Her works range from small-scale intimate box sculptures and collages to assemblage works and altars, to large-scale multimedia installations, such as her 1988 *Mojotech* (List Visual Arts Center, Massachusetts Institute of Technology). Saar describes her art: "I am intrigued with combining the remnants of memories, fragments of relics, and ordinary objects with the components of technology. It's a way of delving into the past and reaching into the future simultaneously. The art itself becomes the bridge."[1]

Born in Los Angeles, California, on 30 July 1926, Betye Brown Saar grew up in Watts, a section of Los Angeles. Saar's father, Jefferson Maze Brown, studied at the University of California, Los Angeles (UCLA), where he met and married Saar's mother, Beatrice Lillian Parson, in 1925. Issues of color and class emerge in many of Saar's works, which are based on her own experience growing up in a racially mixed household of European, African American, and Native American descent. An early artistic influence on Saar was the construction of the *Watts Towers* (1921–25) by Italian-born artist Simon Rodia. This monumental sculpture, which incorporated found objects, demonstrated to Saar the exciting potential of assemblage.

Saar's family life changed dramatically in 1931 when her father died from kidney failure. Saar, with her mother and sisters, moved to Pasadena to live with her great-aunt Hattie Parson Keys and her husband. After high school she attended Pasadena City College, then studied design at UCLA. She initially wanted to attend the Chouinard Art School, a professional art school in Los Angeles (now part of California Institute of Arts), but did not apply because at that time, as a private institution, Chouinard denied admission to African Americans. After graduating from UCLA in 1949, Saar worked as a social worker, simultaneously pursuing her interest in design. She met African American artist Curtis Tann, with whom she started an enamel and jewelry business, Brown and Tann.

In 1952 Betye married Richard Saar, a ceramics manufacturer, and moved to Los Angeles. In addition to raising her daughters Alison and Lezley, and working as an artist, Saar also completed graduate work at the University of Southern California and California State University, Northridge, and taught in both the California State and University of California systems.

In 1967 Saar saw a Joseph Cornell exhibition at the Pasadena Museum of Art. Cornell's utilization of box forms and assemblage greatly affected her, and she began to create box sculptures, including a series on her Aunt Hattie. In 1968, when Saar and her husband divorced, she took a job as a costume designer for the Inner City Cultural Center in Midtown Los Angeles. Her experience as a designer led to her more theatrical works, including freestanding altars and installation pieces.

An active member of both the Feminist and Black Arts movements of the 1970s, Saar addresses a variety of topics in her work, from racial stereotypes to slavery to the Watts riots of August 1965, including the well-known 1972 assemblage *The Liberation of Aunt Jemima* (University of California, Berkeley Art Museum), which deconstructs images of "The Mammy" and Aunt Jemima.

Many of Saar's series celebrate both historical heroines and ordinary women. Her 1979 series on Hattie Parson Keys demonstrates the importance of ancestry and personal history. Ranging from small-scale box sculptures to multimedia collages, the works in this series utilize found objects and photographs, as Saar describes:

> These works are from a nostalgic series that developed from the mementos of my great-aunt, Hattie Parson Keys. The letters, autographs, hankies, scraps of lace, and fabric are fragments from the past, a sort of sentimental journey back when time moved slower and people collected memories.[2]

The multimedia collage *Night Letter: Special Delivery* depicts Hattie juxtaposed with fragments of a letter and bordered by a row of "Special Delivery" stamps. A piece of black veiling covers the portrait against a background of somber blue and purple paper cutouts.

Saar has won many prestigious awards, including two National Endowment for the Arts Fellowships, the Twenty-Second Annual Artist Award from the Studio Museum in Harlem in 1990, and a Guggenheim Fellowship in 1991. At the College Art Association she was honored by the Women's Caucus for Art in 1989 and by the Committee on Women in the Arts in 2004. She has participated in many group exhibitions, as well as solo exhibitions at both the Whitney Museum of American Art in 1975 and the Studio Museum in Harlem in 1980. In 1994, Saar and John Otterbridge represented the United States at the 22nd Biennial of São Paulo in Brazil.

Saar currently lives in the Los Angeles area and continues to mentor successive generations of African American and women artists, including Alison and Lezley Saar. The three often collaborate on projects and participate in group exhibitions, including the 2005 traveling exhibition titled *Family Legacies: The Art of Betye, Alison and Lezley Saar.*[3]

M.R.

BIBLIOGRAPHY

Artist website: http://www.betyesaar.net (27 July 2005)

Carpenter, Jane H. *Betye Saar*. San Francisco: Pomegranate, 2003.

Farrington, Lisa E. *Creating Their Own Image: The History of African-American Women Artists.* Oxford: Oxford University Press, 2005.

Saar, Betye. *Workers + Warriors: The Return of Aunt Jemima.* exh. cat. New York: Michael Rosenfeld Gallery, 1998. With an essay by Arlene Raven.

1. Quoted in Riggs, Thomas, ed. *St. James Guide to Black Artists*. Published in Association with the Schomburg Center for Research in Black Culture. Detroit: St. James Press, 1997, 465.

2. Saar, Betye. "Artist Statement," in *Betye Saar: Collages*. exh. cat. New York: Gallery 62, National Urban League, Inc., 1979.

3. *Night Letter: Special Delivery* is not in the Wein exhibition at Boston University; instead it is included in the exhibition *Betye Saar: Extending the Frozen Moment* held simultaneously at the University of Michigan Museum of Art.

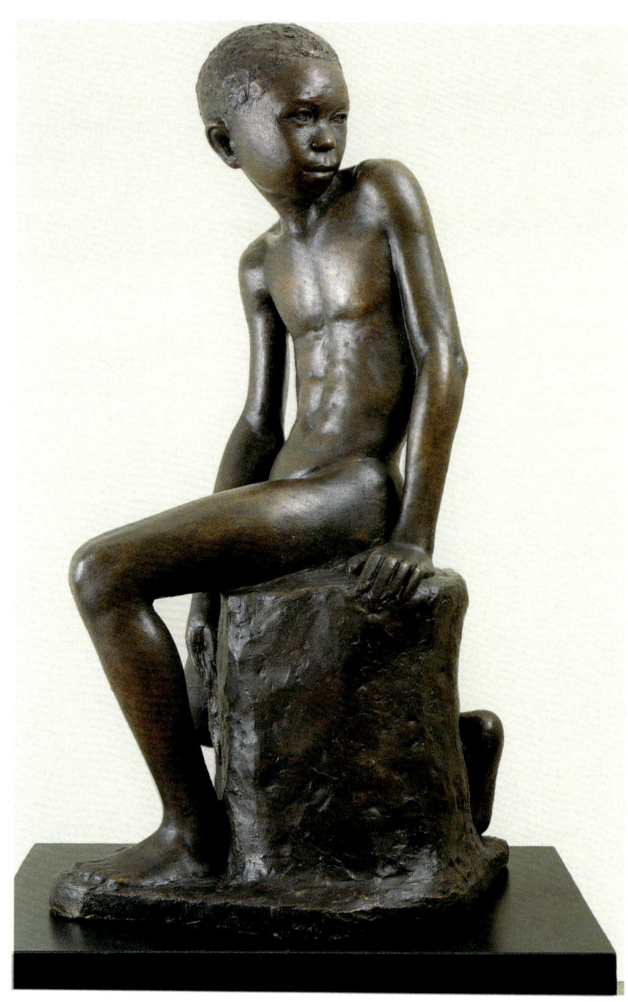

AUGUSTA SAVAGE • (1892–1962)

Young Boy, 1940–42

Bronze reproduction (one of twelve casts) after painted plaster, 33 in. high (83.3 cm)

Augusta Savage was born Augusta Christine Fells on 29 February 1892 in Green Cove Spring, Florida, the seventh child in a poor family of fourteen children. Her father was a fundamentalist preacher, the Reverend Edward Fells; her mother was Cornelia Fells.[1] Information about her early life is sketchy. She married at fifteen and had one daughter, Irene Connie Moore. Within a few years her husband died, and she moved to West Palm Beach with her family. She struggled to teach herself clay modeling, and received encouragement from her high school principal, but was discouraged by her father, who disapproved of "graven images." Nevertheless, she persisted and won a special prize at the West Palm Beach County Fair in 1919. She subsequently moved to Jacksonville in order to pursue a career as an artist.[2]

In 1921 she moved to New York, leaving her daughter with her parents and her second husband, James Savage, whom she subsequently divorced. In New York she enrolled at Cooper Union, studied with George Brewster, and held down part-time jobs. In 1923 she competed for a summer scholarship to an art school located at Fontainebleau, outside Paris. Although she won the scholarship, it was withdrawn when the jurors discovered she was African American. In October of that year she married Robert L. Poston, an associate of Marcus Garvey, but he died the following March. In 1925 she won a tuition scholarship to the Academy of Fine Arts in Rome. W.E.B. Du Bois, then the editor of *Crisis* (the NAACP journal), attempted to raise money for her travel and living expenses abroad, but together they were unable to gather the necessary funds. One of the reasons was the financial drain her family placed on her; when a hurricane hit Florida in 1928, the Red Cross sent members of her family to live with her in New York.[3] Meanwhile, she showed her sculpture in Harmon Foundation exhibitions. In 1932 the Julius Rosenwald Fund awarded her a fellowship (renewed for a second year) to work in France. She studied in Paris with Felix Beauneteaux and Charles Despiau. The Carnegie Foundation then funded her travel for eight months in France, Belgium, and Germany.

Returning to New York in 1932, she found Harlem and the country in the midst of the Depression. She put her energies into helping young black artists. She opened the Savage Studio of Arts and Crafts in a basement apartment on West 143rd Street and taught both children and adults, including Norman Lewis, William Artis, Ernest Crichlow, Elton C. Fax, and Gwendolyn Knight. She helped found the Harlem Artists Guild, of which she became vice president, and she pressed the government to support the artists of Harlem. In 1936 she became an assistant supervisor for the Federal Art Project (FAP) of the Works Progress Administration (WPA) and was appointed the first director of the WPA's Harlem Community Art Center, which opened in December 1937.

She postponed assuming the duties for that job to work on a commission to design and sculpt a work for the New York World's Fair (1939–40) that would be "symbolic of the unique contribution made by the American Negro to the world's music, particularly in song."[4] The final sixteen-foot-tall plaster sculpture, *The Harp*, depicted African American choir singers as the strings of a harp, with the forearm and cupped hand of the Creator as the harp's base. A man kneels in front with outstretched arms holding a plaque inscribed with the musical notes from James Weldon Johnson's famous anthem "Lift Every Voice and Sing." Lacking funds, Savage was not able to cast the plaster into bronze, but a small bronze replica, *Lift Every Voice and Sing*, 1939, survives.

In 1939 Savage had a solo exhibition at the Argent Gallery that was not well received. She also established her own private art gallery, the Salon of Contemporary Negro Art, on 125th Street, where she exhibited the work of her former students, but the gallery failed financially. In 1940 she planned to tour her work throughout the Midwest, but that too was unsuccessful. In the early 1940s Savage continued to be active in artists' organizations, while struggling with the expense of making sculpture. She became embittered because of the lack of recognition and moved to Saugerties, in upstate New York, where she lived in isolation from the art world for the last 17 years of her life. In 1961, her daughter returned the ailing Savage to New York. She died on 27 March 1962.

Despite the troubles of her later life, during the 1930s no other artist in Harlem had quite the single-minded force as Savage. With her encouragement of the young artists she mentored, the Harlem Renaissance can be said to have lasted well into the 1940s. In 1988 the Schomburg Center mounted an exhibition, *Augusta Savage and the Art Schools of Harlem*. After the 1940s much of Savage's work had disappeared or been destroyed, so that only nineteen pieces could be located for the exhibition.

Among Savage's most lyrical works, *Young Boy* is one of the most satisfying three-dimensional sculptural experiences for the viewer. All views have their appeal when one circles around the lithe prepubescent boy who sits with relaxed arms as he turns to look over his left shoulder, with his legs and feet poised for him to spring up if necessary. Because of the fragility of the original painted sculpture owned by the Weins, they had it cast in bronze. A bronze replica is included in the current exhibition.

P.H.

BIBLIOGRAPHY

Bearden, Romare and Harry Henderson. "Augusta Savage," in *A History of African-American Artists from 1792 to the Present*. New York: Pantheon Books, 1993.

Bibby, Deirdre. "Augusta Savage," in *Black Women in America: An Historical Encyclopedia*, vol. 2, Darlene Clark Hine, Elsa Barkley Brown, and Rosalyn Terborg-Penn, eds. New York: Carlson, 1993.

Schomburg Center for Research in Black Culture. *Augusta Savage and the Art Schools of Harlem*. New York: The New York Public Library, 1988. Essay by Deidre L. Bibby; chronology by Juanita Marie Holland.

1. Bearden and Henderson, 168.
2. Information in this brief biography is condensed from the author's entry on Savage for *Dictionary of Women Artists*, vol. 2, Delia Gaze, ed. (London: Fitzroy Dearborn Publishers, 1997), 1234–1236.
3. *Augusta Savage and the Art Schools of Harlem*, 14.
4. *New York Times*, 9 December 1937.

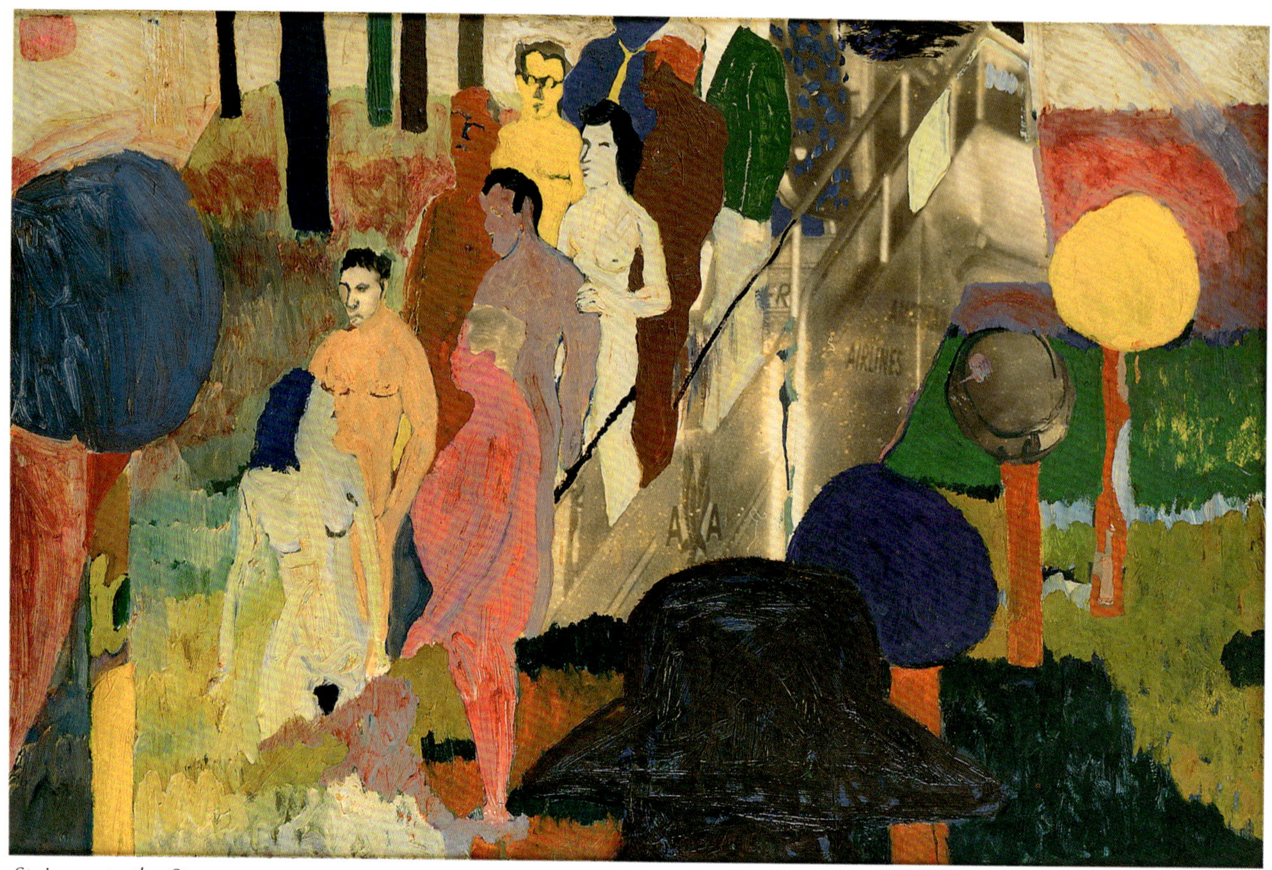

Stairway to the Stars

BOB THOMPSON • (1937–1966)

Stairway to the Stars, n.d.

Paper, oil and photostat on canvas, 40 x 60 in. (101.6 x 152.4 cm)

Untitled (Pink and Blue Figures), 1962

Oil on canvas, 30½ x 38½ in. (77.5 x 97.8 cm)

In a short but intense career, figurative expressionist painter Robert L. (Bob) Thompson produced over 1000 works in eight years. In direct dialogue with the Western canon, many of Thompson's works appropriate and transform well-known paintings into new and startling images. Recognizable by their powerful and sometimes haunting imagery, Thompson's paintings utilize flat, brilliant colors, illogical perspective, compressed space, distorted figures, and strange forms to create unique figurative works. Indeed, as an artist working during the height of Abstract Expressionism in the United States, Thompson's oeuvre provides an excellent example of the persistent interest in figurative and narrative works during the 1950s and 60s.

Born 26 June 1937 in Louisville, Kentucky, Thompson grew up in a middle-class educated household. His father ran the state's only African American–owned dry-cleaning plant and his mother was a graduate of the Kentucky State Normal School. In 1955, after graduating from high school, Thompson enrolled at Boston University, where he intended to study medicine. Poor grades and lack of interest led him to withdraw, however, in 1957 he returned to Kentucky, where he enrolled at the University of Louisville to study art.

Thompson spent the summer of 1958 in Provincetown,

Massachusetts, well known as an artists' colony. Here he met his mentor, figurative expressionist painter Jan Müller, who influenced his work. Müller had studied under painter Hans Hofmann, though in contrast to his teacher, Müller continued to work figuratively, using narrative, dissonant colors, and distorted forms.

In 1959 Thompson moved to Manhattan's Lower East Side, where he met and married Carol Plenda. That year he also had his first solo exhibition at the Arts in Louisville Gallery, and in 1960 he had his first New York show at the Delancey Street Museum. While living in New York he was an active member of the Beat community of the 1950s and 60s, fraternizing with poet Allen Ginsberg and writer LeRoi Jones (later Amiri Baraka), among others. Thompson was one of many painters immersed in the local jazz scene, often going to the club Five Spot to listen to music. In 1959 Thompson also participated in two of the earliest Happenings: Allan Kaprow's *18 Happenings in 6 Parts* and Red Grooms's *The Burning Building*. Like many of the Beats, Thompson lived a hard and fast life immersed in drugs and alcohol, abuses that would lead to his early death.

Thompson was also an expatriate artist. In 1960 he received a grant to travel to Paris, where he lived for two years. From there Thompson and his wife traveled to Ibiza, Spain. They extended their stay in Europe until 1963 with the aid of an Opportunity Fellowship from the John Hay Whitney Foundation. Thompson's works during this period demonstrate his enthusiasm for and interest in European art, of both early modernists and the Old Masters.

Thompson's 1962 *Untitled (Pink and Blue Figures)* exemplifies his increasing interest in almost hallucinatory depictions of carnal desires, sex, and violence, as well as the unconscious. This painting depicts two seemingly mythical figures, perhaps part human, part animal. Painted in vibrant, contrasting colors, the distorted creatures face each other against an abstracted bare landscape. This violent, colorful clashing of forms is typical of Thompson's work from 1962–64: many of his paintings during this period contain brightly colored fantastic beasts and monsters swirling around distorted human forms. Though this untitled work does not depict a specific mythical or religious scene, it does demonstrate Thompson's continual and increasing interest in biblical and mythical themes. Later works, such as his 1963–64 *Nativity* (Collection of John Sacchi), a direct quotation of Piero della Francesca's 1472–74 *Montefeltro Madonna* (Pinacoteca di Brera, Milan), utilize the same bright, flat colors and distorted forms in a powerful appropriation of the biblical scene.

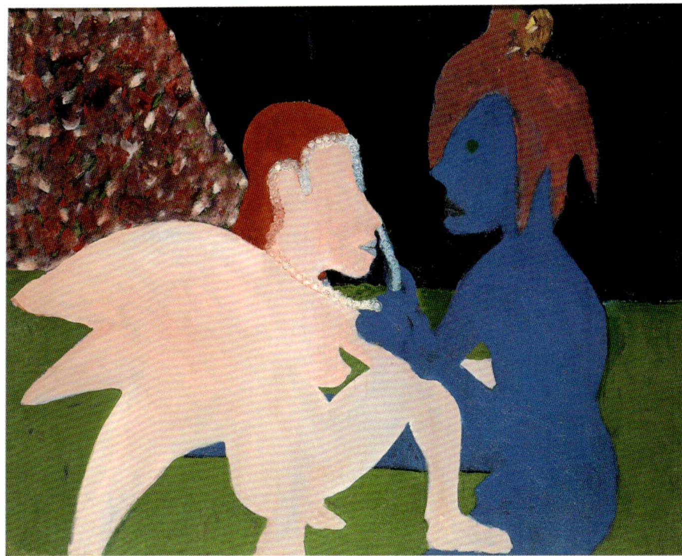

Untitled (Pink and Blue Figures)

The undated *Stairway to the Stars* is a rare example of a multimedia work by Thompson, one that juxtaposes paper cutouts and a large photostat of an American Airlines airplane stairway with multicolored figures rendered in oil paint. The ambiguous narrative, dynamic use of color, and intensity of paint application, along with the appropriation of imagery from contemporary culture, makes *Stairway to the Stars* a striking image.

Thompson continued to paint until his death. Many of his later works deal with themes of death, martyrdom, redemption, and execution, with a large number of them appropriating Renaissance images of Christ. In March 1966, Thompson's alcohol and heroin addictions began to take a serious toll. After a serious gallbladder operation, Thompson was advised to rest, but his excessive lifestyle continued. Thompson died two months later in Rome, of a drug overdose on 30 May 1966. M.R.

BIBLIOGRAPHY

Golden, Thelma. *Bob Thompson*. exh. cat. New York: Whitney Museum of American Art in association with the University of California Press, Berkeley, 1998. With an essay by Judith Wilson and commentaries by Shamim Momin.

Studio Museum in Harlem. *The World of Bob Thompson*. exh. cat. New York: Studio Museum in Harlem, 1978. Preface by Mary Schmidt Campbell; introduction by Gylbert Coker.

Wilson, Judith. "Myths and Memories: Bob Thompson," *Art in America* 71 (May 1983): 139–43.

CHARLES WHITE • (1918–1979)

Skipping, 1960

Crayon on paper, 33½ x 26 in. (85.1 x 66.1 cm)

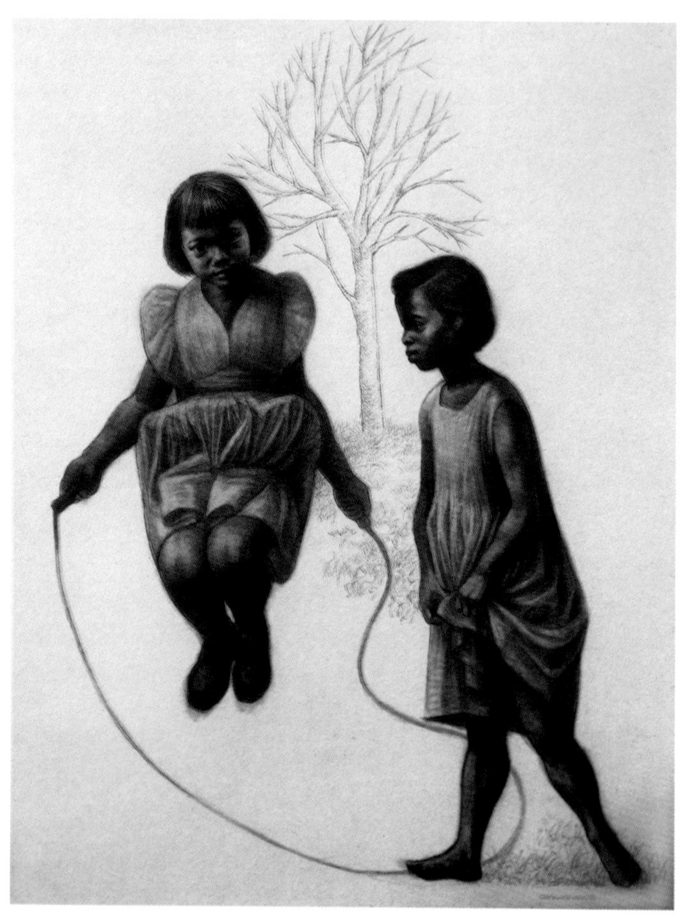

Charles White was one of the best academic draftsmen of the figure that the United States produced in the twentieth century. Early in his career he vowed to make images that would both be technically excellent and also express his unwavering conviction that African Americans—whether well-known or ordinary—are heroic in their struggles for justice and self-esteem. In 1940 he conveyed his views to writer Willard Motley:

> I feel a definite tie-up between all that has happened to the Negro in the past and the whole thinking and acting of the Negro now. Because the white man does not know the history of the Negro, he misunderstands him.
>
> I am interested in the total, even propaganda, angle of painting, but I feel the job of everyone in the creative field is to picture the whole scene. The old masters pioneered in the technical field. I am interested in creating a style that is much more powerful, that will take in the technical and, at the same time, say what I have to say. Painting is the only weapon I have with which to fight what I resent.[1]

Although his style developed over the years, this remained his basic philosophy.

White was born in Chicago, Illinois, on 2 April 1918. His mother, Ethel Gary, who hailed from Yazoo County, Mississippi, had moved north during the Great Migration and found employment as a domestic; his father, Charles White, Sr., of Native American descent, worked as a dining car waiter and construction worker. White's parents never married and separated when he was a toddler. Ethel later married a laborer and postal worker, but left him because of his alcoholism and inability to hold a steady job. She was, however, ambitious for her young son; she bought him an oil paint set and scrimped to pay for ten years of violin lessons for him.

With a talent for drawing he won a competition for free art lessons to the Saturday classes at the Art Institute of Chicago. In the public library he discovered Alain Locke's anthology, *The New Negro*, which, he later recalled, "opened new vistas for me. I never knew before that there were black artists or poets or writers. I was about thirteen years old. . . . It was the most influential book of them [in all] my development."[2] His art teachers encouraged him to enter scholarship competitions to prestigious local art schools, two of which awarded him with scholarships only to reject him because of his race. Eventually he graduated from high school and was accepted to the School of the Art Institute of Chicago, completing the two-year program in one year.

As a professional artist without a job, he was eligible to join the Federal Art Project (FAP) of the Works Progress Administration (WPA), where he met and was influenced by leading FAP Chicago artists Mitchell Siporin, Edward Millman, Aaron Bohrod, David Fredenthal, and Joe Jones, who were also leftist in their political outlook. They introduced White to the work of the Mexican muralists and encouraged White's political outlook. One of his FAP murals depicted the African American leaders Sojourner Truth, Frederick Douglass, George Washington Carver,

Booker T. Washington, and Marian Anderson. The Associated Negro Press commissioned him to paint a mural for the 1940 American Negro Exposition in Chicago.

He met and then married Elizabeth Catlett in 1941. Living in New Orleans where Catlett went to teach at Dillard University, he first experienced southern Jim Crow discrimination. One incident that remained vivid in his memory was a beating he received for entering a New Orleans restaurant. Over a fifteen-year period three of his uncles and two cousins were lynched. These incidents increased his anger at racial injustices. As Romare Bearden and Harry Henderson observed, "But if his dedication was sharpened, so was his sense of the need for a completely disciplined mastery of his art."[3]

When Catlett and White moved to New York in 1942, he began to study with printmaker Harry Sternberg at the Art Students League. Sternberg urged him to focus on the individuality of men and women—and not think of them as just symbols. White turned increasingly to black-and-white drawing, honing his skills in ways akin to the German artist Käthe Kollwitz, whom he admired. With a Julius Rosenwald Fund fellowship, White and Catlett went to Hampton Institute (now Hampton University) where White painted the mural *Contribution of the Negro to American Democracy*, which contained figures from history, such as Crispus Attucks, Peter Salem, Nat Turner, Denmark Vesey, Booker T. Washington, George Washington Carver, and Paul Robeson.

In 1944 White was drafted into the Army and assigned to the South, but was sent to a Veterans Administration hospital the next year when diagnosed with tuberculosis. After World War II he and Catlett left for Mexico, where they became affiliated with the Taller de Gráfica Popular. In 1946 he and Catlett divorced, and that fall he had an exhibition at the A.C.A. Galleries in New York.

In 1950 White married a social worker, Frances Barrett. They traveled to France, Italy, West Germany, and Eastern Europe. White discovered that his reputation preceded him and he was honored in Czechoslovakia, Poland, East Germany, and the Soviet Union. When they returned, White was summoned to appear before the House Committee on Un-American Activities, but several weeks later he was informed that he need not appear.[4] In 1956 the Whites moved to Los Angeles, both for the climate and with hopes that the environment there would be better for an interracial couple. In 1963 the Whites adopted the first of their two children, Jessica and later Ian. In 1965 he started teaching at the Otis Art Institute in Los Angeles. In the late 1950s and early 1960s, White became involved in the Civil Rights movement and produced several series of drawings and portfolios of lithographs that commented on the issues of the times, such as the *J'Accuse* series of drawings and the *Wanted Poster* series of the late 1960s.

During the 1970s he received major prizes and in 1972 was elected to full membership to the National Academy of Design. As a result of his chronic respiratory problems, he died at a Veterans Administration Hospital on 3 October 1979. In 1980 he was posthumously honored by President Jimmy Carter.

White's entire career focused on images of African Americans and African American history. *Skipping* was done in 1960.[5] Using crayon, he achieved rich velvety effects for this spirited image of two girls absorbed in their jumping rope. The child with the rope, however, seems to beckon us to join in. Many of White's works extend that same invitation to the viewer; they stare at us, confront us with their ideas, and welcome us to the struggle. P.H.

BIBLIOGRAPHY

Barnwell, Andrea D. *Charles White*. San Francisco: Pomegranate, 2002.

Bearden, Romare and Harry Henderson. "Charles White," in *A History of African-American Artists from 1792 to the Present*. New York: Pantheon Books, 1993.

Freedom Ways 20, No. 3 (1980) [Issue devoted to Charles White].

1. Quoted in Bearden and Henderson 1993, 408; originally quoted in Willard Motley, "Negro Art in Chicago," *Opportunity* 18 (January 1940): 19–22.

2. Quoted in Bearden and Henderson 1993, 406–07; from an interview dated 23 September 1973.

3. Bearden and Henderson, 409.

4. Barnwell, 50–51.

5. We are grateful to C. Ian White for dating the drawing.

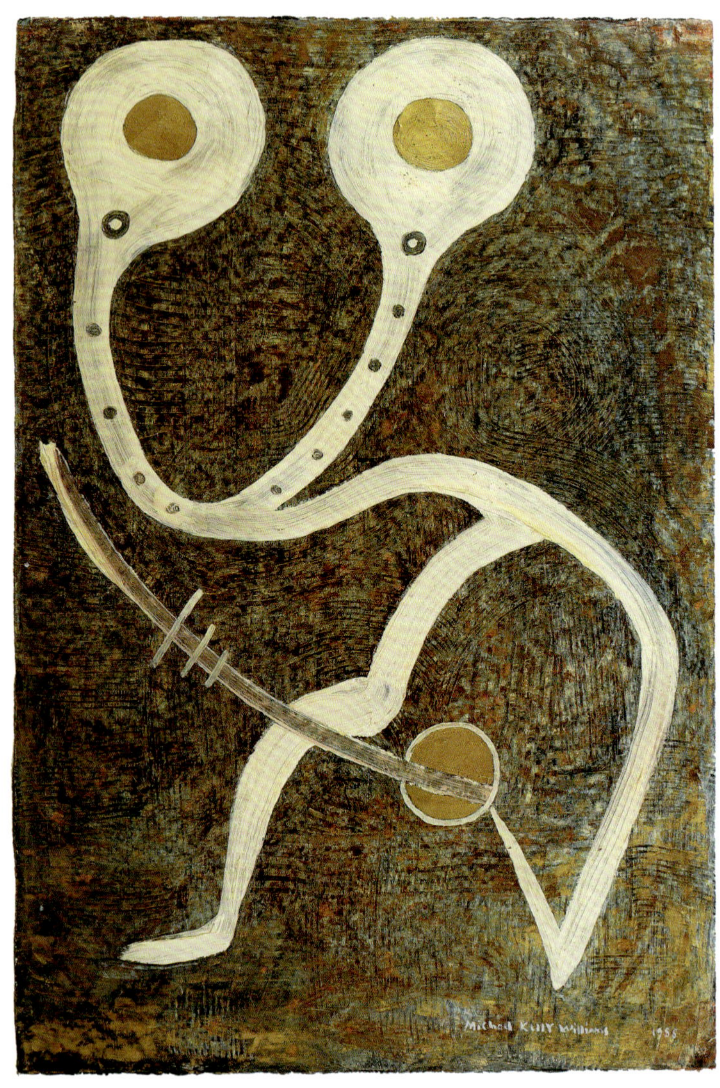

MICHAEL KELLY WILLIAMS • (born 1950)

Ganawa, 1988

Oil on treated paper, 44 x 30 in. (111.8 x 76.2 cm)

Contemporary artist and art educator Michael Kelly Williams works in a variety of media, including printmaking, sculpture, painting, and public art. Williams's father, Kelly Williams, of African American and Cherokee descent, was born in Atlanta, Georgia, and his mother, Elizabeth Ann Swartz, of German and Cree Indian descent, was born in Battle Creek, Michigan. He spent his early years in Neuilly-sur-Seine, France, where he was born on 8 March 1950, while his father studied art abroad on the G.I. Bill. His family returned to the United States when he was five years old, settling in Detroit, Michigan, where his father worked in a car factory while also running a community-based arts program. His mother worked for the Detroit Parks and Recreation Department and later as a School Community Agent. Early on, Williams was influenced by his parents' interest in art and education:

> My father was an artist. I took art for granted when I was growing up. I assumed everyone had access to art materials. It was another language. As far as I can

remember my father had a community-based art school and later gallery. I grew up in this environment so I feel comfortable working in community-based arts organizations and I have worked in many.[1]

Williams's wide variety of educational and artistic experiences began at a young age. At Cass Technical High School he studied engraving, lithography, and sculpture. During his final year at Cass, he represented his school in a special sculpture class held at the Detroit Institute of Arts and taught by Michigan State University professor Robert Wilde. In 1969 Williams went to Michigan State to work with Wilde. From 1971–72 he attended Wayne State University in Detroit and, funded by a grant, he participated in an archaeological dig in Tuscany. At Wayne State Williams also studied woodcut printing with Bob Woodward. In 1973 he enrolled at the University of Michigan, Ann Arbor, graduating cum laude with a B.F.A. in 1975.

Williams went on to study at various prestigious workshops and schools throughout the United States, including a program in Near Eastern Languages and Civilizations at the University of Chicago during 1977–78 and at Krishna Reddy's Color Print Atelier at New York University in 1980. He has won many prestigious fellowships, both in the United States and abroad, including a Residency in Morocco, 1983, a Residency Award from the New York State Council on the Arts, 1984, an Artist-in-Residency grant from the Studio Museum in Harlem, 1986, and a fellowship to attend the Skowhegan School of Painting and Sculpture in Maine, 1988.

Williams cites his parents, art historian Cledie Taylor and sculptor Robert Wilde, as significant influences, but singles out printmaker Robert Blackburn as his most important mentor. Williams attended Blackburn's famous printmaking workshop in New York City from 1979–83 and taught there from 1979–94. Williams states:

> The printmaking workshop had a profound impact on me with artists from all over the world. . . . Printmaking's long history as an art of the people in so many countries interests me. I studied as many of these traditions as I could.[2]

Williams's travels to Italy, Greece, Egypt, and Morocco, as well as his educational and artistic training both at home and abroad, inform many of his works. In *Ganawa*, Williams uses his signature abstracted human forms to depict the music of the Ganawa people. Of this work he recently wrote: "*Ganawa* is about the music of the Ganawa people of Morocco, who play large metal castanets, string instruments and drums. I was given a tape of the music that I listened to while creating the piece. . . . [I was] inspired by the music."[3] Music plays a significant role in Williams's art, both as the subject of many of his works and a part of his art-making process. He often listens to jazz while he works in order to maintain spontaneity, which is clearly evident in the central figure that sways against a vivid background of expressive brushstrokes in brown, green, and yellow tones. Folk art and African art serve as sources of inspiration for Williams; he comments: "The unique flavor of Black Folk Art and the spiritually charged forms of African Art have continued to influence and inspire me. *Ganawa* moves like a Bill Traylor figure, while the mysterious nature of its body, head, eyes, cymbals, and horns are close to some African art work like that of the Makonde."[4]

Williams received an M.F.A. in Sculpture in 1996 from Brooklyn College of the City University of New York and most recently, in 2001, a degree in education from the Hubert H. Lehman College in the Bronx. In addition to practicing art, Williams teaches and leads workshops in a variety of educational settings—at the Bronx Museum in New York, at the Berkshire School of Contemporary Art in North Adams, Massachusetts, and at the Studio Museum in Harlem. He also instructs adults and children in community centers, public schools, and libraries for the Printmaking Workshop's Community Program. In 1992 he worked on a public art project for the Metropolitan Transit Authority's Arts for Transit Program, in which he designed two glass mosaics, *El #1* and *El #5*, for the Intervale Subway Station.

Williams's work has been exhibited at various galleries throughout the United States. Most recently Williams was featured in the 2003 Library of Congress exhibition, *"Creative Space": Fifty Years of Robert Blackburn's Printmaking Workshop*, as well as in the 1994 traveling exhibition organized by the Studio Museum in Harlem, *25 Years of African American Art*. M.R.

BIBLIOGRAPHY

Riggs, Thomas, ed. "Michael Kelly Williams," in *St. James Guide to Black Artists*. Published in Association with the Schomburg Center for Research in Black Culture. Detroit: St. James Press, 1997.

Stanislaus, Grace. *From the Studio: Artist-in-Residence, 1986–87*. exh. cat. New York: Studio Museum in Harlem, 1987.

Taha, Halima. *Collecting African American Art*. New York: Crown Press, 1998.

Website on Robert Blackburn: http://www.loc.gov/exhibits/blackburn/ (27 July 2005).

1. Michael Kelly Williams, e-mail to Melissa Renn, 24 July 2005.
2. Ibid.
3. Ibid.
4. Michael Kelly Williams, e-mail to Melissa Renn, 29 July 2005.

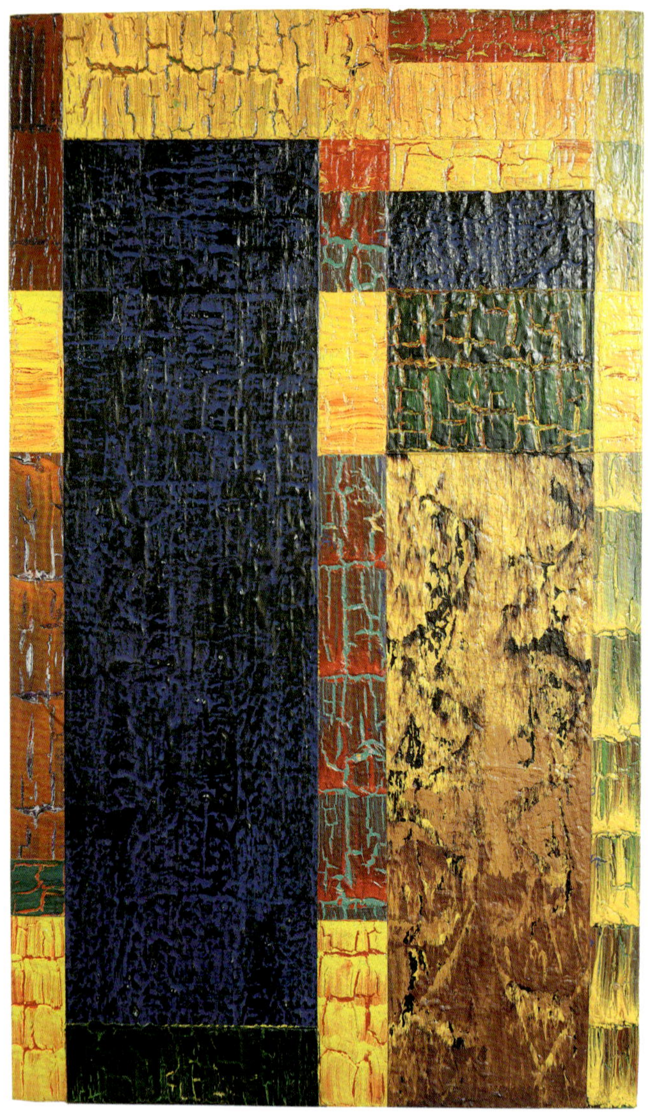

WILLIAM T. WILLIAMS • (born 1942)

Carolina Shout, 1990

Acrylic on canvas, 75 x 44 in. (190.5 x 111.8 cm)

William T. Williams was born on 17 July 1942 in the rural enclave of Cross Creek, North Carolina, to William Thomas Williams and Hazel Davis Williams. His father was drafted into the army during World War II and sent to North Africa, then Italy and France. Following his discharge, in 1946, the family moved to New York City —first to Harlem, then relocated to Queens. In 1950 they moved into a public housing project in Far Rockaway, an integrated neighborhood. Although raised and schooled in New York, Williams returned to North Carolina each summer to stay with his grandparents until he was about fourteen years old. He credits his North Carolina memories for helping to shape his aesthetic preoccupations, even today.

Encouraged by his teachers, he commuted into Manhattan to attend the High School of Industrial Arts (now the High School of Art and Design), which offered an intensive program of art instruction. After two years in a community college he went to Pratt Institute in Brooklyn, where he found supportive teachers—Philip Pearlstein, Alex Katz, and Richard Bove—and where he met and later married fellow art student Pat DeWeese, who today is a quilter. Upon graduating from Pratt in 1966, Williams entered Yale University School of Art and studied primarily with George Wardlaw and Al Held. He received his M.F.A. in 1968.

While still an art student Williams chose to make abstract art, because it allows him to concentrate on the processes of artmaking—to experiment with the properties of color (its hue, weight, and optical movement), with the density of paint (its layers and surface touch), and with composition (the balancing of colored and toned masses and line). Mastering the techniques was the first step toward his goal of conveying his experiences. In a recent interview he recalled: "Early on representational painting was too fussy for me. It was only when I came to abstraction that I really began to enjoy the whole process of painting and began to think of what art could do."[1] In Williams's early paintings he manipulated on canvas quadrangles covered with flat pure colors that tilt into optical space and are intersected by straight or curving bars of contrasting colors, such as *Elbert Jackson L.A.M.F., Part II*, 1969 (The Museum of Modern Art).

The late 1960s were active professional years for Williams on many counts. In 1968 he returned to New York and met Romare Bearden and other artists. He proposed to the trustees of the fledgeling Studio Museum in Harlem an artists-in-residence program, an idea he had developed at Yale. They promptly hired him to implement a plan. He is proud that the program is still going strong.

Meanwhile, his career as a painter gained momentum. In 1969 he showed his work in the Whitney Museum of American Art Biennial and in exhibitions at the Larry Aldrich Museum in Connecticut and the Studio Museum in Harlem. The Museum of Modern Art included him in an exhibition that traveled to Moscow. In 1971 he began teaching art at Brooklyn College, a job he still holds. He has also taught summers at the Skowhegan School of Painting and Sculpture, where he had himself been a summer student.

As an abstract artist, his style has gradually changed over the years. After works like *Elbert Jackson L.A.M.F., Part II,* in the early 1970s he began to paint monochromatically, using only the touch and direction of the brush to give definition to the surface, as in *Equinox*, 1975 (collection of the artist). After a trip to Nigeria in 1977, where he experienced the heat, light, sun, dust, and baked earth of that equatorial country, colors returned and the surface became more densely textured and cracked, as in *Savannah*, 1979. During the 1980s he developed paintings with broad vertical rectangles of contrasting colors laid on with thick acrylic paint, such as *Carolina Shout*.

Williams wants his paintings to express his dual experiences, particularly the contrast of memories of the sounds and texture of his North Carolina summers with his Pratt and Yale training as a modernist artist living and working in New York. He views *Carolina Shout* as an homage to Romare Bearden, who also incorporated his North Carolina memories into his collages, including his own *Carolina Shout*. Both artists, of course, consciously acknowledge the piano composition by James P. Johnson, first recorded in 1921. Williams's *Carolina Shout* can be seen as having analogies to Johnson's piece. It has a basic structure of large and small rectangles, over which are successive layers of acrylic paint, built up and sometimes cracking to reveal the colors of previous layers. The whole was orchestrated over time until Williams achieved to his satisfaction simultaneous effects of harmony and dissonance across the rectangles. But such paintings also recall the piecing, layering, and stitching of quilts. Quilts, Williams recalls, were the first art objects he saw as a small child in North Carolina. Unconsciously he was absorbing Southern cultural practices that included quilts —quilts that had individuality, transmitted traditions, and spoke of human warmth and struggles.[2] Quilts, then, have always been a part of his experiences, as is living with music—with the jazz, blues, and classical guitar he enjoys listening to when painting. He strives for the synthesis of these arts in his painting, as in his life. P.H.

BIBLIOGRAPHY

Anacostia Museum, Smithsonian Institution. *Contemporary Visual Expressions*. exh. cat. Washington, D.C.: Smithsonian Institution, 1986. Essay by David C. Driskell.

Mercer, Valerie J. "Behind Closed Doors: William T. Williams Struggles to Create Paintings that Have a Life of Their Own," *American Visions* 6 (April 1991): 14–19.

Montclair Art Museum. *William T. Williams: Fourteen Paintings*. exh. cat. Montclair, New Jersey: Montclair Art Museum, 1991. Essay by Valerie J. Mercer.

Williams, William T. Transcript of statement for a panel discussion, "When That Time Came Rolling Down: Panel I," 25 March 1984, in *Artist and Influence* (1985), 161–63.

1. William T. Williams, audio tape interview with Patricia Hills, 12 July 2005, and telephone interview, 29 July 2005. Most of the information in this sketch is drawn from these interviews.

2. See the author's "Cultural Legacies and the Transformation of the Cubist Collage Aesthetic by Romare Bearden, Jacob Lawrence, and Other African American Artists," forthcoming in a National Gallery of Art publication.

ELLIS WILSON • (1899–1977)

Hope, n.d.

Encaustic on board, 22½ x 11 in. (57.2 x 27.9 cm)

Born in Mayfield, Kentucky, on 30 April 1899, Ellis Wilson was a figurative painter whose works often depict scenes of African American and Haitian daily life. Raised in an all-black section of Mayfield known as "The Bottom," Wilson attended the Colored Graded School. Wilson's mother, Minnie, founded the Bottom Neighborhood's Second Christian Church and his father, Frank Wilson, who owned his own barbershop, exerted an early artistic influence on his son. In 1933, as a tribute to his father, Ellis Wilson was listed in the Harmon Foundation catalogue directory as the "son of an artist."

After high school Wilson attended a free state school for African Americans in Frankfurt, Kentucky, now Kentucky State College. The school only offered agricultural and educational training, so in 1918–19 Wilson left for Chicago to pursue a degree in art. He enrolled in the School of the Art Institute of Chicago, which at that time was one of the few institutions that accepted black students. At the Art Institute Wilson studied with William McKnight Farrow, an expert etcher and the Institute's first black instructor. Through Farrow, Wilson came into contact with many other black artists, including Richmond Barthé, and also became active in the Chicago Art League. He graduated from the Art Institute in 1923, having won the George E. Hoe and Charles S. Peterson prizes in art. In 1927 Wilson heard Alain Locke speak at Chicago's groundbreaking 1927 exhibition "The Negro in Art Week." Inspired by Locke, he relocated to Harlem, where he became active in the Harlem Renaissance and contributed work to both exhibitions and publications. Two of Wilson's works appeared in Harmon Foundation exhibitions: a figure study in 1930 and an early still life in 1933. Wilson also provided an illustration for the March 1929 issue of *The Crisis*, edited by W.E.B. Du Bois. Wilson was actively involved with many arts organizations, including the Harlem Artists Guild and the Savage School of Arts and Crafts.

In addition to his career as an artist, Wilson worked various jobs. In 1935 he was laid off from his day job at Farroll Brothers Brokerage and went to work for the Federal Art Project (FAP) of the Works Progress Administration (WPA). Under the FAP, Wilson was assigned to a mapping division that created geographical dioramas. While on the WPA he met many artists, including Beauford and Joseph Delaney.

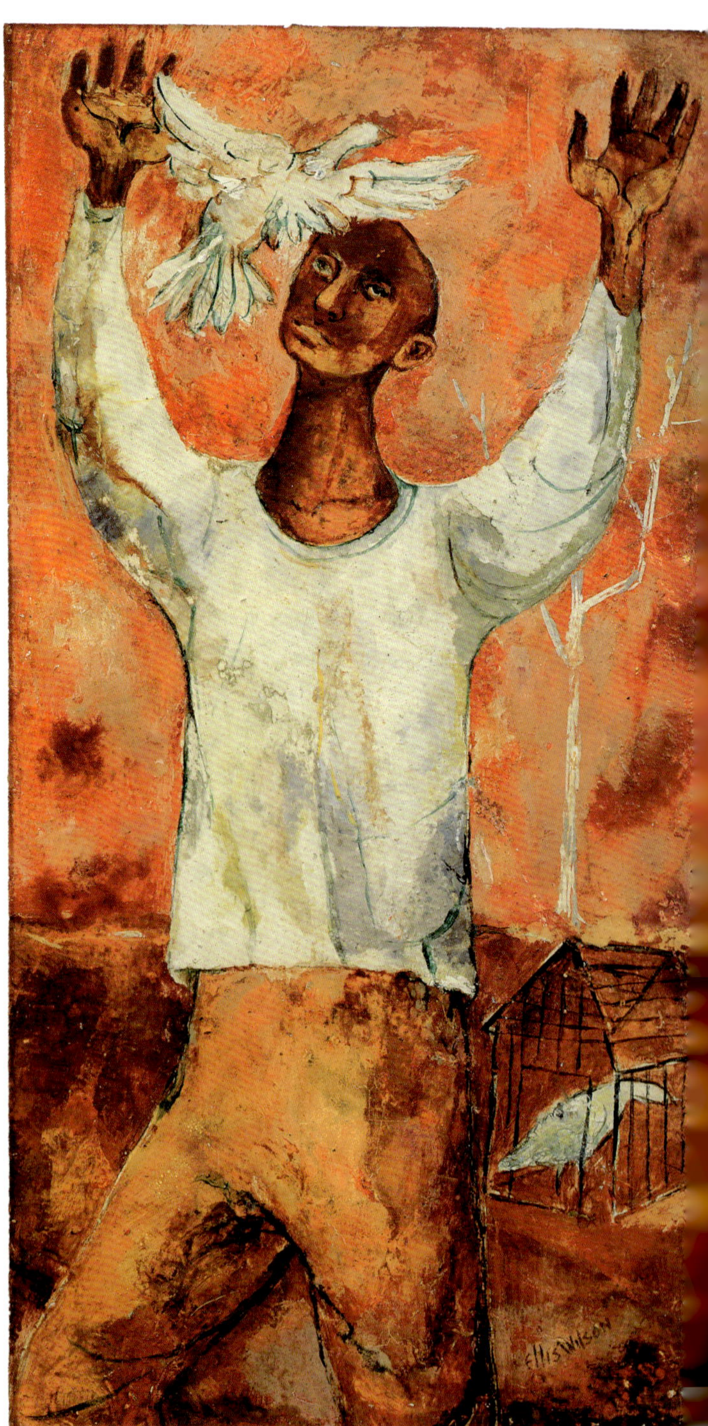

In the early 1940s Wilson went to work for an aircraft engine factory, where he did a series of sketches of the defense workers. In 1944 he won a Guggenheim Fellowship for his drawings of the factory workers and traveled to the South, where he did many sketches and paintings of rural southern black people, both in the open-air markets of Charleston, and of the Gullah people on the Sea Islands off the coast of South Carolina.

In 1952 one of Wilson's sketches from his trip to Charleston won the Terry Art Institute's Prize for Art in Miami. The $3,000 award made it possible for him to travel to Haiti, which was a pivotal moment for Wilson as an artist. As he recalled, upon watching the Haitian peasants and farmers carry goods to the market: "It came to me that at a distance, you see these people coming and going—and you don't see their features. They're black—they're a mass of darkness—so I started painting the faces flat. That was a big step for me!"[1] Wilson's Haitian paintings, characterized by their stylized and elongated figures, flat application of paint, and bright colors, characterize his mature works.

Wilson's paintings consistently celebrate the daily life of African Americans. His style has ranged from realistic portraiture to the stylized forms of his Haitian paintings. Rendered in one of Wilson's rare painting styles, *Hope* is undated, as are most of Wilson's works. According to Wilson scholar Albert F. Sperath, *Hope* was most likely painted in the 1950s, around the time Wilson traveled to Haiti, which is seen in the elongated form of the central figure.[2] However, unlike Wilson's silhouetted, faceless figures from his Haitian series, the man in this image has a detailed face. This uplifting depiction of a man releasing a white bird from its cage serves as a visual metaphor of freedom.

Wilson lived and worked at his East 18th Street studio in Manhattan for forty years. He had few exhibitions during his lifetime, one of the most significant being a hometown exhibition in 1947, which he stated was one of the high points of his life. Just before his death he had a small exhibition at the Second Christian Church in the Bottom Community, which included a tribute to the Mayfield Colored Graded School. Wilson died in New York City in 1977, leaving behind very few written or spoken words about his work. He remained relatively unknown until 1985, when an episode of the television series *The Cosby Show* featured one of his paintings, sparking a renewed interest in his work. M.R.

BIBLIOGRAPHY

Bearden, Romare and Harry Henderson. "Ellis Wilson," in *A History of African-American Artists from 1792 to the Present*. New York: Pantheon Books, 1993.

Sperath, Albert F. *The Art of Ellis Wilson*. With essays by Margaret R. Vendryes, Steven H. Jones and Eva F. King. Lexington, Kentucky: The University Press of Kentucky, 2000.

Wilson, Ellis, Interview with Camille Billops, 25 February 1975, in *Artist and Influence* 13 (1994): 213–24.

1. Bearden and Henderson, 342.
2. Information provided on 8 June 2005 by Albert F. Sperath, who is compiling a catalogue raisonné of Wilson's work.

JOHN WILSON • (born 1922)

Girl in Mirror, 1940s

Oil on board, 28 x 15¼ in. (69.9 x 38.7 cm)

Joyce, 1945

Pencil on paper, 18½ x 15 in. (46.9 x 38.1 cm) [see page 16]

Portrait of Joyce, 1947

Oil on canvas, 23½ x 15½ in. (59.7 x 39.4 cm)

John Wilson, whose career includes teaching at the College of Fine Arts of Boston University from 1965–86, is a leading Boston sculptor. In the 1980s he won competitions to design a statue bust of Dr. Martin Luther King, Jr., for the United States Capitol, and a monumental head of King for the Buffalo Arts Commission. In Boston, his seven-foot bronze head, *Eternal Presence*, unveiled in 1987, graces the grounds of the Museum of the National Center of Afro-American Artists, and *Father and Child (Reading)*, unveiled 1990, is installed at Roxbury Community College.[1]

John Woodrow Wilson was born on 14 April 1922 and raised in Roxbury, Massachusetts, the second of five children of Reginald and Violet Wilson, immigrants from British Guiana (now the Republic of Guyana). Moving to the United States to improve his family's opportunities, Wilson's father worked as a shipping clerk but lost his job with the onset of the Depression. The family was at times on welfare, as were so many during the Depression, and his father became politically critical of the racism the family encountered in Boston. Privately the elder Wilson became an ardent follower of Marcus Garvey, a black nationalist who had organized the United Negro Improvement Association. Wilson recalls growing up with different African American newspapers in his home and political discussions a common occurrence, and he developed a lifelong sensitivity to issues of segregation, justice, and self-esteem.

As with most of the artists in this exhibition, Wilson showed an early talent to draw and make art. He joined the Roxbury Boys Club, which had art classes taught by students from the School of the Museum of Fine Arts; thus, the influence of the Russian émigré artist Alexander Iacovleff, who advocated expressive drawing, filtered through to the youngsters taking the classes. After graduating from Roxbury Memorial High School, where he was editor of the school newspaper, he went on scholarship in 1940 to the School of the Museum of Fine Arts. His teacher there, Karl Zerbe, encouraged him and kept him on course. The other students, such as David Aronson, Reed Kay, Jack Kramer, and Arthur Polonsky, readily accepted him; they would become his future colleagues at Boston University. It was in art school that he began to look for books about African American art, and discovered James Porter and Alain Locke, who "helped to give me a direction."[2] Receiving a diploma in 1945, at the end of World War II, he postponed a fellowship to travel to Europe, and instead enrolled at Tufts, where he took a B.S. degree in art education in 1947.

The sojourn in Paris, 1947–49, and his study with Fernand Léger directed him toward a more modern way of making art. Although he wanted to learn mural techniques, Léger insisted he learn more about composition. The Léger influence showed Wilson that he could use line, color, and monumental forms to express the social reality of the working classes and the oppressed races. While abroad, he also traveled to the great museums of Europe.

After returning to Boston in 1950, he taught briefly at the School of the Museum of Fine Arts before leaving for Mexico on a John Hay Whitney Fellowship with Julie Kowitch, whom he had recently married. In Mexico City they met Elizabeth Catlett and her husband Francesco Mora, both active in the community of leftist artists that had organized the graphic workshop Taller de Gráfica Popular. In Mexico he also learned the art of true fresco, a technique popularized by Diego Rivera, José Clemente Orozco, and David Siqueiros, in which paint mixed with lime water is applied to wet plaster and hence becomes part of the fabric of the wall. He subsequently painted *Incident*, a mural that shows a couple inside a house grimly staring out a window where a group of Ku Klux Klan members are in the process of lynching a young black man. In Mexico, the Wilsons' first-born daughter, Becky, arrived, and they decided to return to the States.

The first job offer Wilson accepted was in Chicago. From there they moved to New York, where Wilson taught at the Pratt Institute Evening School and then in the New York City public school system. In 1964 they returned to

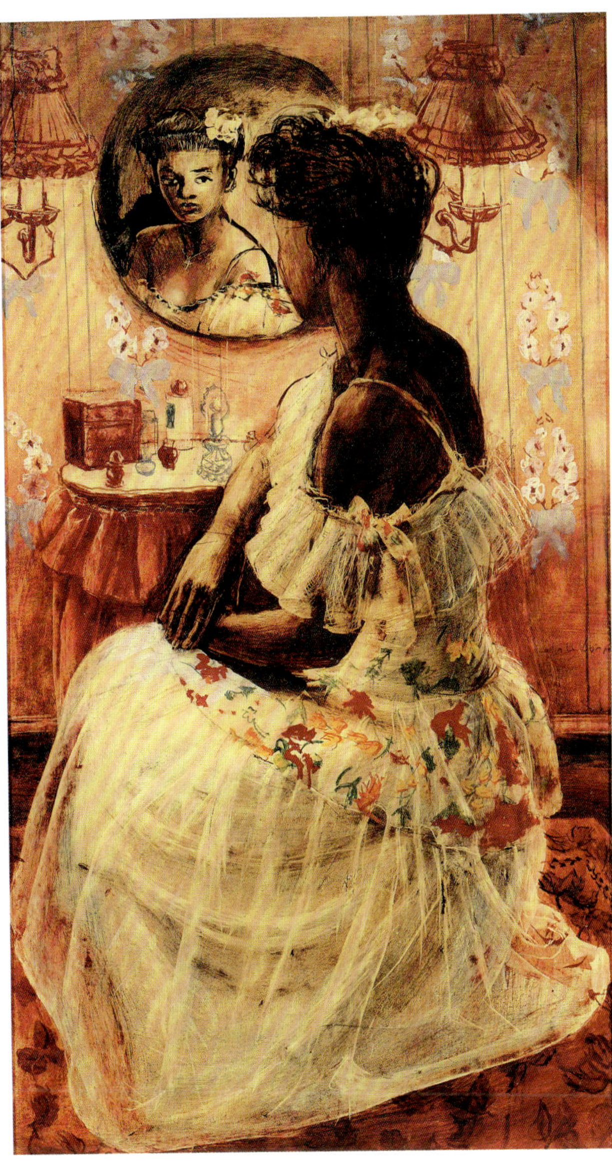

Girl in Mirror

Boston, where David Aronson offered Wilson a job teaching at the School for the Arts (now the College of Fine Arts) at Boston University. A Professor Emeritus since his retirement in 1986, Wilson continues to make drawings and sculpture. He had a major retrospective at the Museum of Fine Arts, Boston, in 1995, and another at Grinnell College, Iowa, in 2004.

The three works by Wilson in the Wein collection are images personal to the artist.[3] The model for *Girl in Mirror* was his sister, Gail, who sits before a vanity and mirror enveloped in flowers—as part of the print of her summer party dress and as a motif of the wallpaper, as well as an actual flower pinned to her hair. The pictures of Joyce depict, of course, Joyce Wein, whom Wilson knew as

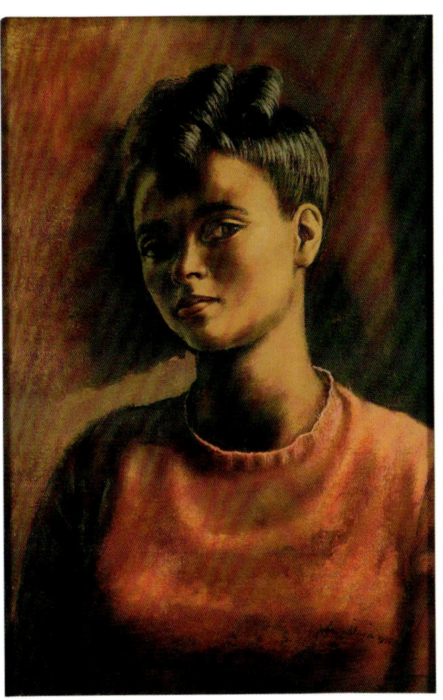

Joyce

Joyce Alexander, a Simmons College student. Wilson recalled Joyce, about five years his junior, as a gregarious person who introduced him to Boston Symphony Orchestra concerts. Because of her, Wilson started listening to classical records. He vividly remembers the oil painting *Portrait of Joyce*. On the eve of his journey to France in 1947 he called his friends and said he wanted to paint their portraits as a going-away gift. He painted Joyce in oil in a red sweater with her hair swept up into a large curl off her forehead. Her expression is subdued and intelligent, as befits a serious Simmons College student interested in both classical music and jazz. P.H.

BIBLIOGRAPHY

Fax, Elton C. *Seventeen Black Artists*. New York: Dodd, Mead and Company, 1971.

Grinnell College. *John Wilson: A Retrospective*. exh. cat. Grinnell, Iowa: Faulconer Gallery, 2004. Curator, Kay Wilson Jenkins. Essays by Pamela Franks, Saadi A. Simawe, and Dave Williams.

Hills, Patricia. "A Portrait of the Artist as an African-American: A Conversation with John Wilson," in *Dialogue: John Wilson/Joseph Norman*. exh. cat. Boston: The Museum of the National Center of Afro-American Artists in association with The Museum of Fine Arts, 1995.

1. See Edmund Barry Gaither and Shelley R. Langdale, "John Wilson/Joseph Norman: An Introduction," in *Dialogue: John Wilson/Joseph Norman*.
2. Hills, 29.
3. John Wilson, telephone interview with Patricia Hills, 21 July 2005.

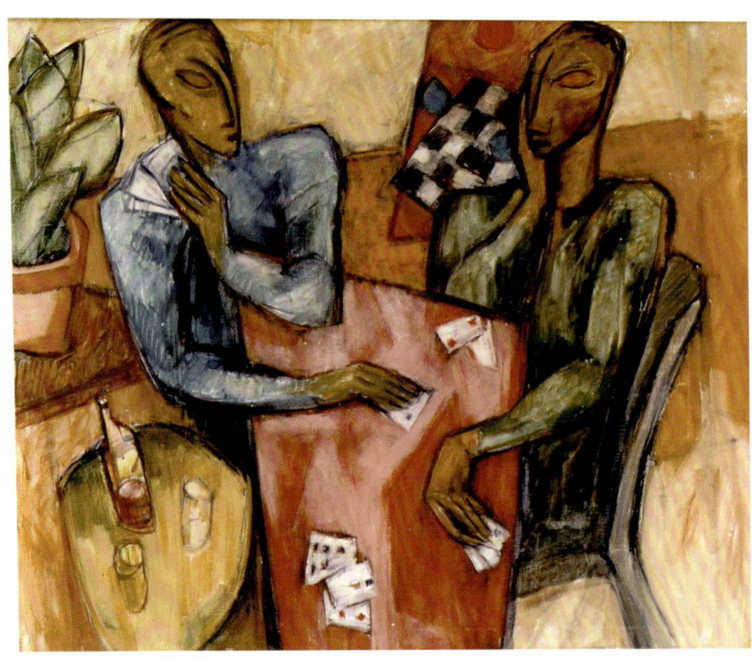

HALE WOODRUFF • (1900–1980)

Card Players, 1970

Oil on canvas, 36½ x 43 in. (92.7 x 109.2 cm)

Artist and educator Hale Aspacio Woodruff was born in Cairo, Illinois, on 26 August 1900 to George and Augusta Bell Woodruff. His father died when he was very young, so Woodruff and his mother moved to East Nashville, Tennessee, where he was raised. Woodruff showed an early interest in drawing and as a teenager designed hand-drawn menus for a local restaurant in Nashville, illustrated cartoons for his high school newspaper, and copied drawings and engravings out of the family Bible. In high school, Woodruff read *The Crisis*, the journal of the National Association for the Advancement of Colored People (NAACP), edited by W.E.B. Du Bois, where he was first introduced to the works of Henry Ossawa Tanner; at this point Woodruff vowed to travel to Paris to meet the renowned African American painter.

In 1918, Woodruff left Nashville and moved to Indianapolis, where he took a part-time job at *The Indianapolis Ledger*, drawing political cartoons that criticized segregation, police brutality, and lynching. In 1920 he enrolled at the Herron Art School, where he studied with William Forsyth. At the John Herron Art Museum (now Indianapolis Museum of Art) Woodruff saw the works of the European masters for the first time and vowed to travel to Europe once again. Lacking the funds to travel abroad, Woodruff enrolled briefly at the School of the Art Institute of Chicago, where he studied part-time.

Woodruff returned to Indianapolis in the mid-1920s, where he continued to paint independently while also working at the Senate Avenue YMCA, run by activist and community leader Fayburn E. De Frantz. Through De Frantz Woodruff met many notable figures active in both the New Negro movement and Harlem Renaissance, including Charles S. Johnson, W.E.B. Du Bois, and Countee Cullen. Inspired by the people he met at the YMCA, Woodruff began to exhibit his art regularly and submitted works to the Harmon Foundation exhibitions, where he won a bronze award for five of his paintings in 1926.

In 1927 Woodruff left for Paris, where he met up with his friend and fellow artist Palmer Hayden. Woodruff initially hoped to study art at the Académie Julian, where Henry Ossawa Tanner had studied, but by 1927 the school's reputation had changed, and with Woodruff's increasing interest in European modernism, he chose instead to study at the Académie Scandinave and the Académie Moderne. At the Académie Moderne, Woodruff painted city scenes, landscapes, and views of Paris and experimented with Impressionistic, Postimpressionistic, and Cubist styles. Woodruff lived the life of a Parisian artist, residing in Montparnasse, visiting the many museums, frequenting shops and galleries where he encountered African art, and painting outdoors along the Seine.

In 1930 Woodruff painted *The Cardplayers*, which demonstrates the influence of French artist Paul Cézanne. Woodruff commented on Cézanne's impact in a 1977 interview. He described how:

> Cézanne opened up new doors for me. . . . In this particular work [Paul Cézanne, *Boy in the Red Vest*, 1893–95] as well as others, I set about trying to find a means by which I could learn from these examples, not to simply paraphrase them and copy them, but to learn their basic ideas beneath them. While I have already begun my own work, I began to assimilate these ideas in my own painting. I understood why Cézanne tilted the tops of his tables, how he brought things forward, how he eliminated so-called optical perspective and used space as surface construction.[1]

Employing multiple perspectives, vivid colors, and thick application of paint, *The Cardplayers* in the Wein Collection demonstrates Woodruff's interest in Cubism and Post-impressionism. His painting, however, makes significant modifications to Cézanne's version, incorporating mask-like faces that recall African art. Indeed, Woodruff had read Alain Locke's essay "The Legacy of the Ancestral Arts," which encouraged African American artists to look to the discipline of African sculpture. He painted additional versions of *The Cardplayers* in the 1970s, as the original 1930 painting was badly damaged. The 1970 painting shown here is a later reworking of his earlier painting with some variations in the color, the positioning of the two central figures, and the objects surrounding them.

When Woodruff returned to the United States he taught at the newly founded Atlanta University in Atlanta, Georgia, where he was professor of art from 1931–45. In 1935 he worked on a series of Federal Art Project (FAP) murals for the Atlanta School of Social Work on the Atlanta University campus as well as a mural series *The Negro in Modern America* for the David T. Howard Junior High School in Atlanta. Many students came to Atlanta University to work with Woodruff, who, in addition to organizing student groups such as The Painters' Guild, brought exhibitions of African art and renowned speakers to the campus. In 1936 Woodruff traveled to Mexico, where he worked with muralist Diego Rivera on a series of frescoes. That experience certainly influenced his *Amistad* mutiny murals at Talladega College in 1939, which depict, with great pictorial clarity and dramatic realism, the Amistad slave mutiny of 1839.

In 1942 Hale Woodruff inaugurated the Atlanta University Exhibitions, which would become nationally recognized exhibitions highlighting art by African Americans. In 1943 and 1944 Woodruff received consecutive Julius Rosenwald Fellowships, which he used to travel to New York, where he set up a studio.

In 1947 Woodruff relocated to New York, where he taught at New York University from 1947–68. During the 1950s Woodruff's works became increasingly abstract, with an emphasis on technique, thick application of paint, expressive use of color, and attention to surface. Though much scholarship centers on Woodruff's earlier career as a teacher, painter, and mural artist, recently more attention has been given to his Abstract Expressionist paintings.[2] In his abstractions, however, Woodruff never completely abandoned subject matter and continually utilized the form, content, and history of African art as sources for his abstract works.

Woodruff was, along with Romare Bearden, one of the founding members of *Spiral*, whose purpose was to address the challenges of being an African American artist. Woodruff also participated in *Spiral's* only exhibition, the 1965 *Works in Black and White*. When he retired from full-time teaching in 1966, New York University gave him a "Great Teacher" award for his contributions as both an artist and an educator. He died 26 September 1980. M.R.

BIBLIOGRAPHY

Bearden, Romare and Harry Henderson. "Hale Woodruff," in *A History of African-American Artists from 1792 to the Present*. New York: Pantheon Books, 1993.

Leininger-Miller, Theresa A. *New Negro Artists in Paris: African American Painters and Sculptors in the City of Light, 1922–1934*. New Brunswick, New Jersey: Rutgers University Press, 2001.

Stoelting, Winifred L. *Hale Woodruff, Artist and Teacher: Through the Atlanta Years*. Ph.D. Dissertation: Emory University, 1978.

Studio Museum in Harlem. *Hale Woodruff: Fifty Years of His Art*. exh. cat. New York: Studio Museum in Harlem, 1979. With essays by Winifred Stoelting and Gylbert Coker, and an interview by Albert Murray; foreword by Mary Schmidt Campbell; introduction by Romare Bearden.

1. Hale Woodruff, taped notes, 28 August 1977. Quoted in Stoelting, 181.

2. See Ann Eden Gibson's *Abstract Expressionism: Other Politics*. New Haven: Yale University Press, 1997.

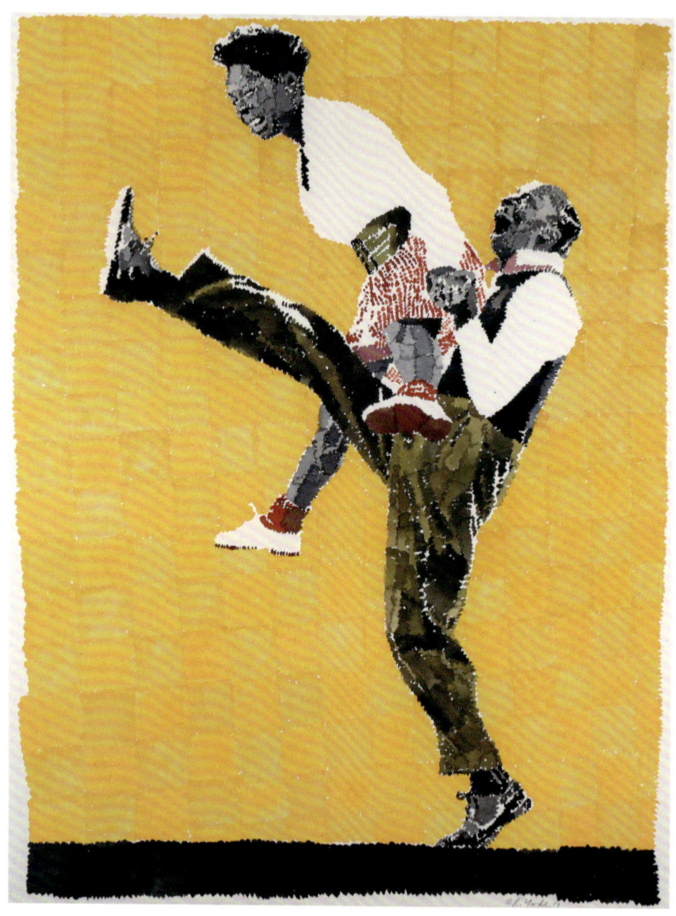

RICHARD YARDE • (born 1939)

Savoy, 1991

Watercolor on paper, 41½ x 29⅝ in. (105.4 x 75.3 cm)

Richard Yarde works in many media, including watercolor, installation art, sculpture, oil painting, and film. His works have dealt with a variety of subjects including his personal family history; a series of memorial portraits of prominent African Americans such as Marcus Garvey and Jack Johnson; an installation of the Savoy Ballroom; and issues of health and healing.

Born in Boston, Massachusetts, on 29 October 1939, Richard Yarde grew up in Roxbury; his parents were originally from Barbados. He credits many members of his family for influencing his development as an artist:

> My first influence was my older brother Edgar, who taught me to draw from comics. My godfather, Amos Gibson, was also an inspiration. He operated a portrait photography studio in Boston's South End. I loved to watch him hand tint black-and-white photographs. I would try to imitate him by adding watercolor to newspaper photographs that interested me. My mother, Enid, supported me in my art by bringing home art materials, even though she had her heart set on my becoming a minister. When I was nine I took Saturday morning classes in watercolor and sculpture at the Museum of Fine Arts in Boston. There I was drawn to William Blake's watercolors. They reminded me of the comic books I loved. The ritual and religion of Blake's work really stuck with me.[1]

After graduating from high school, Yarde enrolled at Boston University where he studied with Reed Kay, Conger Metcalf, and Walter Murch, all of whom had a tremendous influence, especially Metcalf who helped him obtain a scholarship to continue his studies at Boston University. Yarde describes his autobiographical film titled *That's*

Where I'm At, as a turning point in his career as an artist. The film centered on his childhood experiences growing up in Roxbury, and shifted his direction towards increasingly autobiographical content. Yarde graduated with a B.F.A. in 1962 and an M.F.A. in 1964.

Yarde recognizes the significant role art teachers play and values his own role as a mentor. He has taught at many Massachusetts institutions over the past forty years, including Boston University, Wellesley College, and the Boston and Amherst campuses of the University of Massachusetts. He has also been a visiting artist at Amherst College, Mount Holyoke College, and Massachusetts College of Art. The University of Massachusetts, Amherst, recognized his contributions as a faculty member with a 1996–97 Distinguished Teaching Award.

Yarde drew from both history and his own personal experience in his 1982 installation of the Savoy Ballroom. Growing up in the South End of Boston in the 1940s and 1950s, Yarde was aware of the importance of dance in the African American community and has commented on how dancing was a ritualized way of having fun. He also enjoyed Boston's jazz scene, frequenting George Wein's first club, Storyville, in its early days. The large-scale installation *Savoy* recreated the famous ballroom, filling it with life-sized three-dimensional paintings of the dancers. The exhibition toured the country, culminating in a show at the Studio Museum in Harlem where, on opening night, many of the original Savoy dancers walked around the installation interacting with the painted versions of themselves.

Yarde's 1991 watercolor, *Savoy,* builds on themes he earlier explored in his 1982 installation. An excellent example of his large-scale watercolors, the vibrant colors and fluid handling of paint beautifully replicates the energy and dynamism of the Savoy ballroom dancers. Music is extremely important to Yarde, and he describes how "one of the underlying aspects of rhythm in my work is the grid."[2] Yarde uses this figurative element, seen here in a background of repeated yellow squares, to set up a visual rhythm for the subject matter. His painting technique also contributes to the work's sense of immediacy. When he works in watercolor he paints directly on the paper, with no prior sketching. He states: "I just try to draw with the paint. I found that many times when you put down the drawing it is like a straitjacket and you have to respond to that."[3]

In 1991 Yarde began to experience serious health problems due to years of medication for high blood pressure, including a series of small strokes and kidney failure. His experiences with both the medical profession and alternative healing practices have been incorporated into his most recent work, both his 2003 installation at the Worcester Museum of Art, *Ring Shout,* and his 1996–97 series, *Mojo Hand,* organized by the Massachusetts College of Art. Memories, dreams, and personal experiences serve as the sources for these paintings that address issues of mortality and vulnerability, healing and rebirth.

Yarde continues to exhibit widely and has participated in many shows, including *Visionary Anatomies* at the National Academy of Sciences, Washington, D.C., 2004–05, *Pulse: Art, Healing and Transformation* at the Institute of Contemporary Art, Boston, 2003, and in *When The Spirit Moves,* an exhibition organized by the National Afro-American Museum and Cultural Center in Wilberforce, Ohio, 1999. He has received many honors, including being named a 2002 Honoree at the Studio Museum in Harlem Gala, the Commonwealth Award from the Massachusetts Cultural Council in 2001, an honorary Doctorate from the Massachusetts College of Art in 1998, and an Academy Award in Art from the American Academy of Arts and Letters in 1995.

Yarde currently teaches at the University of Massachusetts, Amherst, and lives in Northampton with his wife, writer Susan Donovan. His ongoing interest in the Savoy Ballroom is demonstrated in his most recent project, the illustration of a children's book about the Savoy with writer Bebe Moore Campbell, which will be published by Philomel Books in 2006. M.R.

BIBLIOGRAPHY

Horn, Alona M. "Showing Vital Signs: The Watercolors of Richard Yarde." *American Visions* 13 (February/March 1998).

Riggs, Thomas, ed. "Richard Yarde," in *St. James Guide to Black Artists.* Published in Association with the Schomburg Center for Research in Black Culture. Detroit: St. James Press, 1997.

Shaw, Gwendolyn DuBois. "Mojo Hand: History, Healing and Hoodoo in the Watercolors of Richard Yarde," in *Pulse: Art, Healing and Transformation.* Edited by Jessica Morgan. Germany: Steidl Publishing, 2003.

Yarde, Richard. *Savoy: An Installation.* exh. cat. South Hadley, Massachusetts: The Mount Holyoke College Art Museum, 1982.

1. Quoted in Riggs, 591.
2. Richard Yarde, interview with Melissa Renn, 19 July 2005.
3. Ibid.

SELECTED GENERAL BIBLIOGRAPHY

Amaki, Amalia K., ed. *A Century of African American Art: The Paul R. Jones Collection*. exh. cat. Newark, Delaware: University Museum, University of Delaware; New Brunswick, New Jersey: Rutgers University Press, 2004.

Arnett, William and Paul Arnett, eds. *Souls Grown Deep: African American Vernacular Art of the South*. 2 vols. Atlanta, Georgia: Tinwood Books in association with the Schomburg Center for Research in Black Culture, the New York Public Library, 2000–01.

Artist and Influence: The Journal of Black American Cultural History. Annual publication since 1981 of the Hatch-Billops Collection, Inc., New York (now Emory University, Atlanta, Georgia). Issues from 1981 to present.

Barnwell, Andrea D. *The Walter O. Evans Collection of African American Art*. exh. cat. Seattle: Walter O. Evans Foundation for Art and Literature in association with University of Washington Press, 1999.

Bearden, Romare and Harry Henderson. *A History of African-American Artists from 1792 to the Present*. New York: Pantheon Books, 1993.

Bontemps, Arna Alexander, ed. *Forever Free: Art by African American Women, 1862–1980*. exh. cat. Normal, Illinois: Illinois State University, 1981.

Campbell, Mary Schmidt. *Tradition and Conflict: Images of a Turbulent Decade, 1963–1973*. exh. cat. New York: Studio Museum in Harlem, 1985.

Collins, Lisa Gail, Lisa Mintz Messinger, and Rachel Mustalish. *African-American Artists, 1929–1945: Prints, Drawings, and Paintings in The Metropolitan Museum of Art*. exh. cat. New York: Metropolitan Museum of Art, 2003.

Dallas Museum of Art. *Black Art, Ancestral Legacy: The African Impulse in African-American Art*. exh. cat. New York: Harry N. Abrams, 1989. Curated by Alvia J. Wardlaw and Maureen McKenna; essays by David C. Driskell, Edmund Barry Gaither, Regenia A. Perry, Alvia J. Wardlaw, William Ferris, Ute Stebich, and Robert Farris Thompson.

Davis, Lenwood G. *Black Artists in the United States: An Annotated Bibliography of Books, Articles, and Dissertations on Black Artists, 1779–1979*. Westport, Connecticut: Greenwood Press, 1980.

Driskell, David C. *The Other Side of Color: African American Art in the Collection of Camille O. and William H. Cosby, Jr.* exh. cat. San Francisco: Pomegranate, 2001.

———. *African American Visual Aesthetic: A Postmodernist View*. exh. cat. Washington, D.C.: Smithsonian Institution, 1995.

———. *Two Centuries of Black American Art*. exh. cat. New York: Alfred A. Knopf with the Los Angeles County Museum of Art, 1976.

Du Bois, W.E.B. *The Souls of Black Folk* (1903). New York: New American Library, 1969.

Farrington, Lisa E. *Creating Their Own Image: The History of African-American Women Artists*. Oxford: Oxford University Press, 2005.

Fax, Elton C. *Black Artists of the New Generation*. New York: Dodd, Mead, 1977.

———. *Seventeen Black Artists*. New York: Dodd, Mead, 1971.

Fine, Elsa Honig. *The Afro-American Artist: A Search for Identity*. New York: Holt, Rinehart, and Winston, 1973.

Gaither, Edmund B. *Afro-American Artists: New York and Boston*. exh. cat. Boston: The Museum of the National Center of Afro-American Artists, The Museum of Fine Arts, and The School of the Museum of Fine Arts, 1970.

Gibson, Ann Eden. *Abstract Expressionism: Other Politics*. New Haven: Yale University Press, 1997.

Gibson, Ann. *The Search for Freedom: African American Abstract Painting 1945–1974*. exh. cat. New York: Kenkeleba House, 1991.

Golden, Thelma. *Black Male: Representations of Masculinity in Contemporary American Art*. exh. cat. New York: Abrams and the Whitney Museum of American Art, 1994.

Gwen, Everett. *African American Masters: Highlights from the Smithsonian American Art Museum*. New York: Abrams, 2003.

Harrisburg, Halley K., ed. *African-American Art: 20th Century Masterworks*. Vol. 8. New York: Michael Rosenfeld Gallery, 2001.

———, ed. *African-American Art: 20th Century Masterworks*, Vol. 10. New York: Michael Rosenfeld Gallery, 2003.

Haywood Gallery, London. *Rhapsodies in Black: Art of the Harlem Renaissance*. exh. cat. Berkeley: University of California Press, 1997. Curated by David A. Bailey and Richard J. Powell, with essays by Simon Callow, Andrea D. Barnwell, Jeffrey C. Stewart, Paul Gilroy, Martina Attille, and Henry Louis Gates, Jr.

Harris, Michael D. *Colored Pictures: Race and Visual Representation*. Chapel Hill: University of North Carolina Press, 2003.

Henkes, Robert. *The Art of Black American Women: Works of Twenty-Four Artists of the Twentieth Century*. Jefferson, North Carolina: McFarland & Co., 1993.

Holland, Juanita, ed. *Narratives of African American Art and Identity: The David C. Driskell Collection*. exh. cat. San Francisco: Pomegranate, 1998.

Igoe, Lynn Moody. *250 Years of Afro-American Art: An Annotated Bibliography*. New York: R.R. Bowker Company, 1981.

The International Review of African American Art (formerly *Black Art: An International Quarterly*). Issues from 1976 to present.

Kenkeleba Gallery. *The Search for Freedom: African American Abstract Painting, 1945–1975*. exh. cat. New York: Kenkeleba Gallery, 1991.

King-Hammond, Leslie. *Gumbo Ya Ya: Anthology of Contemporary African-American Women Artists*. New York: Midmarch Arts Press, 1995.

King-Hammond, Leslie and Tritobia Hayes Benjamin. *Three Generations of African American Women Sculptors: A Study in Paradox*. exh. cat. Philadelphia: The Afro-American Historical and Cultural Museum, 1996.

LeFalle-Collins, Lizzetta and Shifra M. Goldman. *In the Spirit of Resistance: African-American Modernists and the Mexican Muralist School*. exh. cat. New York: The American Federation of Arts, 1996.

Leininger-Miller, Theresa A. *New Negro Artists in Paris: African American Painters and Sculptors in the City of Light, 1922–1934*. New Brunswick, New Jersey: Rutgers University Press, 2001.

Lewis, Samella. *Black Artists on Art*. Los Angeles: Contemporary Crafts and Publishers, 1969.

———. *African American Art and Artists*. 3rd ed. revised. Berkeley: University of California Press, 2003.

Lippard, Lucy R. *Mixed Blessings: New Art in a Multicultural America*. New York: Pantheon, 1990.

Livingston, Jane and John Beardsley. *Black Folk Art in America: 1930–1980*. Jackson: University Press of Mississippi, 1982.

Locke, Alain. *Negro Art, Past and Present*. Washington, D.C.: Associates in Negro Folk Education, 1936.

———. *The Negro in Art*. Washington, D.C.: Associates in Negro Folk Education, 1940.

———. *The New Negro: Voices of the Harlem Renaissance* (1925). Introduction by Arnold Rampersad. New York: Athenaeum, 1992.

McElroy, Guy C., Richard J. Powell, and Sharon F. Patton. *African-American Artists, 1800–1987: Selections from the Evans-Tibbs Collection*. Introduction by David C. Driskell. Washington, D.C.: Smithsonian Institution Traveling Exhibition Service in association with University of Washington Press, Seattle, 1989.

Morrison, Keith. *Art in Washington and its Afro-American Presence: 1940–1970*. exh. cat. Washington, D.C.: Washington Project for the Arts, 1985.

Patton, Sharon F. *African-American Art*. New York: Oxford University Press, 1998.

Perry, Regina. *Free Within Ourselves: African American Artists in the Collection of the National Museum of American Art*. Washington, D.C.: Smithsonian Institution, 1992.

Porter, James A. *Modern Negro Art*. New York: Dryden Press, 1943.

Powell, Richard J. *African-American Art: 20th Century Masterworks*. Vol. 2. New York: Michael Rosenfeld Gallery, 1995.

———. *Black Art: A Cultural History*. 2nd ed. London: Thames & Hudson, 2003.

———. *The Blues Aesthetic: Black Culture and Modernism*. exh. cat. Washington, D.C.: The National Museum of American Art, Smithsonian Institution Press, 1991.

Powell, Richard J. and Jock Reynolds. *To Conserve a Legacy: American Art from Historically Black Colleges and Universities*. exh. cat. Andover, Massachusetts: Addison Gallery of American Art; New York: The Studio Museum in Harlem; Cambridge, Massachusetts: Distributed by MIT Press, 1999.

Prigoff, James. *Walls of Heritage, Walls of Pride: African American Murals*. San Francisco: Pomegranate, 2000.

Reynolds, Gary A. and Beryl J. Wright. *Against the Odds: African-American Artists and the Harmon Foundation*. Newark, New Jersey: Newark Museum, 1989.

Riggs, Thomas, ed. *St. James Guide to Black Artists*. Published in association with the Schomburg Center for Research in Black Culture. Detroit: St. James Press, 1997.

Robinson, Jontyle Theresa. *Bearing Witness: Contemporary Works by African American Women Artists*. exh. cat. New York: Spelman College and Rizzoli International Publications, Inc., 1996.

Sims, Lowery Stokes. *Challenge of the Modern: African-American Artists 1925–1945*. New York: The Studio Museum in Harlem, 2003.

Studio Museum in Harlem. *Explorations in the City of Light: African-American Artists in Paris, 1945–1965*. exh. cat. New York: Studio Museum in Harlem, 1996. Introduction by Kinshasha Holman Conwill; essays by Catherine Bernard, Peter Selz, Michel Fabre, and Valerie J. Mercer.

———. *Harlem Renaissance: Art of Black America*. exh. cat. Introduction by Mary Schmidt Campbell; essays by David C. Driskell, David Levering Lewis, and Deborah Willis Ryan. New York: Harry N. Abrams, Inc., 1987.

———. *Ritual and Myth: A Survey of African American Art*. exh. cat. Foreword by Mary Schmidt Campbell; introduction by David C. Driskell; essay by Leslie King-Hammond. New York: Studio Museum in Harlem, 1982.

Taha, Halima. *Collecting African American Art*. New York: Crown, 1998.

Taylor, William E. and Harriet G. Warkel. *A Shared Heritage: Art by Four African Americans*. Indianapolis: Indiana University Press, 1996.

Thompson, Robert Farris. *Flash of the Spirit: African and Afro-American Art and Philosophy*. New York: Random House, 1983.

Thompson, Robert Farris, John Mason, and Judith McWillie. *Another Face of the Diamond: Pathways though the Black Atlantic South*. exh. cat. New York: INTAR Latin American Gallery, 1988.

Vlach, John Michael. *By the Work of Their Hands: Studies in Afro-American Folk Life*. Charlottesville: University Press of Virginia, 1991.

Wein, George. *Myself Among Others*. Cambridge, Massachusetts: Da Capo Press, 2003.

Willis, Deborah. *Reflections in Black: A History of Black Photographers 1840 to the Present*. New York: W.W. Norton, 2000.

IMAGE CREDITS

All photography courtesy of George and Joyce Wein. Photographers include: Pollitzer, Strong & Meyer, NY, Jim Strong, Inc., NY, and Joshua Nevsky.

All works are being lent to the exhibition courtesy of the George and Joyce Wein Collection, with the exception of Norman W. Lewis's *Carneval II*, which is courtesy of the Ed and Patricia Bradley/George and Joyce Wein Collection.

The Boston University Art Gallery would like to thank the following individuals and institutions that have given permission to reproduce the images listed below.

Charles Alston, *Untitled*, 1952. Oil on canvas. 20 x 16 in. (50.8 x 40.7 cm). © Estate of Charles Alston; Courtesy of Michael Rosenfeld Gallery, LLC, New York, NY.

Benny Andrews, *Angel*, 1977. Collage of painted acrylic, canvas, cloth, rope, and terry cloth on canvas. 76 x 45 in. (193.1 x 114.3 cm). © Benny Andrews.

Ernie Barnes, *Song of Myself*, n.d. Oil on canvas. 24 x 36 in. (60.9 x 91.4 cm). © Ernie Barnes, Courtesy of the Company of Art.

Richmond Barthé, *Feral Benga (Benga: Dance Figure)*, 1935. Bronze. 18½ in. high (39.4 cm). © Richmond Barthé Trust.

Romare Bearden, *New Orleans Farewell*, 1974. Collage of painted photostats and acrylic on board. 44 x 51 in. (111.8 x 129.5 cm). Art © Romare Bearden Foundation/Licensed by VAGA, New York, NY.

Romare Bearden, *Profile/Part II, The Thirties: Uptown Sunday Night Session*, 1981. Collage of various papers with foil, paint, ink, and graphite on fiberboard. 44 x 56 in. (111.8 x 142.2 cm). Art © Romare Bearden Foundation/Licensed by VAGA, New York, NY.

John Biggers, *Prempe II*, 1957. Conté crayon. 38¼ x 29⅜ in. (97.7 x 74.6 cm). Art © John T. Biggers Estate/Licensed by VAGA, New York, NY. Estate represented by Michael Rosenfeld Gallery.

Jules Cahn, *New Orleans Jazz Festival: Sister Gertrude, George and Joyce*, 1973. © Jules Cahn Collection. Courtesy of the Historic New Orleans Collection.

Elizabeth Catlett, *Torso*, 1997. Wood (red eucalyptus). 42 in. high (106.7 cm). Art © Elizabeth Catlett/Licensed by VAGA, New York, NY.

Eldzier Cortor, *Nude Dressing*, 1945. Ink on paper. 14 x 10 in. sight (35.6 x 25.4 cm). © Eldzier Cortor; Courtesy of Michael Rosenfeld Gallery, LLC, New York, NY.

Eldzier Cortor, *Room No. 5*, 1948. Oil on board. 37½ x 27 in. (95.3 x 68.6 cm). © Eldzier Cortor; courtesy of Michael Rosenfeld Gallery, LLC, New York, NY.

Allan Rohan Crite, *Tire Jumping in Front of My Window*, 1936/47. Oil on canvas. 23½ x 17½ in. (59.7 x 44.5 cm). © Allan Rohan Crite.

Allan Rohan Crite, *Surely He Hath Borne Our Griefs*, 1948. Lithograph. 12 x 9¾ in. comp (30.5 x 24.8 cm). © Allan Rohan Crite.

Allan Rohan Crite, *Family*, 1980. Pencil on paper. 11¾ x 14¾ in. sight (29.9 x 37.5 cm). © Allan Rohan Crite.

Allan Rohan Crite, *The Teacher*, 1980. Pencil on paper. 11¼ x 14½ in. comp (28.6 x 36.4 cm). © Allan Rohan Crite.

Miles Davis, *Untitled*, n.d. Oil on canvas. 53 x 25½ in. (134.6 x 64.8 cm). © Miles Davis Properties, LLC.

Miles Davis, *Untitled*, n.d. Acrylic on canvas. 57½ x 40½ in. (146.1 x 102.9 cm). © Miles Davis Properties, LLC.

Minnie Evans, *Untitled (Woman's Head with Flowers)*, 1955. Crayon and pencil on paper. 11½ x 9 in. (29.2 x 22.9 cm). © Courtesy Luise Ross Gallery, New York.

Palmer Hayden, *10th Cavalry Trooper*, 1939. Oil on canvas, 20 x 30½ in. (50.8 x 77.5 cm). © Hayden Family Revocable Art Trust. Courtesy of M. Hanks Gallery, Santa Monica, CA.

Palmer Hayden, *The Theatre*, 1950. Oil on canvas. 20 x 26 in. (50.8 x 66.1 cm). © Hayden Family Revocable Art Trust. Courtesy of M. Hanks Gallery, Santa Monica, CA.

Al Hirschfeld, *George Wein*, n.d. Pen on paper. 25 x 19 in. (63.5 x 48.3 cm). © AL HIRSCHFELD/MARGO FEIDEN GALLERIES LTD., NEW YORK. WWW.ALHIRSCHFELD.COM.

Oliver Johnson, *Louis Armstrong*, 1977. Oil on paper. 27 x 22 in. (68.6 x 55.9 cm). © Oliver B. Johnson – Gallery Felicie, Inc.

Wifredo Lam, *Untitled*, 1943. Oil on burlap. 24 x 31 in. (60.9 x 78.7 cm). © 2005 Artists Rights Society (ARS), New York/ADAGP, Paris.

Jacob Lawrence, *Bus*, 1941. Gouache on paper. 17 x 22 in. (43.2 x 55.9 cm). © 2005 The Estate of Gwendolyn Knight Lawrence/Artists Rights Society (ARS), New York.

Jacob Lawrence, *Fulton and Nostrand*, 1958. Egg tempera on hardboard. 24 x 30 in. (60.9 x 76.2 cm). © 2005 The Estate of Gwendolyn Knight Lawrence/Artists Rights Society (ARS), New York.

Hughie Lee-Smith, *Man with Balloons*, 1960. Oil on canvas. 36¼ x 46 in. (92.1 x 116.8 cm). Art © Estate of Hughie Lee-Smith/ Licensed by VAGA, New York, NY.

Hughie Lee-Smith, *The Other Side*, 1960s. Oil on canvas. 36 x 48 in. (91.4 x 121.9 cm). Art © Estate of Hughie Lee-Smith/ Licensed by VAGA, New York, NY.

Hughie Lee-Smith, *End of Act One*, 1987. Oil on canvas. 32 x 34¼ in. (81.3 x 86.9 cm). Art © Estate of Hughie Lee-Smith/ Licensed by VAGA, New York, NY.

Norman Lewis, *Shopping*, 1941. Oil on canvas. 36 x 24 in. (91.4 x 60.9 cm). © Courtesy of Tarin M. Fuller, Iandor Fine Arts, Newark, NJ.

Norman Lewis, *Harlem Jazz Jamboree*, 1943. Oil on canvas. 17¾ x 15½ in. (45.1 x 39.4 cm). © Courtesy of Tarin M. Fuller, Iandor Fine Arts, Newark, NJ.

Norman Lewis, *Street Musicians*, 1945. Oil on canvas. 25¾ x 19¼ in. (65.4 x 48.9 cm). © Courtesy of Tarin M. Fuller, Iandor Fine Arts, Newark, NJ.

Norman Lewis, *Cosmopolitan*, 1946. Oil on canvas. 35 x 20 in.

(88.9 x 50.8 cm). © Courtesy of Tarin M. Fuller, Iandor Fine Arts, Newark, NJ.

Norman Lewis, *Promenade*, 1950. Oil on canvas. 39¼ x 29¼ in. (99.7 x 74.3 cm). © Courtesy of Tarin M. Fuller, Iandor Fine Arts, Newark, NJ.

Norman Lewis, *Carneval II*, 1962. Oil on canvas. 64 x 52 in. (162.6 x 132.1 cm). © Courtesy of Tarin M. Fuller, Iandor Fine Arts, Newark, NJ.

Norman Lewis, *Triumphal*, 1972. Oil on canvas. 87 x 73 in. (220.9 x 185.4 cm). © Courtesy of Tarin M. Fuller, Iandor Fine Arts, Newark, NJ.

Faith Ringgold, *Matisse's Chapel: The French Collection Part 1: #6*, 1991. Acrylic on canvas; printed, tie-dyed, and pieced fabric. 74 x 79½ in. (187.9 x 201.9 cm). Faith Ringgold © 1991.

Betye Saar, *Night Letter: Special Delivery*, 1977. Mixed media collage on paper. 15 x 20¾ in. (38.1 x 52.7 cm). © Courtesy of Michael Rosenfeld Gallery, LLC, New York, NY.

Bob Thompson, *Stairway to the Stars*, n.d. Paper, oil, and photostat on canvas. 40 x 60 in. (101.6 x 152.4 cm). © Courtesy of Michael Rosenfeld Gallery, LLC, New York, NY.

Bob Thompson, *Untitled (Pink and Blue Figures)*, 1962. Oil on canvas. 30½ x 38½ in. (77.5 x 97.8 cm). © Courtesy of Michael Rosenfeld Gallery, LLC, New York, NY.

Charles White, *Skipping*, 1960. Crayon on paper. 33½ x 26 in. (85.1 x 66.1 cm). © Charles White Archives, 1960.

Michael Kelly Williams, *Ganawa*, 1988. Oil on treated paper. 44 x 30 in. (111.8 x 76.2 cm). © Michael Kelly Williams.

William T. Williams, *Carolina Shout*, 1990. Acrylic on canvas. 75 x 44 in. (190.5 x 111.8 cm). © William T. Williams.

John Wilson, *Girl in Mirror*, 1940s. Oil on board. 28 x 15¼ in. (69.9 x 38.7 cm). Art © John Wilson/Licensed by VAGA, New York, NY.

John Wilson, *Joyce*, 1945. Pencil on paper. 18½ x 15 in. (46.9 x 38.1 cm). Art © John Wilson/Licensed by VAGA, New York, NY.

John Wilson, *Portrait of Joyce*, 1947. Oil on canvas. 23½ x 15½ in. (59.7 x 39.4 cm). Art © John Wilson/Licensed by VAGA, New York, NY.

Hale Woodruff, *Card Players*, 1970. Oil on canvas. 36½ x 43 in. (92.7 x 109.2 cm). © Estate of Hale Woodruff/ Elnora, Inc.; Courtesy of Michael Rosenfeld Gallery, LLC, New York, NY.

Richard Yarde, *Savoy*, 1991. Watercolor on paper. 41½ x 29⅝ in. (105.4 x 75.3 cm). © R. Yarde.

After pursuing copyright permissions with due diligence, the Boston University Art Gallery regrets the unintentional omission of any holders from this list.

BOSTON UNIVERSITY ART GALLERY
855 Commonwealth Avenue
Boston, Massachusetts 02215
617/353–3329
www.bu.edu/art

Design and printing by
THE STINEHOUR PRESS
Lunenburg, Vermont

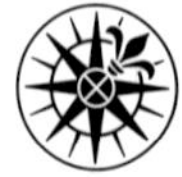

Bound by
ACME BOOKBINDING
Charlestown, Massachusetts